LIBRARY OF NEW TESTAMENT STUDIES

390

Formerly the Journal for the Study of the New Testament Supplement series

Editor

Mark Goodacre

'WHO IS THIS SON OF MAN?'

The Latest Scholarship on a Puzzling Expression of the Historical Jesus

EDITED BY
Larry W. Hurtado
AND
Paul L. Owen

t & t clark

Copyright © Larry W. Hurtado, Paul L. Owen and contributors, 2011

Published by T&T Clark International
A Continuum imprint
The Tower Building, 11 York Road, London SE1 7NX
80 Maiden Lane, Suite 704, New York, NY 10038

www.continuumbooks.com

British Library Cataloguing-in-Publication Data
A catalogue record for this book is available from the British Library

ISBN: HB: 978-0-567-52119-4

Typeset by Pindar NZ, Auckland, New Zealand
Printed and bound in Great Britain

Contents

PREFACE
THE SON OF MAN DEBATE: WHAT'S THE PROBLEM?

Paul L. Owen

The present volume seeks to advance scholarly discussion pertaining to the usage of the expression ὁ υἱος τοῦ ἀνθρώπου ('the son of man') in the Greek gospels. Those four words have accrued a significance in theological studies, both critical and confessional, far out of proportion to their length. Such a seemingly inauspicious way of speaking about Jesus has been the conduit of scholarly energy for a variety of reasons.

The phrase 'son of man' is strikingly frequent as a means of self-expression on the part of Jesus in the Synoptic Gospels. Given its frequency on the lips of Jesus, in combination with its rarity in the epistolary writings of early Christianity, it is by all accounts the 'title' for Jesus with the most convincing credentials of authenticity. Nearly all scholars admit that this *manner of speaking* goes back to the historical Jesus. Whereas other titles like *Son of God*, *Messiah*, and *Lord* clearly functioned later as means of confessional expression in the early church, 'son of man' does not seem to have been picked up and utilized in the same manner. What are we to make of this?

This leads us to an important question. Should 'son of man' even be treated as a title for Jesus at all? Is it possible that ὁ υἱος τοῦ ἀνθρώπου in Greek translates an original Aramaic expression which designated Jesus in a non-titular manner? It has been suggested by some that Jesus used this expression in Aramaic as a humble substitute for the personal pronoun 'I'. Others have argued that it stood generically for humankind in general, or a particular class of people ('a man in my situation'). Still others have suggested that it stood in place of an indefinite pronoun, simply meaning 'someone'.

To what literary materials should we turn to determine the answers to such questions? Nowhere in Aramaic texts dating from around the time of Jesus do we find any individual being referred to as '*the* son of man' (בר אנשא). While there is a handful of texts which use 'son of man' (בר אנש) to assert things about a person, what is the significance of such examples, since they always lack the definite article we find in the Greek gospels? And what are we to make of the evidence found in later Aramaic materials drawn from rabbinic and Targumic texts? What might we glean from their use of the same language and expression thought to underlie ὁ υἱος τοῦ ἀνθρώπου in the New Testament? Is there a way to ensure that we are reaching conclusions based on linguistic evidence from the proper time period and geographical range?

Another issue is the connection between Jesus' employment of the expression 'son of man' and Dan. 7.13, which provides the probable textual origin for at least some of the 'son of man' sayings in the Gospels. Are those ('apocalyptic') Synoptic sayings which make use of Dan. 7.13 in order to assert something about the son of man's role in the final judgement to be attributed to Jesus himself, or are they best seen as theological elaborations by the early church? This then raises questions about the meaning of the vision of the 'son of man' in the book of Daniel. Is the cryptic figure described there to be understood as an angel, a symbol of the people of God, or an apocalyptic Messiah? And how are we to understand other apocalyptic texts which appear to appropriate the Danielic material in their own messianic rhetoric? What of those Synoptic sayings which are less direct in their appropriation of Daniel (the so-called 'suffering' and 'earthly' son of man)? Are they any more (or less) likely candidates for authenticity than are the apocalyptic sayings? How should they be understood by critical scholars who seek to distinguish the thoughts of Jesus from those of his devoted followers? And what role did the early transmitters and translators of the Jesus tradition play in passing on such sayings within the developing hermeneutic of Christian devotion?

These sorts of questions have received an array of competing answers, and it is to the furtherance of such discussions that the present collection of essays is directed. The following chapters deal with a range of issues related to linguistics, the Aramaic evidence, the historical Jesus, and the influence of Daniel 7 in early Judaism and Christianity. First, the history of the 'son of man' discussion will be surveyed by Albert Lukaszewski, who provides a formidable overview of the numerous methodological and linguistic issues involved in tackling the problem. Then, Paul Owen, David Shepherd and Peter Williams engage, at various levels, the work of Maurice Casey, who has devoted an enormous amount of energy to the debate in modern scholarship. Finally, Darrell Bock, Benjamin Reynolds and Darrell Hannah explore the use of the 'son of man' expression, and the appropriation of Daniel 7, at Jesus' trial, in John's Gospel, and within the *Parables of Enoch* (*1 Enoch* 37–71) respectively. The 'son of man' debate serves as a conduit for discussions about method in Aramaic studies, the process whereby the oral teaching of Jesus took written form in the Greek gospels, the development of messianic hope(s) in the Second Temple period, the influence of Daniel 7 in Jewish apocalyptic texts, the self-understanding of the historical Jesus, and the relationship of Jesus' modes of speech to the content of early Christian faith and devotion. It is our hope as editors that this collaboration will make a fresh and fruitful contribution to the ongoing discussion of these matters in New Testament scholarship.

Bibliographical and general

ABD	David Noel Freedman (ed.), *The Anchor Bible Dictionary* (6 vols; New York: Doubleday, 1992)
AcOr	*Acta Orientalia*
ÄF	Äthiopistische Forschungen
AThANT	Abhandlungen zur Theologie des Alten und des Neuen Testamentes
BBET	Beiträge zur biblischen Exegese und Theologie
BBR	*Bulletin for Biblical Research*
BECNT	Baker Exegetical Commentary on the New Testament
BETL	Bibliotheca ephemeridum theologicarum lovaniensium
Bib	*Biblica*
BSR	Biblioteca di Scienze Religiose
BZNW	Beihefte zur *ZNW*
CBQ	*Catholic Biblical Quarterly*
CBQMS	*Catholic Biblical Quarterly*, Monograph Series
ch.	chapter
chs.	chapters
CSCO	Corpus scriptorum christianorum orientalium
DJG	Joel B. Green, Scot McKnight, I. Howard Marshall (eds), *Dictionary of Jesus and the Gospels* (Downers Grove, IL: InterVarsity, 1992)
DSD	*Dead Sea Discoveries*

ETL	*Ephemerides theologicae lovanienses*
EvQ	*Evangelical Quarterly*
ExpTim	*Expository Times*
FZPhTh	*Freiburger Zeitschrift für Philosophie und Theologie*
HSS	Harvard Semitic Studies
HTR	*Harvard Theological Review*
JBL	*Journal of Biblical Literature*
JNES	*Journal of Near Eastern Studies*
JSHRZ	Jüdische Schriften aus hellenistisch-römischer Zeit
JSNT	*Journal for the Study of the New Testament*
JSNTSup	*Journal for the Study of the New Testament*, Supplement Series
JSOTSup	*Journal for the Study of the Old Testament*, Supplement Series
JSP	*Journal for the Study of the Pseudepigrapha*
JSS	*Journal of Semitic Studies*
JTS	*Journal of Theological Studies*
KJV	King James Version
LHBOTS	Library of Hebrew Bible/Old Testament Studies
LNTS	Library of New Testament Studies
MPAT	*Manual of Palestinian Aramaic Texts*
MT	Masoretic Text
n.	note
nn.	notes
NovTSup	*Novum Testamentum*, Supplements
NT	New Testament
NTAbh	Neutestamentliche Abhandlungen
NTS	*New Testament Studies*
OT	Old Testament
QD	Quaestiones disputatae
RAC	*Reallexikon für Antike und Christentum*
RSV	Revised Standard Version
SBLDS	SBL Dissertation Series
SBLMS	SBL Monograph Series
SBLSCS	SBL Septuagint and Cognate Studies

SBLSymS	SBL Symposium Series
SBT	Studies in Biblical Theology
SNTSMS	Society for New Testament Studies Monograph Series
SSEJC	Studies in Scripture in Early Judaism and Christianity
STDJ	Studies on the Texts of the Desert of Judah
SUNT	Studien zur Umwelt des Neuen Testaments
SVTP	Studia in Veteris Testamenti pseudepigrapha
TANZ	Texte und Arbeiten zum neutestamentlichen Zeitalter
TLZ	*Theologische Literaturzeitung*
TynB	*Tyndale Bulletin*
v.	verse
vv.	verses
WUNT	Wissenschaftliche Untersuchungen zum Neuen Testament
ZNW	*Zeitschrift für die neutestamentliche Wissenschaft*

Ancient sources

Josephus

Ant.	*Antiquities of the Jews*

Philo

Vit. Mos.	*De vita Mosis*

Mishnah, Talmud and related literature

Ber.	*Berakot*
Kil.	*Kilayim*
Taanit	*Taanit*
Tan.	*Tanhuma*
Sanh.	*Sanhedrin*
Suk.	*Sukkah*
Yoma	*Yoma*

Targumic texts

Tg-Jonathan	*Targum Pseudo-Jonathan*
Tg-Onkelos	*Targum Onkelos*

Other Rabbinic literature

Num. Rab.   *Numbers Rabbah*

Early Christian literature

Adv. Haer.   Irenaeus, *Adversus Haereses*
Adv. Marc   Tertullian, *Adversus Marcionem*
Barn.   *Barnabas*
Dial.   Justin Martyr, *Dialogue with Trypho the Jew*
Ignatius, *Eph.*   Ignatius, *Letter to the Ephesians*

Darrell L. Bock is Research Professor of New Testament Studies at Dallas Theological Seminary. He has written full commentaries on Luke and Acts, as well as a technical study *Blasphemy and Exaltation in Judaism and the Jewish Examination of Jesus* (Mohr/Siebeck, 1998). He has just edited a major historical Jesus study with Robert Webb, *Key Events in the Life of the Historical Jesus* (Mohr/Siebeck, 2009) and is associate editor on a new project on Second Temple background to the gospels with Bruce Chilton, *A Comparative Handbook to the Gospel of Mark* (Brill, 2009). He has been a Humboldt scholar for two sabbaticals at the University of Tübingen.

Darrell D. Hannah is Rector of All Saints Parish Church in Ascot, England. He is the author of *Michael and Christ: Michael traditions and Angel Christology in early Christianity* (Mohr Siebeck, 1999), and a forthcoming commentary on the *Epistula Apostolorum* (Oxford). He has published articles in the *Journal of Theological Studies*, *Vigiliae christianae*, *Zeitschrift für die neutestamentliche Wissenschaft*, and *New Testament Studies*.

Larry W. Hurtado is Professor of New Testament Language, Literature and Theology in the University of Edinburgh (New College, School of Divinity). He is a Fellow of the Royal Society of Edinburgh, and President of the British New Testament Society (2009–12). Among his publications are *Lord Jesus Christ: devotion to Jesus in earliest Christianity* (Eerdmans, 2003), and *How*

*on Earth did Jesus Become a God? Historical questions about earliest devo-
tion to Jesus* (Eerdmans, 2005). His latest book is *'God' in the New Testament*
(Abingdon Press, 2010).

Albert L. Lukaszewski is co-chair of the Hellenistic Greek Language and
Linguistics section for the international meeting of the Society of Biblical
Literature. He has previously served as general editor of the Lexham Syntactic
Greek New Testament and researcher at the Comprehensive Aramaic Lexicon.
In addition to his doctoral work on language dynamics at the time of Jesus
and his grammatical research on Qumran Aramaic, he was also a National
Endowment for the Humanities fellow in Aramaic.

Paul L. Owen is Associate Professor of Biblical and Religious Studies at
Montreat College in North Carolina. His previous research has appeared in
a number of venues, including the *Journal of Biblical Literature*, the *Journal
for the Study of the New Testament*, and the Library of Second Temple Studies
within the monograph *Of Scribes and Sages: early Jewish interpretation and
transmission of scripture* (Continuum, 2004).

Benjamin E. Reynolds is Assistant Professor of Religious Studies at Tyndale
University College in Toronto, Ontario, Canada. His publications include
The Apocalyptic Son of Man in the Gospel of John (Mohr Siebeck, 2008) and
articles in *Biblica, Neotestamentica,* and *Henoch*.

David Shepherd is Senior Lecturer in Hebrew Bible and Jewish Studies at the
University of Chester. His work in biblical studies and languages has appeared
in various periodicals, including the *Journal of Jewish Studies, Journal for the
Study of the Pseudepigrapha,* and *Journal for the Study of the New Testament*,
and his doctoral work on the Aramaic version of Job from Qumran was published in the Studia Semitica Neerlandica as *Targum and Translation* (Van
Gorcum, 2004). He has served on the Board of the International Organization
of Targum Studies since 2007.

P. J. Williams is Warden of Tyndale House in Cambridge. His doctoral work
at Cambridge was on the Syriac Old Testament, and he has also been Senior

Lecturer in New Testament at the University of Aberdeen. His books include *Early Syriac Translation Technique and the Textual Criticism of the Greek Gospels*, and he is editor of the *Tyndale Bulletin*.

Issues Concerning the Aramaic Behind ὁ υἱὸς τοῦ ἀνθρώπου: A Critical Review of Scholarship

Albert L. Lukaszewski

The issues pertaining to the Aramaic behind ὁ υἱὸς τοῦ ἀνθρώπου have been discussed with a growing pace in recent years. No scholarly study exists in a vacuum, however, and those that address the Son of Man problem are no exception. Consequently, the Aramaic issues surrounding the Son of Man debate are best understood in their historical settings.

The following review of the debate may be divided into three parts, the first starting with Tertullian's allusion to Daniel in the second century and running to Fiebig's comprehensive treatment in 1901, the second commencing with the resumption of the debate after the Second World War until Sjöberg's study in 1951, and the third being heralded by Geza Vermes' presentation at Oxford in 1965 and continuing to the present.

The Debate Part 1: To the Early Twentieth Century

Foundational to any modern study of the Son of Man sayings is the linguistic background to the term 'Son of Man'. Ever since the second century, exegetes have drawn a correlation between Daniel's vision and Jesus' Son of Man sayings in the Gospels.[1] But the expression was typically treated in linguistic isolation, being understood only as a Greek expression until the Reformation. A Hebraic background for the phrase was then posited by Ulrich

---

1. Tertullian, *Adv. Marc.* 4.10.

Zwingli.[2] It was not until about 100 years later, however, that Johannes Coccejus commented on Mt. 8.20 by positing an Aramaic background to the phrase.[3] Since that time, the majority of scholars have assumed the correctness of Coccejus' basic linguistic position and have subsequently disputed about what that Aramaic background actually was.

The argument that the phrase 'Son of Man' derived from an Aramaic expression still had its advocates, even through a rather languid period for philological studies of the matter in the eighteenth and most of the nineteenth centuries.[4] Nevertheless, this period saw a dramatic rise in the variety of interpretations offered for the term 'Son of Man'.[5] Then, on the cusp of the twentieth century, several landmark studies brought greater prominence to the position that the background lay in some Aramaic expression. In *Israelitische und judische Geschichte*, Julius Wellhausen posited Jesus' use of Aramaic בר אנשא to mean 'I'.[6] Nathaniel Schmidt argued for a non-titular, idiomatic usage meaning

---

2.   Delbert Burkett, *The Son of Man Debate* (SNTSMS, 107; Cambridge: Cambridge University Press, 1999), p. 14. This view was argued as recently as 1923; it has, however, decreased in popularity since then. For a list of scholars who take this position, see Burkett, p. 14 nn. 2–3.

3.   Johannes Coccejus, *Opera omnia*. vol. 4 (Amsterdam: Someren, 1701), p. 15.

4.   For example, '. . . erst Jesus adelte den בר נש = υἱὸς τοῦ ἀνθρώπου' (Paul de Lagarde, *Gesammelte Abhandlungen* [Leipzig: F.A. Brockhaus, 1866], p. 25, n. 3). The lack of any philological pursuit in addressing the problem during this period has been described thus: '[T]here appeared many studies indeed, which in one way or another, touched upon this question, but . . . these discussions inevitably suffered from the obsession of the times and the philological issue was drowned by other interests' (Chrys C. Caragounis, *The Son of Man* [WUNT, 38; Tübingen: Mohr, 1986], p. 11).

5.   The variety was so great that Lietzmann writes: 'Was hat nicht alles "Menschensohn" bedeuten sollen! Idealmensch, der die Menschennatur verherrlicht; messias, aber im Geensatz zum Gottessohn der Juden, als armer, niedriger mensch; Messias als Träger aller Menschenwürde und Menschenrechte; Messias als präexistenter himmlischer Mensch; Messias als Organ zur Verwirklichung des durch ihn zugleich dargestellten Menschheitsideales in der Welt; Messias – ohne Nebenbedeutung; Bezeichnung des Berufes Jesu, wie sich derselbe durch seine Menschwerdung bedingte; Messias im Sinne des "Idealmenschen" als Gegensatz gegen den national beschränkten "Davididen"; Messias, als Erzeugter eines Menschen der Gattung Mensch angehörig; schliesslich soll es Messiasbezeichnung im Sinne eines im starken Glauben erhobenen Anspruches sein' (Hans Lietzmann *Der Menschensohn* [Freiburg i.B.: Mohr, 1896], pp. 23–24).

6.   Julius Wellhausen *Israelitische und judische Geschichte* (Berlin: Georg Reimer, 1894), p. 312, n. 1. While his note brought greater prominence to Aramaic theory, Wellhausen would later abandon this view [Burkett, *Son of Man Debate*, p. 84].

'man'.[7] Arnold Meyer then argued in *Jesu Muttersprache* for retroverting ὁ υἱὸς τοῦ ἀνθρώπου as the phrase ההוא בר אנשא, 'that Son of Man'.[8] Meyer's use of the pronoun ההוא was roundly rejected by his contemporaries, however, in particular Lietzmann and Dalman.[9]

Hans Lietzmann's overriding criticism of Meyer's work was that it was insufficiently systematic:[10] 'But all these latter papers do not provide so much a systematic working-through of all this material but rather only hints in what direction the solution of the question is to be sought.'

He then surveys the ways the phrase 'Son of Man' was used in Aramaic and Greek as they were known in the late nineteenth century. Lietzmann insisted that Aramaic grammar did not allow the term בר אנשא to be used for a specific individual.[11] Further, given the lack of the phrase among the rabbis,[12] he concluded that the phrase 'Son of Man' was a technical term developed out of 'Hellenistic' Christian theology.[13]

Dalman contested Meyer's grammatical constructions as unattested, stating, 'There is no example that ההוא אֱנָשָׁא or ההוא בַר אֱנָשָׁא would have been

---

7. Nathaniel Schmidt, 'Was בר נש a Messianic Title?' *JBL* 15(1/2) (1896), pp. 36–53. Schmidt takes significant issue with the selection of options presented by other scholars: נש בר, בר נש, בר אנשא, בר אנשא. Rather, Schmidt notes, several other options exist in Syriac (ברה דאנשא), Christian Palestinian Aramaic (ברה דבר נשא), and other corpora (p. 45).

8. Arnold Meyer, *Jesu Muttersprache: das galiläische Aramäisch in seiner Bedeutung für die Erklärung der Reden Jesu und der Evangelien überhaupt* (Freiburg i.B.: Mohr, 1896), p. 96.

9. Hans Lietzmann *Der Menschensohn*, (Freiburg i.B.: Mohr, 1896), p. 84; Gustav Dalman, *Die Worte Jesu*. vol. 1: *Einleitung und Wichtige Begriffe* (Darmstadt: Wissenschaftliche Buchgesellschaft, 1965 [1st ed. 1898]), p. 205. Lietzmann further rejects the Aramaic theory of the phrase's origin, alleging that the equivalent phrase for ὁ υἱὸς τοῦ ἀνθρώπου does not exist in Aramaic. Rather, בר אנשא simply means 'the man' (ὁ ἄνθρωπος) (*Menschensohn*, p. 85). This conclusion was subsequently challenged by Dalman, who argues for בר אנשא as applicable to a definite individual despite its not appearing in the primary source literature as such (Dalman, *Worte Jesu*, pp. 195–208).

10. 'Alle die zuletzt genannten Abhandlungen aber bieten nicht sowohl eine systematische Durcharbeitung des gesamten vorliegenden Materials, als vielmehr nur Andeutungen, in welcher Richtung die Lösung der Frage zu suchen sei.' (Lietzmann, *Menschensohn*, p. 28). It is worth noting that Leitzmann's criticism is not directed at Meyer alone, but at the work of Uloth, de Lagarde, Wellhausen, Eerdmans, and van Manen, as well.

11. Lietzmann, *Menschensohn*, p. 84.

12. Lietzmann, *Menschensohn*, p. 50.

13. Lietzmann, *Menschensohn*, p. 95.

used in the same way. Still less would mere אֱנָשָׁא בַר have been possible.'[14] Surveying the use of בַר אֱנָשָׁא and its cognates in several corpora of both Hebrew and Aramaic,[15] Dalman concluded that the phrase is well-attested as referring to a single, specific individual.[16]

Shortly after the first edition of Dalman's *Die Worte Jesu* was published, Paul Fiebig published *Der Menschensohn*, the results of which corroborate Dalman.[17] Dialoguing with Lietzmann, Meyer and Wellhausen, Fiebig first surveyed the sundry forms of both אנש and בר across the earlier literature in which compounds with בר are not found frequently and the later literature in which they are; his point is to clarify the meanings and uses of the various words in question before considering them in construct.[18] Fiebig finds no detectable difference of meaning in the uses of אנש, אנשא, (א)נש בר and בר נשא.[19] Further, Fiebig discounts the mistranslation theory espoused by Meyer and, at first, by Wellhausen as 'to be completely excluded'.[20] He then concludes: 'ὁ υἱὸς τοῦ ἀνθρώπου is = the Man from Dan. 7.13 = the Messiah. Is it

---

14. 'Es giebt aber kein Beispiel dafür, dass הָהוּא אֱנָשָׁא oder הָהוּא בַר אֱנָשָׁא in der gleichen Weise gebraucht worden wäre. Noch weniger wäre blosses בַר אֱנָשָׁא dafür möglich gewesen' (Dalman, *Worte Jesu*, p. 205).

15. Dalman compares the use of Aramaic בַר אנש and Hebrew בֶן אדֶם across Biblical Hebrew, Biblical Aramaic, Mishnaic Hebrew, the Targumic Aramaic of Onqelos, the Aramaic of the Samaritan Pentateuch Targum, the Targum of the Prophets, the Christian Palestinian lectionaries, Aramaic recensions of Tobit, and both Palmyrene and Nabataean inscriptions [*Worte Jesu*, pp. 191–97].

16. Dalman, *Worte Jesu*, p. 197.

17. Paul Fiebig *Der Menschensohn: Jesu Selbstbezeichnung mit besonderer Berücksichtigung des aramäischen Sprachgebrauches für 'Mensch'* (Tübingen: Halle a. S.: 1901). Dalman, *Worte Jesu*, pp. 191–219.

18. The corpora of the former are addressed in the first half of the first part (pp. 8–25) and include: the Biblical Aramaic corpus, Targum Onqelos, the Samaritan Aramaic corpus, the Targum to the Prophets, and Aramaic inscriptions. The latter corpora (pp. 26–53) include: the Sword of Moses, Talmud Yerushalmi, the Midrashim, Talmud Bavli, the Christian Palestinian Aramaic lectionaries, the Syriac corpus of the time, Targum Pseudo-Jonathan (referenced as 'Targum jeruschalmi I und II'), and the Targum of the Writings.

19. Fiebig, *Menschensohn*, pp. 59–60. He concludes: 'Wir sehen: keiner der vier Ausdrücke ist eindeutig und sie alle berühren sich in ihren Bedeutungen mannigfach unter einander. Das ist den bisherigen Erörterungen über den sprachlichen Thatbestand gegenüber besonders zu betonen; denn Lietzmann, Dalman und Wellhausen heben die Mehrdeutigkeit der einzelnen Ausdrücke nicht hervor' (p. 60).

20. 'völlig ausgeschlossen'. Fiebig, *Menschensohn*, p. 74.

right that "the Man" as self-reference to Jesus = the Man from Dan. 7.13 = the Messiah is . . .'[21]

Without a doubt, Fiebig's analysis is the most comprehensive treatment of the Son of Man problem of his generation. As a consequence of his work, Dalman's retroversion of ὁ υἱὸς τοῦ ἀνθρώπου to בר אנשא prevailed for the next 50 years as the mainstream solution to the linguistic aspect of the problem.[22]

The debate Part 2: after the Second World War

Renewed interest in the linguistic approach to the Son of Man debate arose after the Second World War with the publication of three major studies that presented alternatives to Dalman's conclusions. In the year following the first edition of Matthew Black's *An Aramaic Approach to the Gospels and Acts*, J. Y. Campbell argued for a misunderstanding and subsequent mistranslation by those who rendered into Greek the supposed Aramaic *Vorlage* of the Son

21.   'ὁ υἱὸς τοῦ ἀνθρώπου ist = der Mensch aus Daniel 7.13 = der Messias. Ist es richtig, dass der Mensch als Selbstbezeichnung Jesu = der Mensch aus Daniel 7.13 = der Messias ist . . .'. (Fiebig, *Menschensohn*, p. 75). This statement is reiterated and emphasized later in the thesis as well (pp. 119–21).

22.   This is not to suggest that Dalman's work lacked its detractors; however, what criticisms of his work there were did not gain adherents and were poorly conveyed. One notable exception to the unusual lack of debate in the first half of the twentieth century is Nathaniel Schmidt's vitriolic 'Recent Study of the Term "Son of Man"' *JBL* 45(3/4) (1926), pp. 326–49. The author decries Dalman's study as unscientific and 'a mistaken estimate based on questionable data'. The main criticisms are Dalman's tendency to weigh textual evidence – especially Palmyrene and Nabataean – without due consideration of the genres involved: 'A philological observation may furnish a significant clue, but it must be followed through all the literary data, with due regard for the necessary criticism of sources and the main theories propounded in this field. Historical methods must be applied in the sifting of the material and the search for ascertainable facts' (p. 327). For all of Schmidt's rhetorical vigour, however, the article lacks any substantial rebuttal to Dalman's detailed discussion in *Die Worte Jesus*.

It is worth noting that, while Meyer's Aramaic argument was rejected, the understanding of the phrase that he espoused continued to find favour. We know of the dissent largely after the fact, by way of the posthumous publication of A. J. Wensinck's notes on the matter. Wensinck agrees that the phrase referenced 'man' but dissents from its being a form of self-reference. Despite the presence of this view, Dalman's view certainly had the greater number of adherents and was regarded as the authoritative position. So Matthew Black. *An Aramaic Approach to the Gospels and Acts* (3rd edn, Peabody, MA: Hendrickson, 1998), p. 296: 'Gustaf Dalman, hitherto the recognized authority on the subject [of the Aramaic backgrounds to the New Testament]'.

of Man passages. He contested Dalman's late dating of an indefinite sense for בַּר אֲנָשׁ, suggesting that the argument was self-fulfilling – one naturally finds later phenomena in sources of late dating. Campbell instead argued that an indefinite phrase may be made to carry a definite sense at any time.[23] He further posited that such a reference in Aramaic was probably accompanied by a demonstrative adjective: הַהוּא בַּר אֲנָשׁ.[24] That demonstrative was unnecessary in Greek and was probably dropped. He concludes that the phrase was thus misunderstood by the translators and was thought to be a title.

Shortly after Campbell argued for a mistranslation, John Bowman attacked Dalman's arguments directly, employing both Targum Onqelos (on which Dalman relied for his work in *Die Worte Jesu*) and the Palestinian Targums from the Cairo Genizah. In the latter, Bowman found instances of both בַּר נַשׁא and בַּר נַשׁ with an indefinite, general sense.[25]

In 1950, Erik Sjöberg revised Dalman's conclusions.[26] Sjöberg, like Fiebig and Dalman, surveys a vast array of ancient Near Eastern texts.[27] With Fiebig and Dalman, he finds that בַּר נַשׁ(א) was probably used often in the Galilean Aramaic of Jesus' time. Against Dalman and Fiebig, however, he finds that the phrase is not self-referential but pronominal, suggesting 'a man' or 'someone'. While much of the corpora that Sjöberg used are today of questionable relevance for the present study, his was the first to attempt a large-scale diachronic analysis by broadening his scope to non-biblical works that preceded Jesus' time by several centuries.

---

23. In support of this, Campbell cites Paul's self-reference in 2 Cor. 12.2-3: 'οἶδα ἄνθρωπον ἐν Χριστῷ . . .'.

24. The phrase may also be בַּר אֲנָשָׁא הַהוּא in Campbell's view.

25. See Gen. 4.14 and 9.5-6.

26. Erik Sjöberg, 'בֶּן אָדָם und בַּר אֱנָשׁ im Hebräischen und Aramäischen', *AcOr* 21 (1950–51), pp. 57–65, 91–107.

27. In the broad range of corpora used were Targum Onqelos, Targum to the Prophets, Elephantine Papyri, Nabataean inscriptions, Palmyrene inscriptions, Christian Palestinian Aramaic, and the Syriac corpus. It is worth noting that the diachronic range of the corpora used by Sjöberg is extraordinarily wide, extending from sixth century BCE to – at the earliest – sixth century CE.

The debate Part 3: after Qumran

After Sjöberg's study, the field lay fallow for 15 years. In 1965, Geza Vermes gave a lecture in Oxford that was subsequently published in the third edition of Matthew Black's *An Aramaic Approach to the Gospels and Acts*.[28] After surveying the literature of the debate, Vermes states:[29]

> [I]t may safely be accepted that (אׁ)שׁנ בֹר was in common use, both as a noun and as a substitute for the indefinite pronoun, in the early as well as in the later stages of the development of the Galilean dialect, and that the employment of the definite or indefinite forms does not substantially affect the meaning.

Vermes then takes as the points of contention the use of the phrase as a circumlocution for the first person and the possible messianic connotation behind its use (*viz.* Dan. 7.13).

Vermes' study took the debate forward in that his was the first study to use the fragments from the Cairo Geniza that Paul Kahle published and the five columns of the Genesis Apocryphon published by Avigad and Yadin.[30] In addition, his corpora of comparison included Talmud Yerushalmi, the Aramaic of the Genesis Rabba, Codex Neofiti, Targum Pseudo-Jonathan, the fragmentary Jerusalem Targum, the Palestinian Talmud, and the Babylonian Talmud.[31] He thus concludes that (אׁ)שׁנ בֹר is a Western Aramaic circumlocution for the first person and is used to indicate humility, humiliation, danger or death. Noting readily that the phrase is not well-attested, he posits that this is not a reflection of the rarity of the phrase: 'It is more likely due to the rarity in the extant Aramaic sources of the sort of idiomatic setting in which such a grammatical phenomenon might normally occur'.[32] This rarity, however, does not affect

---

28.   Geza Vermes, 'The Use of שׁנ בֹר / אׁשׁנ בֹר in Jewish Aramaic' Appendix E in Black, *An Aramaic Approach*, pp. 310–30.

29.   Vermes, 'Use', p. 314.

30.   Paul Kahle, *The Cairo Geniza* (Oxford: Blackwell, 1959); Nahman Avigad and Yigael Yadin, *Genesis Apocryphon* (Jerusalem: Magnes Press, 1956).

31.   It is worth noting that, aside from the Genesis Apocryphon and Codex Neofiti, Vermes' corpora date at least 300 years later than the time of Jesus and the earliest Christians.

32.   Vermes, 'Use', p. 327.

Vermes' conclusion that, because none of the instances he uncovered were messianic in character, בר נש(א) was unsuitable as a name or title.[33]

Finally, for ὁ υἱὸς τοῦ ἀνθρώπου to become the term of honour that it did in Christianity and not have been a creation of the same, Vermes posits a conundrum. If the phrase was translated into Greek from Aramaic, then it was, according to Vermes' argument, something 'other than a title'. If it was natively Greek, one is confronted with the question of why a Hellenist would create 'so alien an idiom'.[34]

Reaction to Vermes' argument was swift and critical.[35] Overall, respondents noted that all of Vermes' examples were generic in nature and could thus include the speaker; one could not therefore be certain of the referent's specificity. As Jeremias notes in reply, ההוא גברא means 'Myself and none other' where בר נשא denotes 'The Man, so myself'.[36] Vermes' response to these criticisms in 1978 was that he was misunderstood; the circumlocution was not necessarily a direct synonym for direct speech but an evasive way of making a roundabout reference. Fitzmyer further noted that Vermes' corpus consisted largely of later Aramaic texts.[37] Later Aramaic dropped the initial א. As a consequence, the morphological aspect of Vermes' study is skewed.[38]

Despite the lateness of the corpora and the morphological problems observed by Fitzmyer, Vermes' argument was taken up, albeit with modification, by

33.   Vermes, 'Use', pp. 327–28. In support of his conclusions, Vermes finally refers to Syriac and Christian Palestinian Aramaic, wherein the expression ὁ υἱὸς τοῦ ἀνθρώπου is rendered severally as ברה דגברה, ברה דברנשא, ברה דאנשא.

34.   Vermes, 'Use', p. 328.

35.   See Frederick H. Borsch, *The Son of Man in Myth and History* (London: SCM Press, 1967); Joachim Jeremias, 'Die alteste Schicht der Menschensohn-Logien', *ZNW* 58 (1967), pp. 159–72; and several works by Joseph A. Fitzmyer: Review of Matthew Black's *An Aramaic Approach to the Gospels and Acts* (3rd edn) in *CBQ* 30 (1968), pp. 417–28; 'The Contribution of Qumran Aramaic to the Study of the NT', *NTS* 20 (1974), pp. 382–407; 'Methodology in the Study of the Aramaic Substratum of Jesus' Sayings in the NT' in *Jesus aux origines de la christologie* (ed. J. Dupont; BETL, 40; Gembloux: Ducoulot, 1975), pp. 73–102. An additional, later, critique of Vermes is found in Bruce Chilton, 'Son of Man: Human and Heavenly', in *The Four Gospels* (ed. F. Van Segbroek, et al.; BETL, 100; Leuven: Leuven University Press, 1992), pp. 203–18.

36.   'Ich und kein anderer' and 'Der Mensch, also auch Ich', respectively. Joachim Jeremias, 'Die alteste Schicht der Menschensohn-Logien', *ZNW* 58 (1967), pp. 159–72 (165, n. 9).

37.   See Note 31.

38.   Joseph Fitzmyer, *A Wandering Aramean* (Missoula: Scholars Press, 1979), pp. 143–60.

Barnabas Lindars and Maurice Casey.[39] Lindars' methodology was manifestly weak and his conclusions have been discounted widely as a result.[40] Of the two, only Casey pursued the philological aspects of the Son of Man problem at length.

Over the course of several studies,[41] Casey carries Vermes' study on בר נשא forward, agreeing with his conclusion and employing it even when reverse translating large sections of Mark's Gospel and Q.[42] From Vermes' work and his own, Casey concludes that '(א)נש(א) בר is a normal term for "man"'.[43]

---

39.   Barnabas Lindars, *Jesus Son of Man* (London: SPCK, 1983); Maurice Casey, *Son of Man: The Interpretation and Influence of Daniel 7* (London: SPCK, 1979).

40.   Lindars analysed a portion of Vermes' corpus and concluded three means of self-reference involving the third person:

1. a generic statement in which the speaker is included with the hearers
2. an exclusive reference by which the speaker alone is referenced
3. a gentilic use of a generic article by which the speaker references a class of persons.

His conclusions, however, have been refuted by several scholars. See Matthew Black 'Aramaic Barnāshā and the Son of Man', *ExpTim* 95 (1984), pp. 200–206; Richard Bauckham, 'The Son of Man: "A Man in My Position" or "Someone"?', *JSNT* 23 (1985), pp. 23–33; Reginald Fuller, 'The Son of Man: A Reconsideration' in *The Living Text: Essays in Honor of Ernest W. Saunders* (ed. Dennis E. Groh and Robert Jewett; Lanham, MD: University Press of America, 1985), pp. 207–17; Caragounis, *The Son of Man*, pp. 29–33. Lindars himself characterizes his conclusions as 'a matter of guesswork' (p. 53) and a 'necessarily speculative reconstruction' (p. 73). Casey would further omit the volume completely from his 'State of Play' review of the literature in *Aramaic Sources of Mark's Gospel* (SNTSMS, 102; Cambridge: Cambridge University Press, 1998), only referencing it later *en passant* (p. 163, n. 17).

41.   Casey, *Son of Man*; 'General, Generic and Indefinite: The Use of the Term "Son of Man" in Aramaic Sources and in the Teaching of Jesus', *JSNT* 29 (1987), pp. 21–56; 'Method in our Madness, and Madness in their Methods', *JSNT* 42 (1991), pp. 17–43; *From Jewish Prophet to Gentile God* (Louisville, KY: Westminster, 1991); 'The Use of the Term (א)נש(א) בר in the Aramaic Translations of the Hebrew Bible', *JSNT* 54 (1994), pp. 87–118; 'Idiom and Translation: Some Aspects of the Son of Man Problem' *NTS* 41 (1995), pp. 164–82.

42.   *Aramaic Sources of Mark's Gospel* (SNTSMS, 102; Cambridge: Cambridge University Press, 1998); *An Aramaic Approach to Q* (SNTSMS, 122; Cambridge: Cambridge University Press, 2002). The several and severe methodological problems with Casey's retroversions in particular have been taken up in detail in my own 'A Viable Approach to the Aramaic of the New Testament' (unpublished doctoral dissertation; University of St Andrews, 2005), pp. 88–99.

43.   *Aramaic Sources*, p. 111.

Following Fitzmyer,[44] he observes that the first Aramaic reference similar to that under consideration is in the third Sefire inscription, a diplomatic treaty dating from the middle of the eighth century BCE that includes the use of בר אנש.[45] Casey then references Aramaic phrases that involve the use of בר as a *nomen regens* and a form of אנש as a *nomen rectum* which he translates as 'Son of Man' and as equivalent to ὁ υἱὸς τοῦ ἀνθρώπου. These 'examples' include a plethora of forms from disparate dialects and dates: בר אנוש, בר נש, בר אנש, בר נשא, ברנשא and בר אנשא.[46]

Casey treats the linguistic issues inherent in the diachrony of these several forms with little regard.[47] Rather, he states that once 'we have reviewed the range of usage of בר (א)נש(א) in natural Aramaic, we can proceed to the reconstruction of Jesus' Son of man sayings'.[48] Given that the range of sources used in his survey extends from the Sefire inscription c.750 BCE to possibly as late as 1200 CE, the latest dating for the writings of Christian Palestinian Aramaic, one may conclude that Casey views Aramaic grammar as being

44.   Fitzmyer, *A Wandering Aramean*, p. 147. Fitzmyer notes that בר אנש is used in the third inscription in the same way that אנש is used in the second (Sf II B 16). The context in which בר אנש occurs, in a list of treaty stipulations, is clearly not poetic. *Contra* Fitzmyer, however, it should be noted that diplomatic treaties typically do not reflect 'the ordinary daily usage of the time' (p. 147). Therefore, while the phrase is clearly attested in a non-poetic document, it cannot be said therefore to represent the common vernacular. Further, Fizmyer discounts any difference between the aforementioned Hebraism, which is prefaced by a negative ל א in the text, and the use of the Aramaic phrase in Sefire III. The textual data, however, do not afford one perspective on whether the phrases בר אנש and ל א אש are not idiomatic ways of referencing two slightly different entities.

45.   Sf III 16–17.

46.   Forms are presented in the order presented by Casey, *Aramaic Sources*, pp. 111–121. It is worth noting that Casey himself cites this discussion as illustrative of his assessment of the evidence related to בר (א)נש(א) and the Son of Man problem to date (*Aramaic Approach*, p. 133).

47.   Casey conflates the issues of lexicography and grammatology. In his methodology for rendering Greek into Aramaic, Casey maintains that one must turn to any dialect anywhere for words that are lacking in the provenance under consideration. Even on a lexicographical level, this methodology is flawed due to considerations of external influence and diachrony that must be addressed whenever comparing Semitic dialects and languages – none of which Casey addresses adequately. Carrying that lexicographical misunderstanding into the grammar behind one's translations renders Casey's retroversions speculative at best.

48.   *Aramaic Sources*, p. 111.

almost completely static for nearly two millennia.[49] He maintains this view against massive textual evidence and several major studies to the contrary,[50] and it is this relatively static view of Aramaic that he uses to support his several retroversions of Greek into Aramaic, including ὁ υἱὸς τοῦ ἀνθρώπου.

Despite his manifest view that one can retrovert Greek using 'Aramaic of any period and dialect' to develop a lexical register, Casey does not define the corpus from which his grammar is developed. Representing the morphological variety attested in the literature with the grammatically ambiguous construction (א)שנ(א) רב, Casey reconstructs ὁ υἱὸς τοῦ ἀνθρώπου with similar variety

49. 'Aramaic Idiom and the Son of Man Problem: A Response to Owen and Shepherd', *JSNT* 25 (2002), pp. 3–32 (5): 'Aramaic was a relatively stable language over a period of centuries.' Casey's perspective ignores the plethora of linguistic changes that have occurred and continue to occur in Aramaic as a living language with an ancient history. Indeed, Casey's attempted justification of his dialectal conflation by citing words found in both the Talmud and the Sefire inscription is comparable to saying that an English speaker of the twentieth century would understand an English speaker of the eleventh because they both use the word 'good' (albeit spelt differently).

50. See Fitzmyer, *A Wandering Aramean*, pp. 57–84; Klaus Beyer. *Die aramäischen Texte vom Toten Meer* (Göttingen: Vandenhöck & Ruprecht, 1984), pp. 23–155; Lukaszewski, 'Viable Approach', pp. 12–32, 103–240. Finally, one may refer to perhaps the most comprehensive treatment on the sundry differences between the Aramaic periods and dialects in Franz Rosenthal, *Die aramäistische Forschung* (Leiden: Brill, 1964).

Extant Aramaic texts date as early as the first half of the tenth century BCE (Fitzmyer, *A Wandering Aramean*, p. 60). Prior to the mid-eighth century BCE, Aramaic is likely to have been relatively indistinguishable from Ammonite – thus the ongoing dispute over the language of the Deir 'Alla inscription. From that point until the late seventh century BCE, the language became progressively standardized as it grew in popularity, eventually displacing Akkadian as the diplomatic language of choice. It is only at this point that the textual evidence allows one to assemble more than a patchwork of grammatical phenomena.

This relative standardization of Aramaic lasted to the end of the third century BCE, when Greek replaced Aramaic as the diplomatic language of choice and the various Aramaic speech communities became increasingly Balkanized. The grammatical trends of the dialects thus grew more disparate with time. The resulting differences in speech were increasingly manifest in written communication. At the time of Jesus, five different dialects of Aramaic are attested: Nabataean and Judaean in the west and Hatran, Palmyrene, and Edessene in the east. These represent the major areas of Aramaic usage under the former period which then became the regional centres of their respective dialects. Their grammatical differences are manifest in later dialects, Edessene through later Syriac and Judaean through later Jewish Literary Aramaic.

The third century CE then sees the beginning of the Late Aramaic period, wherein Aramaic shifts from being a native dialect to being increasingly a learned second language in the latter centuries, after being supplanted by Arabic. Arabic gradually influenced even this usage of Aramaic to the point that Kurds and other minorities in the modern Near East speak an Arabicized dialect commonly called Neo-Aramaic.

as בר אנש, בר נש,[51] בר אנשא, and then בר נש again without justifying any of them.[52]

The anachronism of בר נש is worth noting in light of the aleph dropping from the phrase much later than our period.[53] The remaining two reconstructions, however, illustrate Casey's perspective on the coalescence of the emphatic and absolute states. This ultimately represents Casey's understanding of how the construct phrase was formed at the time.[54]

It was this understanding that was addressed by Paul Owen and David Shepherd in 2001.[55] In a carefully nuanced argument, the authors address Casey's assertion that the emphatic and absolute had coalesced in form and, therefore, meaning. In a survey of the Aramaic of 11Q10 (*TgJob*) and 1QGenesis Apocryphon, the authors note several times in Qumran Aramaic when the emphatic has a definitive force.[56] Further, they note that 'the distinction between the absolute, construct and determined forms was maintained' in the Palestinian Targum fragments found in the Cairo Geniza which would have been written much later.[57] Consequently, Casey's ambiguity between the absolute and emphatic forms is concluded to be unsupported.

Casey subsequently responded to Owen and Shepherd in 2002.[58] In his reply, he appears to have noted their textual data but refuses to address the problems of method noted by his opponents. Attacking Owen and Shepherd as approaching the problem too traditionally and rigidly, Casey again cites a series of references to support his position: four from Talmud Yerushalmi (*y.Ber.* 2.8/3, 2.8/10, 2.8/12, *y.Kil.* 9.4/4), two from Talmud Bavli (*b.Suk.* 53a, *b.Sanh.* 107b), two from Targum Neofiti (Gen. 9.6, 40.23), one from the Sefire treaty (3.14-17),

51.   *Aramaic Sources*, p. 138.

52.   In *Aramaic Sources*, see respectively pages 121, 138, 194, and 220.

53.   The aleph in בר אנש(א) did not coalesce into the נ in Western Aramaic until the rabbinic writings (post-200 CE). See Fitzmyer, *A Wandering Aramean*, p. 149.

54.   As will be noted, Casey's grammatical register is, at best, unduly ambiguous, possibly even confused. See Note 47.

55.   'Speaking Up for Qumran, Dalman and the Son of Man: Was *Bar Enasha* a Common term for "Man" in the Time of Jesus?', *JSNT* 81 (2001), pp. 81–122.

56.   The authors further observe Casey's lack of attention to dialectal and diachronic issues ('Speaking Up', pp. 95, n. 61; 105, n. 93).

57.   'Speaking Up', p. 95, n. 60. The statement is made with reference to S. Fassberg, *A Grammar of the Palestinian Targum Fragments from the Cairo Genizah* (HSS, 38; Atlanta: Scholars, 1990), pp. 136–37.

58.   'Response to Owen and Shepherd'.

two from 11Q10 (9.9, 26.2-3), and one from 1QGenesis Apocryphon (21.13). Casey thus concludes that the emphatic has coalesced with the absolute, thus legitimizing his use of either when reconstructing the Son of Man sayings.

Justifying an Aramaic Vorlage

As is plain in the brief review above, scholars have approached the Son of Man problem from a myriad of angles even within the usually narrow confines of philology. Was ὁ υἱὸς τοῦ ἀνθρώπου coined by the early Christians as a titular term? Or was it adopted from the apocalyptic vision of Daniel 7, complete with apocalyptic and messianic trappings? Or was it adopted from the Hebrew of Ezekiel? Was it common first-century idiom in either Judaea or Galilee? If so, was it a direct substitute for the third person, a more general substitute, or a circumlocution for the first person? For such a breadth of alternatives to arise from four Greek words is no less than astounding. Such a multitude of choice arises more from methodological issues than ambiguity in the sources, unfortunately.

In the early twentieth century, J. H. Moulton commented on the sundry studies that appeared at the turn of the century and the sundry problems of method: 'The fascinating pursuit of Aramaic originals may lead to a good percentage of successful guesses; but they are mere guesses still, except when a decided failure in the Greek can be cleared up by an Aramaic which explains the error, and this acts as corroboration.'[59] This statement crystallizes the most fundamental problem with any attempt to assert that ὁ υἱὸς τοῦ ἀνθρώπου is appropriated from a non-Greek language. While the phrase is used in an obvious titular fashion in the Gospels and may therefore seem unusual – even stilted – in certain contexts, it remains grammatically consonant with known Greek of the time. Consequently, the first question that must be answered by any attempt to revert the phrase into any hypothetical source language is: Why must it *not* be Greek in origin? Before any meaning of the phrase can be asserted, one must establish the context from which a meaning is to be distilled.

As noted above, the majority of scholars who have written on this topic have accepted Coccejus' assertion of an Aramaic, rather than Hebrew, origin

---

59. *A Grammar of New Testament Greek.* Vol. 2: *Accidence and word-formation* (Edinburgh: T&T Clark, 1920), p. 16.

of the phrase. However, the only scholar since Coccejus that has taken up the question to the point of writing an explanation is Maurice Casey. To be sure, Coccejus' assertion was made in passing, but Casey's apology reads with dogmatic force. Working under the constraints of a four-language paradigm, he concludes the following:

1. Jesus is not likely to have known Latin.
2. Greek, where used among the Jews, would have been used only by the aristocracy.
3. Hebrew was a literary language, not a living one.
4. Aramaic was the lingua franca of Jews in Israel.

It naturally follows, according to Casey, that Aramaic must be associated with any phrases posited to be authentically from Jesus. This paradigm is flawed on several levels, not least of which is the number of languages involved. In Coele Syria, the textual record bears witness to not four but five languages in use: Latin, Greek, Hebrew, Aramaic, and the pre-Arabic dialects.[60]

Latin was used not only by the Roman imperials, but also by those Jews who worked in their households.[61] Nonetheless, Jonathan Price has noted: 'Those who lived within the administrative confines of the Roman Empire had few regular or sustained contacts with the Latin language.'[62] Greek, on the other hand, had a much stronger influence on Eretz Israel and Coele Syria as a whole. With the conquest of Alexander, Koine Greek became the administrative language throughout the region, effectively supplanting Aramaic for cross-border trade and any non-parochial purpose. Consequently, the average resident in Coele Syria would have needed to know a not insignificant amount of Greek just to interact with their government, never mind traders.

Nazareth was perhaps five kilometres from Sepphoris and was not a mere

---

60. On the use of Arabic, Ammonite, and Ashdodite in Coele Syria at this time, see Lukaszewski, 'Viable Approach', p. 10, n. 31. See also Chaim Rabin, 'Hebrew and Aramaic in the First Century' in *The Jewish People in the First Century* (ed. Samuel Safrai, et al.; CRINT, 2; Amsterdam: Van Gorcum, 1975), pp. 1010–11.

61. Jonathan J. Price, 'The Jews and the Latin Language in the Roman Empire' in *Jews and Gentiles in the Holy Land* (ed. Menachem Mor et al.; Jerusalem: Yad Ben-Zvi Press, 2003), pp. 165–67.

62. Price, 'The Jews and the Latin Language', p. 165.

satellite village, but a significant thoroughfare for trade. The two formed the most direct trade route between the port at Ptolemais and the central city of Scythopolis and the south. It is therefore increasingly likely that its inhabitants would need to have more than a passing knowledge of Greek.[63] As this knowledge seems particularly strong in Jerusalem,[64] the need for familiarity increases due to trade in both directions. Consequently, the likelihood of Jesus being conversant with and even teaching in Greek is quite high. As Greenfield noted, '[T]here were surely those, even in the rural areas, who could speak Greek freely, just as there were many natives who lived in urban areas who could speak only Aramaic or Hebrew or perhaps in the South, an Arabic dialect.'[65]

On the use of Hebrew, Casey's position is simply untenable in light of the textual evidence. The documentary record shows that Hebrew stayed in use for writing throughout the Hellenistic Period. Further analysis, however, also shows that Hebrew never ceased to be spoken in Judaea from the Exile to the Mishnaic period.[66] Given the aforementioned effects of trade routes and the effect of pilgrimages by conservative Jewish parents such as Mary and Joseph, one cannot rule out a significant level of Hebrew knowledge in Galilee, as well.

As Aramaic is a common point of assent, the place of the pre-Arabic dialects must also be considered for the sake of completeness. Eretz Israel largely

---

63. The route from Sepphoris to Scythopolis via Esdrelon contains several milestones, thus indicating that the route was relied upon significantly and was not the equivalent of a country backroad.

64. Cf. Gerard Mussies, 'Greek in Palestine and the Diaspora' in *The Jewish People in the First Century*, pp. 1040–106; Jonas Greenfield, 'The Languages of Palestine, 200 BCE–200 CE' in *Jewish Languages: Theme and Variations* (ed. H. H. Paper; Cambridge, MA: Association for Jewish Studies, 1978), p. 150; Stanley Porter, 'Did Jesus Ever Teach in Greek?', *Tyndale Bulletin* 44(2) (1993), pp. 199–235; Jan N. Sevenster, *Do You Know Greek? How Much Greek Could the First Jewish Christians Have Known?* (NovTSup 19; Leiden: Brill, 1968).

65. Greenfield, 'Languages', p. 145.

66. Cf. Gary Rendsburg, *Diglossia in Ancient Hebrew* (New Haven, CT: American Oriental Society, 1990); See also Greenfield, 'Languages', p. 151 and Rabin, 'Hebrew and Aramaic', pp. 1007–39. For the Hebrew of Ben Sira as representing a diachronic development between Late Biblical Hebrew and Mishnaic Hebrew, see Avi Hurvitz, 'The Linguistic Status of Ben Sira as a Link between Biblical and Mishnaic Hebrew: Lexicographical Aspects' in *The Hebrew of the Dead Sea Scrolls and Ben Sira* (ed. T. Muraoka and J. F. Elwolde; STDJ 26; Leiden: Brill, 1997), pp. 72–86.

derived its commerce from traders travelling from Egypt and Arabia to India or the northern regions of the empire, and vice versa. Several of the pre-Arabic dialects are therefore attested in Eretz Israel at this time, including Thamudic in the Transjordan.[67] There are also several Arabic names among the Greek and Latin inscriptions found in south-east Syria and Transjordan.[68]

Consequently, when seeking foreign sources to a Greek phrase, one is faced with several candidates. The necessary way forward, as Moulton noted, is that of negative proofs. Given the aforementioned language candidates, any attempt to unearth the Aramaic behind ὁ υἱὸς τοῦ ἀνθρώπου must first justify why an Aramaic source – as opposed to Hebrew or Greek – is necessary. One consequently needs a grammatical touchstone against which to test the phrase.

A touchstone traditionally used to quantify the 'correctness' of a Greek phrase is classical Attic. The trouble with doing so is that the Attic in question predates the time of Jesus by 500 years. Five centuries before the date of this article marks the beginning of the Elizabethan period in English literature – a period coinciding with the English Renaissance.[69] One of the religious highlights of that time is Saint Thomas More's *Dialogue of Comfort against Tribulation* (written 1534). In the 1951 republication of More's work, the editor notes that major redaction was necessary to render the work's language to be 'more like that of today'. Consequently, it would be widely recognized as absurd to try to judge modern English usage by a grammar deduced from a text of that era.[70]

---

67.   Thamudic belongs to the proto-Arabian subgroup and is written in a script that comes from the Arabian Peninsula. The presence of the dialect in the Transjordan suggests migration, presumably by traders.

68.   Rabin, 'Hebrew and Aramaic', pp. 1009–10.

69.   Ellen Crofts, *Chapters in the History of English Literature: From 1509 to the Close of the Elizabethan Period* (London: Rivingtons, 1884).

70.   The note reads: 'The first plan was to change only the spelling. It soon became evident that the punctuation would have to be changed to follow present usage. The longest sentences were then broken up into two or three, and certain others were rearranged into a word order more like that of today' [see the Project Gutenburg version of the work at www.gutenberg.org/files/17075/17075-8.txt (viewed 20 July 2009)]. The situation does not improve if one moves forward by a century, to the King James Version of the Bible in 1611, or even two centuries (300 years ago), to the publication of Defoe's *Robinson Crusoe* in 1719. Descriptions of ancient languages as static – even relatively so – are as groundless as any assertion of the same about English or any other modern language (*Contra* Casey, 'Response to Owen and Shepherd', p. 5).

Consequently, one must try to use a grammar of a more relevant timeframe and provenance. This pursuit, however, leads to several Greek grammars that are distilled from the New Testament. The most recent of these in English was published nearly 50 years ago; the most recent in German is 30 years old; none has been distilled comprehensively. Given these dated and limited treatments, one can say little authoritatively about the Greek aspects of our phrase except to say that it is consonant with the basic rules of Greek grammar. A search through the New Testament reveals that the structure is quite common.[71] The problem with the phrase thus becomes one of context and the religious meaning intended.

As a consequence of this lacklustre sourcing of Greek, philological studies on the Semitic background to the present Greek phrase are forced to assume an origin such as they endeavour to uncover. This is true regardless of whether one attempts to revert the phrase to Aramaic or Hebrew. If (as Casey states) the phrase is not 'natural Greek', why must it be 'natural' Aramaic?[72]

The expression must be demonstrated to be dissonant in relation to the bulk of Greek usage at the time.[73] Once shown to be discordant with Greek, a scientific approach would require analysing the phrase through the known grammatical phenomena and, if possible, grammars of the other languages in use in the same region and time. For ὁ υἱὸς τοῦ ἀνθρώπου, this means considering the Aramaic, Hebrew and pre-Arabic evidence.

In doing so, however, one must first consider translation technique in

71.   Outside the Gospels and Acts, Revelation tops the frequency list for occurrences of the structure article-noun-article-noun (genitive) in which the genitive modifies or otherwise relates directly to the preceding noun. It contains 219 such occurrences. However, the frequency cannot be said to relate to its style. Romans has 91, Hebrews 62, 1 Corinthians 60, 2 Corinthians 57, 1 John 31, and Galatians 30. James, an epistle clearly written by a bilingual author with high Greek skills, has the construction only 13 times. It is worth noting that none of this data was available in the grammars. Rather, it is distilled from my work incorporated in the *Lexham Syntactic Greek New Testament* (Bellingham, WA: Logos Research Systems, n.d.).

72.   Casey notes: 'It is widely agreed that [ὁ υἱὸς τοῦ ἀνθρώπου] is not natural Greek, and that it represents some form of the Aramaic (א)שנ(א) בר' ('Response to Owen and Shepherd', 3). As Moulton's comment on this subject implies, however, it is agreed so widely because it is so widely assumed (*A Grammar of New Testament Greek*, vol. 2, p. 16). In fact, the philological evidence for this point of the debate has never been developed sufficiently to support agreement much beyond assumption. See also Lindars, *Jesus Son of Man*, p. 17.

73.   To ascertain this, a bell curve approach works best to classify superior Greek and inferior Greek relative to the form and syntax employed by the majority of language users.

antiquity. In the literature surveyed above, the only scholar again who has taken up the matter of translation technique is Maurice Casey. Unfortunately, Casey consistently relies on translation studies that analyse modern languages and then extrapolates from those studies to address the problem of retroversion, summarizing the Septuagint's translation techniques only in terms of overliteral translation to the point of transliteration.[74] This does not do justice to the vast array of translation techniques manifest in the Septuagint and further anachronistically interjects modern language issues into a strange milieu. Ancient translations are known to have ranged from the very literal (so the LXX Pentateuch) to the very fluid (the rendering of Ben Sira from Hebrew).[75] At most, translators in antiquity are thought to have used a primitive glossary; there is no concrete evidence for the use of dictionaries or word lists.[76] The literalness of the translation in the first books of the LXX is recognized as not indicative of highly developed translation techniques. Rather, as Olofsson and others have noted, it indicates reverence for the text.[77] Consequently, the literalness of any retroversion of ὁ υἱὸς τοῦ ἀνθρώπου into Aramaic needs to be justified by the level of authority accorded to the text and the strictness required.

Historically, Hebrew has been viewed as a second-string source for the phrase – even when understood to be still in use colloquially during Jesus' time. The known Hebrew speech centres are located in Judaea.[78] The understanding follows that, because Jesus came from Galilee, he would have been conversant in Aramaic alone, not Hebrew. Therefore, if the Son of Man sayings are to relate back to Jesus, they must originate from his mother tongue, Galilean Aramaic.

---

74.   Casey, *Aramaic Sources*, pp. 93–98.
75.   Cf. Benjamin G. Wright, *No Small Difference: Sirach's Relationship to its Hebrew Parent Text* (SBLSCS 26; Atlanta: Scholars Press, 1989), p. 26; Erik W. Larson, The Translation of Enoch: From Aramaic into Greek (unpublished doctoral dissertation; New York University, 1995); Vincent T. M. Skemp, *The Vulgate of Tobit Compared with Other Ancient Witnesses* (SBLDS 180; Atlanta: Scholars Press, 2000); Étienne Nodet, 'Jewish Features in the "Slavonic" *War* of Josephus' (paper presented at the annual meeting of the SBL, Nashville, TN, 21 November 2000), p. 26.
76.   Staffan Olofsson, *The LXX Version: A Guide to the Translation Technique of the Septuagint* (Stockholm: Almqvist & Wiksell, 1992), p. 7.
77.   Olofsson, *The LXX Version*, pp. 33–34. For more on the literalness of translation as correlative to the authority of the text, see Lukaszewski, 'Viable Approach', pp. 72–75.
78.   Greenfield, 'Languages of Palestine', pp. 145–50.

This, however, underscores a second assumption necessary for retroverting the phrase to Galilean Aramaic: a *Sitz im Leben* of Galilee. Two dynamics of the problem mitigate against this influence, however.

First, if one accepts the Son of Man phrases as authentic, one may also accept Jesus' quotations from the Old Testament as authentic and statically handed down as part of the Jesus tradition. This being the case, Jesus is then seen to be quite conversant with Hebrew, preferring it over any Aramaic paraphrase. When combined with the Son of Man sayings in Ezekiel, there is both a religious and linguistic framework on which to argue for a Hebrew background.

Second, while Jesus spent a significant amount of his ministry in Galilee, his last days and the earliest years of the post-resurrection Christian community were based in Judaea. Consequently, even if the phrase comes from Galilee, it was formalized in Judaea and was subjected to linguistic pressure from the speakers there.[79]

Consequently, one cannot rule Hebrew out of the linguistic milieu behind the Son of Man sayings.[80] Rather, a scientific enquiry into the linguistic origins and possible nature of the saying must reason from the grammatical practices manifest diachronically in the texts from the Dead Sea: Qumran, Masada, Wadi Murabbaʿat, Naḥal Ḥever, Naḥal Ṣeʾelim, and Naḥal Mišmar.[81] The phrase 'Son of Man' is heretofore unknown from those corpora and such a study is outside the realm of this discussion. But there is a need for an assessment based on the grammar (especially the construct phrases) therein attested, to provide the scientific underpinning of any alleged Aramaic forerunner to ὁ υἱὸς τοῦ ἀνθρώπου.

A similar study is necessary with respect to the pre-Arabic dialects manifest in Judaea and the Transjordan. Again, attestation of the precise phrase 'Son of

---

79. For this reason, attempts at reconstructing a Galilean form of the phrase appear unnecessary and may be misguided.

80. The fact that Babatha's archive does not include Hebrew texts should not be misconstrued as a comprehensive reflection of the linguistic milieu of the region. See Lukaszewski, 'Viable Approach', p. 8, n. 25.

81. For a sketch of Hebrew as found in the scrolls from the Dead Sea, see T. Muraoka. 'Hebrew' in *Encyclopedia of the Dead Sea Scrolls* (ed. Lawrence H. Schiffman and James C. VanderKam; Oxford: Oxford University Press, 2000), pp. 340–45. See also E. Y. Kutscher, *The Language and Linguistic Background of the Isaiah Scroll (1Q Isaa)* (STDJ 6; Leiden: Brill, 1974), pp. 23–30.

Man' is not necessary as much as the morphological and syntactic dynamics of the attested genitival expressions. An awareness of genitival expressions in other Semitic languages contributes to the degree to which one can attribute the phrase to one of them, none of them, or all of them.

After excluding the phrase from Greek and justifying its origin as being particular to the Aramaic of the time, it is necessary to justify one's chosen morphology. As noted above, studies as recent as 1965 showed an unnecessary reliance on Jewish Palestinian Aramaic and sources well outside the period of the earliest Christians.[82] Again in 1979, Fitzmyer drew from a text of the eighth century BCE to illustrate the earliest occurrence of the phrase in Old Aramaic.[83] While the latter is helpful for reasons of historicity, such an instance does not necessarily reflect the way a similar, diplomatic text would have been worded 800 years on, never mind the way a religious text would have been phrased. Rather, one must restrict one's corpus to the closest dialects possible and as close as possible to the same or similar genres.[84]

As Fitzmyer has noted, the time of Jesus and the earliest Christians is in the period of Middle Aramaic, a period from about 200 BCE to about 200 CE. These dates are certainly not firm,[85] but the relevance of the texts even within that range, never mind outside it, varies considerably. The texts from Coele Syria with provenance closest to the earliest attested post-resurrection communities are of three kinds: texts from Qumran, the Bar Kokhba letters, and the epigraphic material. Obviously, accepting the post-resurrection Church as the approximate centre, the relevance of each text is in direct correlation to its proximity in terms of date, geography and genre. The nature of the epigraphic material renders it unsuitable for the present problem except to clarify how

---

82.   Vermes, 'Use', pp. 310–30.

83.   Fitzmyer, *A Wandering Aramean*, p. 147.

84.   For this reason, the Aramaic from 11Q10 is not as relevant to the present problem as it may seem. There is no indication that such a form as that evinced in 11Q10 26.3 (בר אנש) was the only way that the phrase could be constructed.

85.   Fitzmyer, *A Wandering Aramean*, p. 77, n. 32. It is worth noting that the natural start for Middle Aramaic is around 300 BCE, with the conquest of Alexander the Great. However, as Fitzmyer here notes, the Aramaic of Daniel suggests a degree of persistence in the older form called Biblical Aramaic. The degree to which this linguistic conservatism is a forerunner of the Atticising school of the second century CE is unclear.

fluid the linguistic environment was.[86] The Bar Kokhba letters appear around 60 years later than the source material for the Son of Man sayings, and after the revolt of 66 and the subsequent destruction of the temple in 70 as well as during the upheaval of the Bar Kokhba rebellion. Where it contradicts earlier material, therefore, the relationship of that evidence to the earlier texts must be clarified before it can be applied to the present problem. Consequently, to use the corpus closest in provenance to the earliest post-resurrection Christian communities without equivocations one necessarily turns to Qumran Aramaic.

Whereas the Bar Kokhba material is well outside the period in which the Son of Man sayings came to be used among Christians, Qumran Aramaic existed in parallel. The earliest dating given to any of the Aramaic texts from Qumran is the first half of the second century BCE. The terminus for the community as 68 CE, however, closely parallels the writing of the earliest Gospels. Consequently, the role of Qumran Aramaic as the primary source for any philological enquiry about Aramaic and the New Testament is beyond dispute. The question of the Aramaic behind ὁ υἱὸς τοῦ ἀνθρώπου thus moves from a concern about the genitival expression according to an allegedly homogeneous Aramaic, or even the more precise Middle Aramaic, to the construct phrase in Qumran Aramaic specifically.

'Natural' Aramaic

As with Biblical Aramaic, the Aramaic from Qumran evinces more than one way to form the construct relationship. Where Biblical Aramaic reflects three different ways,[87] however, Qumran Aramaic (QA) manifests up to seven.[88] A scientific approach to the problem must justify its choice of form then, otherwise

---

86. One of the primary ways the presence of Judaea-based Arabians are known to us is through the names included in this material.

87. F. Rosenthal, *A Grammar of Biblical Aramaic* (Wiesbaden: Harassowitz, 1995), p. 29 (§48).

88. Lukaszewski, 'Viable Approach', pp. 199–201 (§9.1.2.2). This is not at all unusual. T. Muraoka and B. Porten find six different forms of the construct phrase in the Elephantine Papyri (*A Grammar of Egyptian Aramaic* [Leiden: Brill, 2nd edn, 2003], p. 216 [§60*b*]). F. Schulthess finds four ways in the Christian Palestinian Aramaic corpus from centuries later than our period (*Grammatik des Christlich-Palästinischen Aramäisch* [Hildesheim: Olms, 1965], pp. 81–82 [§157]).

the debate lapses unnecessarily into generalizations such as בַר (אֱ)נָשׁ(אֱ),
which do little to further the discussion beyond a lexemic level.

The most definitive conclusion from that reconstruction is the use of the
construct for the *nomen regens*, but this is an assumption given the lack of
pointing for the word בַר. In fact, not all attested forms of the construct in QA
have a *nomen regens* in the construct state, as the prevailing reconstructions
of Dalman, Vermes, and Casey suggest. Rather, 3.5 per cent of the construct
phrases from Qumran use the absolute state for the *nomen regens*.[89] When
retroverting a phrase that accounts for even less than that among the articulated
genitival relationships of the New Testament,[90] that is not an insignificant
amount.

The following constructions reflect the ways the construct relationship is
expressed in the Aramaic documents from Qumran:[91]

1. *construct + emphatic* (שְׂעַר יֹמְמָא 4Q209 7 2.5; לְבַב נוּנָא 4Q197 4 1.12)
2. *construct + absolute* (אֵל עֶלְיוֹן 1QapGen 22.21; בַר עֶלְיוֹן 4Q246 2.1)[92]
3. *emphatic + emphatic* (מָרֵה שְׁמַיָּא 1QapGen 22.21)[93]
4. *absolute + relative particle + absolute* (עָרְקָא דְמַסָּן 1QapGen 22.21)
5. *construct + relative particle + absolute* (דְּבַר דִּי עָן 4Q197 4 3.11, 4Q205
   2 1.26)

---

89. Lukaszewski, 'Viable Approach', p. 200, n. 32.

90. The phrase ὁ υἱὸς τοῦ ἀνθρώπου occurs 84 times among the 6,847 articulated
genitival noun relationships attested in the Gospels and Acts (i.e., 1.23 per cent).

91. For a fuller discussion on the construct phrase in Qumran Aramaic, see Lukaszewski,
'Viable Approach', pp. 199–201. For confidence markers relative to any passage here cited,
see the chrestomathy in Lukaszewski, 'Viable Approach', pp. 241–412.

The data presented here is based on readings taken from high-resolution photographs in
consultation with the relevant *editio princeps*. These readings were then verified against the
texts themselves, as necessary, in a research visit to Jerusalem undertaken in 2002. Thanks
again are due to the Russell Trust Foundation, Emanuel Tov and Weston Fields of the Dead
Sea Scrolls Foundation, and Hava Katz of the Israel Antiquities Authority for being supportive
of that research.

92. The Aramaic of the Targum of Job is necessarily questionable on grounds of genre,
dating and issues of linguistic milieu (i.e. the Aramaic–Hebrew interplay). However, 11Q10
26.3 does offer בַר אֱנָשׁ for consideration.

93. There is the possibility that the *nomen rectum* of this phrase should rather be understood to function adjectivally – so *heavenly lord*. However, it is more commonly rendered *the
Lord of the Heavens*.

6. *emphatic + relative particle + emphatic* (ימא רבא דן די מלחא 1QapGen
21.16)

7. *construct with proleptic suffix + relative particle + absolute* (ברה די אל
4Q246 2.1)[94]

To bring these grammatical constructions into the present context, a retroversion of ὁ υἱὸς τοῦ ἀνθρώπου into Qumran Aramaic can be one of the
following, respectively:[95]

1.   בר אנשא

2.   בר אנש

3.   ברא אנשא

4.   בר די אנש

5.   בר די אנש

6.   ברא די אנשא

7.   ברה די אנש

Contrary to the forms espoused by Vermes and as Fitzmyer has previously
noted, the initial aleph of אנש has not yet disappeared in Qumran Aramaic.
The only exception to this is the plural absolute of the lexeme, נשין (1QapGen
20.7; 4Q201 3.14; 4Q202 2.18).[96]

As noted above, the matter of the definiteness of the emphatic form has
recently been a matter of debate.[97] The definiteness of the emphatic form within
the construct phrase, however, is a slightly different matter. As shown in the

94.   It is worth noting that, while unlikely, this may be an emphatic *nomen regens*. In
Qumran Aramaic aleph is the primary indicator of the emphatic state but has not completely
replaced *he*. See Lukaszewski, 'Viable Approach', pp. 109–110; H. H. Rowley, 'Notes on the
Aramaic of the Genesis Apocryphon' in *Hebrew and Semitic Studies Presented to Godfrey
Rolles Driver* (ed. D. W. Thomas and W. D. McHardy; Oxford: Clarendon Press, 1963), p. 119.
He, however, remains the sole indicator of the third masculine singular pronominal suffix
[Lukaszewski, 'Viable Approach', pp. 155–56]. See, e.g. form number 2.

95.   The present retroversions use the same lexemes as used in earlier cognates of the
form in Daniel 7.13 and the third Sefire inscription. The consistency with which אנש is used
where the phrase 'Son of Man' occurs in the whole of Aramaic literature argues against any
form of גבר.

96.   Other examples are in the most poorly preserved columns of the Genesis Apocryphon:
1QapGen 6.8 and 6.10.

97.   Owen and Shepherd, 'Speaking Up'; Casey, 'Response to Owen and Shepherd'.

passages cited above, the emphatic *nomen rectum* in QA does not always reflect a definite connotation but may reflect indefiniteness.[98] As a consequence, an emphatic *nomen rectum* is not necessary for a reconstruction. The consequence of this is considerable for the syntactic force of any hypothetical construct phrase said to represent ὁ υἱὸς τοῦ ἀνθρώπου in the Aramaic of Jesus' time. Any definiteness would be implied by the speaker and inferred by the hearer, but would not necessarily be manifest in the grammar of the language.

The choice of form is made even more difficult by the presence of two different construct forms in synonymous relationship in 4Q246 2.1: 'יקרונה ברה די אל יתאמר ובר עליון' *The son of God will be proclaimed and the son of the Most High will be named.*[99] The use of both options (Nos. 2 and 7) in parallel suggests that the second and seventh options of the above list were understood as stylistically equal.[100] The apocalyptic nature of this context naturally supports the use of either option in similar terms and in addition to the fifth form, found in the Enochic literature (4Q205).

Which of the above forms are most likely to be correct thus remains a matter for discussion. The first and second options have received the greatest support in studies to date. They are the most frequently attested in the QA corpus.[101]

---

98.   Of the emphatic forms cited, the only one about which one can speak with certainty of a definite *nomen rectum* is 1QapGen 22.21: מרה שמיא *the Lord of the heavens*. Also included in this pattern is יד ימא *the shore of the sea* in 1Qap Gen 21.16. At other times, however, the same form is of questionable definiteness. The phrase לבב נונא in 4Q197 4 1.12 may be read as *the heart of a fish* or *the heart of the fish*, either works equally well in context. Similarly, the aforementioned construct phrase in 1QapGen 21.16 begins a chain of construct phrases that contains ימא רבא דן די מלחא *this great sea of salt*. The ambiguity of the emphatic *nomen rectum* and the fact that this construction is a modified form of the ancient name for the Dead Sea justifies several alternative translations: *this Great Sea of Salt* or, more commonly, *this Great Salt Sea*. Additionally, one is unclear about whether עליון in 4Q246 2.1 should be understood as a reverential superlative-degree combination (i.e. *the son of the Most High*) or as a technical reference to ʿElyon as a proper noun synonymous with God (i.e. *the son of Elyon*). The evidence thus suggests that definiteness was clearly present in cases where the emphatic occurs as a *nomen rectum*, but it may not *always* be present.

99.   Translation mine. For the implications of this passage relative to the New Testament, see Fitzmyer, *A Wandering Aramean*, pp. 102–107.

100.   All of the options for expressing the genitival relationship would be syntactically equivalent. Their exact usage with regard to genre and other literary concerns, however, suggests that certain forms would be more common in certain circumstances.

101.   Nearly 96 per cent of the construct phrases in Qumran Aramaic do not use the relative particle. See Lukaszewski, 'Viable Approach', p. 200 (§9.1.2.2).

The first form is also supported as an option by Fitzmyer's observation that the earliest occurrence of a phrase 'Son of Man' in the Aramaic literature is in the third inscription from Sefire. It is then echoed in the Aramaic of Dan. 7.13.

The diachrony of linguistic development, however, suggests that the other options are very much in use. As Vermes observes, later dialects from the region use the relative particle exclusively and especially when rendering the phrase ὁ υἱὸς τοῦ ἀνθρώπου into either Syriac or Christian Palestinian Aramaic. For the former, this is consonant with the strong use of די outside Eretz Israel between the tenth and sixth centuries BCE.[102]

Consequently, after one has legitimized the need for retroverting ὁ υἱὸς τοῦ ἀνθρώπου into Aramaic, one is left with three possibilities for an apocalyptic setting. The presence of several forms of the construct phrase in the non-apocalyptic Genesis Apocryphon and Tobit, however, leaves the available formations open to the seven listed above. Currency of one form over another may be argued by both frequency and dating, but the collection of the documents together at Qumran suggests that each was as intelligible as the other to the community.

In conclusion, investigation into the linguistic origins and consequent meaning or meanings of the phrase ὁ υἱὸς τοῦ ἀνθρώπου requires the following steps:

1. Development of a grammatical touchstone of Hellenistic Greek syntax that is *au courant* with current studies and that differentiates it from Attic while also being aware of the potential for geographic differences in style.
2. Recognition that the position that odd Greek equates to non-Greek origins is an assumption that does not hold up all of the time. Therefore, ὁ υἱὸς τοῦ ἀνθρώπου could simply be a unique phrase that does not have non-Greek roots. While this argument seems weak, it is presumptuous to dismiss it out of hand.

---

102. W. Randall Garr, *Dialect Geography of Syria-Palestine: 1000–586 BCE* (Winona Lake, IN: Eisenbrauns, 2004), pp. 85–87. This is not to suggest the preferred formation of the construct phrase in these regions. Rather, the ancient prevalence of the relative particle די in areas outside Eretz Israel suggests that its adoption as a matter of style would not be as common within the region. The occurrences of the different construct phrase formations in Qumran Aramaic support this suggestion.

3. Recognition that non-Greek origins for ὁ υἱὸς τοῦ ἀνθρώπου could be from one of the three other dialectal collections in use in first-century Eretz Israel: Hebrew, Aramaic, and the pre-Arabic dialects. We do not have enough of the last to forge a way forward, so the most promising way forward at present is Hebrew and Aramaic. However, because ὁ υἱὸς τοῦ ἀνθρώπου is non-Greek does not make it either; it simply becomes a Semitism.[103]

4. Establishment of a grammatical touchstone of Hebrew syntax against which one can say that Son of Man fits with Hebrew or does not. We do not currently have a grammar of first-century Judaean Hebrew. Rather, the closest we can come is first century BCE.[104] Given a lack of better resources, one can use this, but it would be better to map a trajectory of Hebrew's syntactic development from the sectarian Qumran Scrolls, through what there is among the Bar Kokhba letters, and finish with the Mishnah. This would thus give a spectrum against which to judge the possible development of the phrase.

5. If ὁ υἱὸς τοῦ ἀνθρώπου is thought to be not Greek and not Hebrew, this does not necessarily mean that it comes from Aramaic. Rather, one must use a grammatical touchstone of Aramaic syntax against which one can say that ὁ υἱὸς τοῦ ἀνθρώπου fits with Aramaic or does not. It is widely recognised that the written dialect closest to that of the early church is Qumran Aramaic. Therefore, such a touchstone has been established to a certain extent.[105]

Ultimately, just because the phrase does not fit with one language does not mean it belongs to another. The way forward is to use negative proofs to show where it is not likely to belong.

After proceeding through these steps, one is in a position to critically evaluate the phrase ὁ υἱὸς τοῦ ἀνθρώπου against the wider linguistic milieu. If all options are exhausted and ὁ υἱὸς τοῦ ἀνθρώπου resonates rightly with no

---

103.   On this point we are indebted to the excellent work of Max Wilcox who has continued to work in this area since his thesis under Matthew Black on Semitisms in Acts.

104.   Cf. Elisha Qimron, *The Hebrew of the Dead Sea Scrolls* (HSS 29; Atlanta: Scholars Press, 1986).

105.   See this author's *Viable Approach*.

known language, one must say that we cannot know more at the present time, pending further research into the syntax of the languages involved. Until the linguistic data has been mined to this extent, however, no further clarification seems possible with respect to a form, never mind definition, of an Aramaic Son of Man.

2

PROBLEMS WITH CASEY'S 'SOLUTION'

Paul L. Owen

In scholarly discussion of the 'son of man' problem, there can be no doubt as to the weight of the contributions of Maurice Casey.[1] Through a series of articles and monographs, he has carefully advanced a range of evidence for his views, drawn from fields such as Aramaic research, apocalyptic literature, historical Jesus studies, translation theory and linguistics. Casey has robustly argued for a rather simple hypothesis: the actual Aramaic expression בר אנשא lying behind the gospels expression 'son of man', which appears as a title for Jesus in the Greek gospels, was simply an ordinary term for 'man'. Hence, by way of implication, the only 'son of man' sayings in the gospels which can be accepted as likely authentic must be drawn from a pool of sayings which are capable of being understood in generic terms – applicable to Jesus, but also to a broader group of people. In this chapter, I will interact with some of his most recent works in this area,[2] and hope thereby to carry the argument forward in several important respects.

---

1. The most thorough history of the 'son of man' discussion thus far must surely be attributed to Mogens Müller, *The Expression 'Son of Man' and the Development of Christology: A History of Interpretation* (London: Equinox Publishing, 2008).

2. The two works which will be the focus of discussion here are: Maurice Casey, 'Aramaic Idiom and the Son of Man Problem: A Response to Owen and Shepherd', *JSNT* 25 (2002), pp. 3–32; and *The Solution to the 'Son of Man' Problem* (London: T&T Clark, 2007).

The development of the Aramaic language

One of the central pillars in Casey's defence of his proposals in his 2002 *JSNT* article, is the appeal to the stability of the Aramaic language (pp. 5–12). If Aramaic is shown to be a relatively stable language, then this will justify his utilization of texts ranging over a period of around a thousand years to establish the probable speech patterns of Jesus in first-century Judea. Casey tells us: 'Aramaic was a relatively stable language over a period of centuries. It was especially stable after being spread in standard form by the Persian bureaucracy. Even before this, it had features that are found later in the Talmuds and in Jewish midrashim' (p. 5). But the evidence that Casey then compiles in support of this observation amounts to an extended exercise in obfuscation, for they involve an appeal to examples that no scholar would think of contesting. For example, the Sefire inscriptions 'contain words' found in later midrash and Talmud (p. 5). And 'many words' which appear in the Qumran texts also show up in the Talmuds (p. 6). Just as trivial is the observation that: 'Syntactic features common for centuries include the narrative use of the participle' (p. 6). How any of these mundane linguistic notes advance the current discussion is difficult to understand.

The argument of Owen and Shepherd[3] certainly did not require the accept-ance of complete instability in all features of Aramaic syntax and vocabulary. Obviously, in any given language, some things will necessarily remain constant through an extended period of time. The fact that certain lexical and syntactic items can be traced through different bodies of Aramaic texts over several centuries is exactly what one would expect of any language. By focusing on such minutiae, Casey manages to ignore the central issues in the discussion, which he chose to side-step. Namely: (1) The emphatic state appears to have remained in force in Western Aramaic well beyond the time of Jesus, which undermines the idea that Jesus' own use of the emphatic state could not have borne a definite and specified meaning with an individual referent. (2) The generic use of the emphatic singular אנשא בר for 'man' is nowhere attested in Aramaic texts predating or contemporary with the time of Jesus, and even the use of the singular absolute אנש בר is not clearly attested anywhere in such

---

3. Paul Owen and David Shepherd, 'Speaking Up for Qumran, Dalman and the Son of Man: Was *Bar Enasha* a Common Term for "Man" in the Time of Jesus?' *JSNT* 81 (2001), pp. 81–122. Referred to below in the body of the text as 'Owen and Shepherd'.

texts with a generic, abstract meaning.[4] It appears but rarely with an indefinite meaning, and always due to some apparent contextual influence. (3) In Aramaic texts close to the time of Jesus, the generic idea is always employed by the use of the plural construction 'the sons of men' (בני אנשא) or simply 'man' (אנשא). Therefore, Jesus, in the expression he employed in the 'son of man' sayings, did not in fact use the most natural idiom for generic statements about human beings.

Why then did he speak of himself so often as 'a son of man' (if employing the absolute בר אנש) or 'the son of man' (if employing the emphatic בר אנשא)? These remain the most likely linguistic explanations for why the expression 'son of man' appears so frequently on the lips of Jesus in the Greek gospels. The most likely answer, which is entirely consistent with the actual Aramaic evidence from Jesus' time period, remains one of the following. Either: (1) Jesus spoke of 'the Son of Man' as a messianic agent of God, and derived this term from Dan. 7.13, though he did not claim to be that agent during his earthly ministry.[5] The post-Easter Church made that identification. (2) Jesus spoke of himself (perhaps employing the indefinite expression in Aramaic) as a 'son of man' and intended his expression as an enigmatic allusion to the language of the vision of Dan. 7.13.[6] Later Christians then turned the expression into a title for Jesus to remove all ambiguity. Or (3) Jesus spoke of 'the Son of Man' as a way of speaking of the figure mentioned in Dan. 7.13, and viewed himself as the present and future fulfilment of that vision.[7]

Casey also appears to miss the methodological point when he insists that Owen and Shepherd hold a 'dogmatic commitment to using only earlier source material' (p. 7). This is by no means the case. The issue is not simply the date of the material, but rather a need to pay careful attention to developments evidenced within the history of the Aramaic language. If it is indeed the case that Western Aramaic retained its determinative force in emphatic nouns even well beyond the time of Jesus, that point is certainly crucial in the present debate

---

4.   As opposed to a concrete meaning, equating to an indefinite pronoun.
5.   This can be referred to as the Bultmann hypothesis. It has been adopted more recently by John J. Collins.
6.   This can be called the Jeremias hypothesis. It has also been adopted by Matthew Black and Richard Bauckham.
7.   This can be called the Dalman hypothesis. It has been defended most recently by Paul Owen and David Shepherd.

about the 'son of man' expression, and should caution scholars in their appeal to later evidence. Likewise, if (as Dalman argued) Middle Aramaic avoided the singular 'son of man' terminology in generic statements (expressing this through plural constructions), whereas the generic usage of the emphatic singular became common only in the later period, such an observation would need to be carefully weighed in the handling of documentary material from the time of Jesus. In other words, in the context of this discussion, the problem *is not a lack of evidence* for how the 'son of man' terminology was used in Jesus' time, which needs to be supplemented by later material; the problem is that there is plenty of evidence from the time of Jesus, and it all runs directly counter to Casey's proposals.

This also goes to demonstrate that Casey's discussions of matters pertaining to dialect (p. 8) and date (p. 9) in Aramaic texts are beside the point. Nobody would contest the fact that the boundaries between the Aramaic dialects and time periods are somewhat fluid, which means that evidence from various sources *can* indeed be fruitfully compared (with due care) in linguistic study. The point which Casey ignores is that when there are demonstrable differences in dialectal usage (such as the case with the use of the emphatic state in Eastern and Western Aramaic), and shifts in terminology over time (such as the much later use of the singular in the emphatic state (בר אנשא) to make generic statements in the Talmuds and Jewish midrash), then those shifts must be accounted for. Again, the issue is not the use of later texts of various dialects to supplement our knowledge of the language of Jesus;[8] it is the use of later texts to impute linguistic usage which is *contradicted* by the sources contemporary to the time in question.

Generic and optional use of the emphatic state

Casey takes Owen and Shepherd to task (pp. 14–18) for their handling of the use of the emphatic state with generic nouns. He has three primary complaints. First, he complains about their 'standard of judgment' (p. 14). Essentially, he grants that they are correct in arguing that 'the absolute state was still in normal

---

8. Casey's examples to this effect (on pp. 10–11) are all therefore interesting, but likewise irrelevant.

use' in the Dead Sea Scrolls (which date near the time of Jesus), but then insists 'I have not however suggested otherwise' (p. 15). It is not clear what he is trying to establish here. Certainly, Owen and Shepherd understand that Casey sees the breakdown between the states as a somewhat gradual process.[9] The issue at stake is simply this. Did the emphatic state retain its determinative force in Aramaic usage during the time of Jesus? After all, we are discussing what Jesus' use of בר אנשא would have meant to an Aramaic speaker, are we not?

Casey has insisted that the breakdown between emphatic and absolute was so pronounced, that it *could not* have been understood to refer to one particular man (*the* son of man, identified by some Jews as the apocalyptic agent of God), but could *only* have borne the generic meaning of 'man'.[10] This is because the term itself simply meant 'man', and the interchangeable relationship of the states was such that no further nuance *could* have been added by the employment of the emphatic state. But if the states were in normal use in the time of Jesus, and determination *was* still being expressed through the emphatic state, then in fact the Greek-speaking church need not be said to have misunderstood the meaning of the expression בר אנשא by rendering it as a proper title for Jesus. It is only if the emphatic state lost its determinative force that one would expect to see בר אנשא appearing at times in generic expressions pertaining to people (which is precisely what we do see, only in later Aramaic texts). This is clearly central to the whole discussion.

Second, Casey criticizes Owen and Shepherd for their over-reliance upon 'existing' (p. 15), 'traditional' (p. 17) and 'antiquated' (p. 18) secondary literature. (Why 'existing' should be a negative qualifier is especially difficult to decipher.) He complains particularly of their repeated citation of the work of such specialists as E. Y. Kutcher, T. Muraoka and B. Porten, S. A. Kaufman, and F. Rosenthal. Since Casey has produced no meaningful scholarship in the area of Aramaic grammar, one is at a loss as to what to make of his somewhat casual dismissal of others who are widely recognized for their particular

---

9.   See Owen and Shepherd, 'Speaking Up', p. 89, n. 36.

10.   'The nature of the idiom is such that this variation *could not* affect the meaning' (Maurice Casey, *Son of Man: The Interpretation and Influence of Daniel 7* [London: SPCK, 1979], p. 228 emphasis added). Casey is adamant that the absolute and emphatic states of בר אנש(א) were already being used by the time of Jesus 'without *any difference* of meaning' (Casey, *Son of Man*, p. 228, emphasis added).

expertise. Casey himself is unable to appeal to any existing body of scholarship in Aramaic studies to counter the established positions Owen and Shepherd documented through citation of the standard literature. He is content merely to offer his own isolated conjectures based on individual examples, as a substitute for the detailed studies of those who have published widely in the field. This is certainly a curious method of argumentation.

Other observations

Casey's reply to Owen and Shepherd contains some other problems, which can be set forth without the need for lengthy discussion.

Problems with the evidence

Casey reduces the argument of Owen and Shepherd to the mundane observation that אנשא בר is not used to make generic statements about people in Middle Aramaic. 'The trouble with this is that the quantity of Aramaic text that survives from this time is too small for such inferences to be valid' (p. 18). But the trouble with Casey's response (as Owen and Shepherd have documented), is that *there are* plenty of generic references to humankind in Middle Aramaic. They just do not employ בר אנשא.[11]

Normal and common

Casey complains that Owen and Shepherd confuse 'normal' and 'common' when discussing בר אנשא (p. 19). But it should be obvious from their discussion that by 'common' they mean 'ordinary', not necessarily 'frequent'. Hence his complaint is a needless rabbit trail.

Qumran evidence

Casey dismisses Owen and Shepherd's discussion of the Qumran terminology with three responses (pp. 20–21). He says that sometimes authors simply chose to use different terminology than בר אנשא. He says that the choice of one expression does not indicate the unwillingness to use another expression. And he says that the usage of one author should not be casually attributed to

---

11. Owen and Shepherd, 'Speaking Up', pp. 104–20 for details.

another author. Hence, the idiomatic expressions employed by the Qumranites do not necessarily tell us much about the speech patterns of Jesus (who spoke Galilean Aramaic). In response, we can only insist that such a neglect of the actual data does not carry the discussion forward. When writers of a given time period consistently employ certain sets of terminology and avoid others, that means something. And to complain about the use of the Dead Sea Scrolls to make generalizations about the language of Jesus, when Casey himself employs *much* later Aramaic texts to that end, is somewhat astonishing.[12]

Inadequate discussions

Casey's discussion of the five examples of בר אוש (pp. 27–30) is quite inadequate. It leaves out the fact that in Dan. 7.13, the expression 'son of man' stands in place of the expected description of an angelic appearance (a 'son of God') in the heavenly court (cf. Dan. 7.10 and 3.25).[13] It ignores the repeated use of the term 'son' in Sefire 3.14-17, which provides the context for understanding the use of the term 'son of man' to describe the death of any *future heir* to the royal throne.[14] His discussion of *1QapGen* 21.13 ignores the distinction between abstract and concrete references. The text anticipates the concrete instance of some particular man attempting to count Abraham's seed. It employs בר אוש, therefore, in a purely indefinite but concrete, and not a generic, abstract sense.[15] Furthermore, the imagined 'counter' is likely described as a 'son of man' because it is the *future descendants* of Abraham who are in view per the context. And his discussion of *11QTgJob* 9.9 and 26.2-3 stumbles on the simple fact that

---

12.   Especially when Casey says in the same article: 'Qumran Aramaic can safely be used in the reconstruction of sayings of Jesus' ('Aramaic Idiom and the Son of Man Sayings', p. 7). And again: 'We must suppose that Jesus spoke Galilean Aramaic, but hardly any Galilean Aramaic of the right period survives. This difficult situation has been quite transformed by the discovery of the Dead Sea Scrolls, which provide us with a large slice of Aramaic vocabulary, and standard syntax, from shortly before the time of Jesus' (*Solution*, p. 117).

13.   Alternatively, 'one like a son of man' may be a way of identifying the humanlike figure with one of the angels (cf. Dan. 8.15; 10.5).

14.   Casey says this 'excludes the death of the king himself, as mentioned in lines 14–15, from voiding the treaty' ('Aramaic Idiom and the Son of Man Sayings', p. 29). As if the king himself was not also a son!

15.   It is true, as Casey points out ('Aramaic Idiom and the Son of Man Sayings', p. 28), that indefinites can also be generic. But it does not follow from this that all indefinites *are* generic. Some indefinites simply refer to a particular person or thing, equivalent to an indefinite pronoun.

these are translations of an underlying Hebrew expression (בֶּן אָדָם), which add nothing to the present debate (beyond the fact that the emphatic בַּר אֲנָשָׁא, which could have been used, is consistently avoided).

General issues of dispute

In this next section of the essay we will look at Casey's contribution to the 'son of man' question from a more general framework. Whereas the specific matters discussed above focused upon his 2002 journal article, the following section will focus upon his 2007 monograph (*The Solution to the 'Son of Man' Problem*). Not only are there serious questions from the standpoint of his appeal to the Aramaic expression, but there are also problems with his hypothesis as a whole, in terms of its overall explanatory power.

The meaning of Daniel 7

One of the claims which underlies Casey's point of view is that Daniel 7 is best understood, not as a reference to a particular person, but as a symbol of the elect people of God.[16] Therefore, any later messianic reading of this apocalyptic vision (such as became common in Christianity) would be contrary to the intent of the passage itself. But this reading of the text is open to serious scrutiny.[17]

Daniel 7 opens with a dream-vision in which four beasts are depicted as exerting consecutive rule upon the people of Israel. Though the historical identity of the beasts is open to question,[18] it is clear that the fourth beast is of a unique character (7.19), and significance (cf. 7.7-8, 19-21). This beast has ten

16.   See Casey, *Solution*, pp. 82–91.
17.   Cf. the lucid discussion of Eugen J. Pentiuc, *Jesus the Messiah in the Hebrew Bible* (New York: Paulist Press, 2006), pp. 52–56, including his intriguing etymological suggestions.
18.   Cf. discussion in Tremper Longman, *Daniel* (Grand Rapids: Zondervan, 1999), pp. 176–86; Louis F. Hartman and Alexander A. Di Lella, *The Book of Daniel* (AB, 23; New York: Doubleday, 1978), pp. 211–14; and John J. Collins, *The Apocalyptic Imagination* (Grand Rapids: Eerdmans, 1998), pp. 85–99. We leave aside here discussions of the date of Daniel. A second-century BCE setting for the final canonical form of Daniel would by no means preclude the shaping and collection of much earlier material stemming from the memoirs and experiences of an historical Jewish exile named Daniel. Neither does the language of Daniel preclude such a possibility. See Zdravko Stefanovic, *The Aramaic of Daniel in the Light of Old Aramaic* (JSOTSup, 129; Sheffield: Sheffield Academic Press, 1992).

horns, representing rulers who implement the authority of the kingdom (7.24). Among the horns sprouts a 'little one', who usurps the authority of 'three of the first horns' (7.8). We are told in the vision that this horn has eyes 'like the eyes of a man', and a boastful mouth (v. 8). This horn, 'made war with the saints and prevailed over them' (7.21). Clearly, the little horn represents an individual opponent of God, whose kingdom is destined to be crushed in the end days (cf. 7.24-26). All of this sets the context for the appearance of God's agent of justice in 7.9-14.

In 7.9-10 the Ancient God takes his seat of judgement (on earth?), attended by his court of countless angels, as 'the books' are opened. Dominion has been taken away from the four beasts (v. 12), and the fourth is now burned in the fire of divine wrath (v. 11). The focus then shifts to an adjacent scene in verses 13-14. Daniel recounts: 'I saw in the night visions, and behold, with the clouds of heaven there came one like a son of man, and he came to the Ancient of Days and was presented before him.' And we are now told, that the kingdom, which was taken from the grip of the little horn, is given to this 'son of man' (v. 14), to the end that 'all peoples, nations, and languages should serve him.' The universal sphere of the little horn's tyranny, which embraced the whole earth (cf. 7.23), is now placed in the hands of this 'son of man'.

The most natural way to read this passage is as a description of a transfer of power from one individual (the little horn), to another (the son of man).[19] There is no overriding reason to reject the natural sense of the passage, in order to constrict the meaning of the vision to the triumph of elect Israel in the end days.[20] It is true that 7.22 speaks of judgement being given 'for the saints of the most high', and 7.27 says that the kingdom is given to 'the people of the saints of the most high'. But if the 'son of man' whom Daniel first sees in 7.13 is in fact an anointed ruler of the people of God (cf. Dan. 9.25-26), the transfer

---

19.   Cf. the discussion of Chrys C. Caragounis, *The Son of Man: Vision and Interpretation* (WUNT, 38; Tübingen: Mohr Siebeck, 1986), pp. 35–81.

20.   That Daniel describes the figure coming 'with the clouds of heaven', and appearing '*like* a son of man', also points to his supernatural and heavenly origin. Such language most likely applies to an angel or some other supernatural being with a human appearance or nature.

of power to his hands would of course include all those for whose cause he advocates.[21]

It is also important to note that only of the 'son of man' is it said that 'all peoples, nations, and languages should *serve him*' (7.14). All 'peoples' would include Israel. Another problem for Casey, which he sidesteps, is that 7.27 shifts to the singular at the end of the verse: '*his* kingdom shall be an everlasting kingdom, and all rulers shall serve and obey *him*' (א לה יפלחון וישתמעון מלכותה מלכות עלם וכל שלטני).[22] This seems like a rather obvious echo of the tribute paid to the son of man in verse 14, which tells us the kingdom to be possessed by Israel will be subject to the authority of another. The eschatological kingdom which the saints will enjoy is most likely the one *given to them* by the son of man.

This suggestion is bolstered by the conceptual links between Daniel 7 and Daniel 9.[23] In both cases, the end days are characterized by the tyranny of an earthly opponent of God.[24] In chapter 7 a 'little' horn wages war (vv. 8, 24), oppresses the righteous (vv. 21, 25), and seeks to 'change the times and the law' (v. 25). In chapter 9 a 'prince' destroys the city of Jerusalem and the sanctuary (v. 26), puts 'an end to sacrifice and offering' (v. 27), and makes the Temple 'desolate' (v. 27). The likelihood that these are descriptions of the same figure

---

21. Casey's discussion of this passage is curious. He spends some ten pages discussing Daniel 7, to the effect that: (1) The parallels between 7.14 and 27 show in an 'absolutely clear' and 'decisive' manner that the son of man in the vision is to be interpreted as the people of Israel (*Solution*, p. 85); and (2) Within the Syrian Christian tradition, some took the son of man as a symbol of the triumph of the children of Israel under the Maccabees, and Jerome's polemic shows that this was also the view of Porphyry (pp. 86-91). There are some fairly obvious replies to this: (1) The parallels within chapter 7 would be expected if the son of man were to share his kingdom with the people of God; (2) All of the Syrian interpreters see the vision as pointing beyond the Maccabees and the children of Israel to Jesus as the true fulfilment (hardly helpful to Casey); and (3) On pp. 7–10 Casey dismissed the Syrian Fathers' understanding of the 'son of man' expression as being of 'limited value', due to their Christian assumptions. Apparently, the Syrian Fathers are trustworthy interpreters of the Bible only when they offer some modest help to Casey's position.

22. My translation. Casey renders the end of 7.27 'all dominions will serve and obey it' (*Solution*, p. 85). This avoids the problem, but appears to be an intentional obscuring of the allusion back to the ruler anticipated in 7.13-14.

23. Cf. André Lacocque, *The Book of Daniel* (trans. by David Pellauer; Atlanta: John Knox, 1979), p. 126.

24. The definitive language of 7.14 and 9.24 makes it clear that in both instances we are dealing with eschatological scenarios.

is bolstered by the fact that chapter 7 places these actions within the time frame of 'a time, times, and half a time' (v. 25), or, most likely, three and a half years.[25] Likewise, in chapter 9 the prince's awful actions are apparently enacted during a three-and-a-half-year period.[26] And both chapters anticipate a divine counterpart to the eschatological tyrant, identifying him as a 'son of man' (7.13), and 'Messiah, the ruler' (9.25) respectively.[27]

Memory of the early church

Casey's position essentially entails the retention of only about a dozen authentic 'son of man' sayings.[28] This means that the majority of the 51 (excluding parallel occurrences) sayings employing this expression are the creations of the early church.[29] Furthermore, in those instances where authentic sayings have been preserved, they were misunderstood from a very early period by the Greek-speaking church, and the originally generic Aramaic expression for 'son of man' was transformed into a messianic title for Jesus.[30] This means that precisely *none* of the son of man sayings of the historical Jesus survived to be incorporated into the Christian gospels with their meaning intact.

There are a number of reasons to call this into question in general terms. First of all, it is methodologically dubious to dismiss the authenticity of most 'son of man' sayings because they cannot be understood in the purely generic sense (applicable to mankind or a group of men) Casey demands. We have seen that the evidence for such generic usage of בר אנשא is entirely absent

---

25.   Cf. discussion in John Goldingay, *Daniel* (WBC, 30; Waco: Word, 1989), p. 181, though he takes a different view.

26.   Three and a half years being half of the seven-year 'week' mentioned in 9.27. Of course this reading of the texts in question is open to serious debate. Nothing here rests upon the accuracy of such details. For discussion see Harold W. Hoehner, *Chronological Aspects of the Life of Christ* (Grand Rapids: Zondervan, 1977), pp. 115–39 and Goldingay, *Daniel*, p. 262.

27.   Of course, one might want to argue that the 'son of man' and 'Messiah, the ruler' in these texts should be linked with historical figures like Judas Maccabeus, Zerubbabel, and/or Joshua the high priest, and Onias III (cf. Goldingay, *Daniel*, pp. 169–70, 261–62). In Christian interpretation both texts have been glossed and applied to Jesus. The point being made here does not depend on any specific understanding of the referents.

28.   See Casey, *Solution*, pp. 116–211.

29.   For the listing of the data, see J. Jeremias, *New Testament Theology. I. The Proclamation of Jesus* (London: SCM Press, 1971), pp. 259–60.

30.   See Casey, *Solution*, pp. 246–73.

from any surviving Middle Aramaic texts, which makes it a rather thin basis of judgement. Second, it requires us to assume that the early church invented the 'son of man' title, put it on the lips of Jesus in the gospel sayings, and then utterly abandoned the expression elsewhere. It does not appear outside the gospels as a designation for the Messiah.[31] If the Greek-speaking church, misunderstanding the literal translation practices of earlier Aramaic-speaking Christians, invented this title for Jesus, then why are the Greek letters of Paul, Peter, James, John and Jude utterly ignorant of this now popular Christological convention? And, third, how is it that such a gap was so quickly created between the memory of the earliest Christians and the penning of the gospels? According to Casey, Jesus *never* spoke exclusively of himself using the 'son of man' expression. Yet in our gospels, all penned within 40–50 years of Jesus' ministry, 'son of man' has become *the* overwhelmingly characteristic and distinctive way in which Jesus chose to speak *exclusively* of himself. Is that credible?[32]

Authenticity of the son of man sayings
Casey's way of framing the matter leads him to dismiss the authenticity of a large number of 'son of man' sayings on questionable grounds. We will discuss some of these examples below.

Mt. 24.27, 30, 37, 39, 44
Casey's argument against the authenticity of this discourse in Matthew 24 amounts to two points. First, the material reflects 'the interests of the early church rather than the preaching of the historical Jesus'.[33] And, second, the sayings in this section which employ the 'son of man' expression reveal the influence of Dan. 7.13.[34] Both assertions beg the question, though. Why should

---

31. With the exception of Acts 7.56 and Rev. 1.13. Both of these being instances of heavenly visions, clearly drawing from the imagery of Dan. 7.13.

32. See the discussion of Larry W. Hurtado, *Lord Jesus Christ: Devotion to Jesus in Earliest Christianity* (Grand Rapids: Eerdmans, 2003), pp. 303–306 and James D. G. Dunn, *Jesus Remembered* (Grand Rapids: Eerdmans, 2003), pp. 759–61.

33. Casey, *Solution*, p. 212.

34. Casey, *Solution*, pp. 215, 216, 219, 220.

we just assume that Jesus did not predict an apocalyptic scenario?[35] And why was the early church so capable of applying Dan. 7.13 to Jesus in the context of eschatology, but we are to believe Jesus himself was incapable of drawing such connections?[36]

There are at least three points to be made in favour of the general authenticity of this material. First, the occurrence of the 'son of man' expression, in conjunction with 'end of the world' subject matter, is characteristic of Jesus according to Mark (13.26), Q (Mt. 24.27//Lk. 24), and L (Lk. 17.22, 30). Second, within this block of material there is the potentially embarrassing claim that the Son is ignorant of the timing of the end (Mt. 24.36). Would the early church create such a suggestion? But if they have faithfully passed on the message of Jesus on such a point, why should we be generally sceptical of the eschatological discourse and its 'son of man' sayings? Third, in none of the 'son of man' sayings in this discourse is it obvious that Jesus is speaking about himself as he looks to the future, though the early church obviously identified Jesus as the son of man. Rather, Jesus appears to be speaking of the figure in Daniel's apocalyptic vision throughout this section. It is only because of Matthew's opening explanatory material in 24.1-3 that such a connection must be made ('What will be the sign of *your* coming?'). If such sayings were invented by the early church, why then would they not have Jesus, in replying to the disciples' questions about *his* coming, speak directly of himself in the first person? The best explanation for why Jesus would be depicted as speaking in such a manner (in the third person) is because that is how his sayings were preserved in the earliest memory of the church.

---

35.   On the general point see Dale C. Allison, *Jesus of Nazareth: Millenarian Ascetic* (Philadelphia: Fortress Press, 1998), pp. 95–171; G. R. Beasley-Murray, *Jesus and the Kingdom of God* (Grand Rapids: Eerdmans, 1986), pp. 313–37; and N. T. Wright, *Jesus and the Victory of God* (Philadelphia: Fortress Press, 1996), pp. 320–68 (though Wright interprets Jesus' eschatological language much differently).

36.   Although John J. Collins does not believe Jesus applied the language of Dan. 7.13 to himself, he rightly insists concerning the interpretation of Daniel's vision as it is attested in *1 Enoch* and *4 Ezra*: 'There is no reason in principle why Jesus should not have made similar use of Daniel 7' (Collins, *The Apocalyptic Imagination*, p. 263).

Lk. 17.22, 26, 30; 18.8

Four additional 'son of man' sayings which are rejected by Casey appear in Luke 17–18.[37] The first two occurrences appear within the same unit of text (17.22-37). There is no compelling reason to reject this material out of hand.[38] The expression 'days of the Son of Man' in 17.22 and 26 is unusual in the New Testament, but has Jewish parallels in the Mishnah and *4 Ezra* as a designation of the messianic era.[39] The story of Sodom and Gomorrah (17.28-30) was among the stock of Old Testament materials from which Jesus sometimes drew according to Q (Mt. 10.15//Lk. 10.12); M (Mt. 11.23-24); and L (Lk. 17.29). And, again, Jesus refers to the future Son of Man as though he were speaking of a third party, which is more likely due to the memory of the early church than something put onto the lips of Jesus.

In 18.1-8, the bold comparison of God to an unjust judge of bad character was potentially shocking to Jewish ears, and would be no less unsettling to Christians. It appears within a parable, which is widely acknowledged as one of the most distinctive modes of communication employed by the historical Jesus.[40] And the topic of widows was characteristic of the concerns of Jesus according to Mark (12.42); L (18.3); and Q (Mt. 12.42-43//Lk. 21.2-3). There is no occasion to be sceptical about the dominical origin of this material.

But what of Casey's objection that these units address the problem of the delay of the Parousia? According to Lk. 17.25, the only thing which *must* happen prior to the revealing of the Son of Man is the anticipated suffering of Jesus in Jerusalem. Such a scenario fits the situation at the end of Jesus' life quite comfortably, but would offer little resolution to a church struggling with angst over the delay of the Parousia many decades later.

37. Lk. 17.24 is a parallel of Mt. 24.27, drawn from Q.

38. Casey insists: 'This straightforwardly describes the period during which the parousia was expected and did not come. It is presented as a prediction of Jesus, so that Christians of Luke's time could be reassured that Jesus knew the parousia would not happen as soon as they had hoped, and that their predecessors had been mistaken to expect it' (*Solution*, p. 223).

39. See the discussion of Darrell L. Bock, *Luke 9:51-24:53* (BECNT, 3b; Grand Rapids: Baker, 1996), p. 1427.

40. 'Even scholars who are persuaded that the Gospel parables include additions by the early church still view the parables as providing some of the most authentic and reliable teaching from Jesus' (K. R. Snodgrass, 'Parable', in *Dictionary of Jesus and the Gospels* [eds. Joel B. Green, Scot McKnight, I. Howard Marshall; Downers Grove: InterVarsity Press, 1992], p. 600).

Lk. 21.36 is also rejected by Casey, though without any clear explanation as to why.[41] It appears within a unit of material distinct to Luke (21.34-36), but with several signs of authenticity. The warning to the disciples not to be weighed down with 'drunkenness and cares of this life' (21.34) is hardly flattering them in the eyes of the church. The theme of drunkenness was characteristic of Jesus' teaching according to Q (Mt. 24.49//Lk. 12.45); L (Lk. 21.34); and perhaps M (Mt. 11.19).[42] And the theme of worry was certainly characteristic of Jesus, according to L (Lk. 10.41); Mark (4.19); and Q (Mt. 6.31//Lk. 12.29).

Mt. 10.23[43]

Although it is possible that Matthew has crafted this material and inserted it into the present context, in order to apply the missionary instructions of Jesus to the ministry of the church in his own day, it is also possible that he found it somewhere in his source material. The content itself bears every sign of authenticity. The prediction that the Son of Man would return before the disciples had finished their travels through 'all the towns of Israel' is not likely to have been invented by the early church, since it is certainly open to the suggestion that Jesus was wrong in his expectation. Nor did it find confirmation in the experience of the Christian community at any point in the first century. The unit within which this saying is contained is full of marks of dominical teaching. The expectation of persecution on the part of Jesus is found here in M (Mt. 10.17-18); in Q (Mt. 5.11//Lk. 6.22); and in Mark (13.9). The inspiration of the Spirit when called to give witness is found here in M (Mt. 10.19-20); in Mark (13.11); and possibly L (Lk. 12.11-12).[44] The citation of Micah 7.6 is found here in M (Mt. 10.21); in Mark (13.12) and again in Q (Mt. 10.35-36// Lk. 12.52-53). And Jesus once more speaks of the coming Son of Man as though he would be a figure distinct from himself (Mt. 10.23), which is more likely due to the preservation of Jesus' manner of speaking than the creativity of the early church.

41.   Casey, *Solution*, p. 230.

42.   It is unclear if the differences between Mt. 11.16-19//Lk. 7.31-35 are due to redactions of Q, or whether they are drawing off of two different traditions. See Darrell L. Bock, *Luke 1:1-9:50* (BECNT, 3a; Grand Rapids, Baker, 1994), pp. 660–61.

43.   See Casey, *Solution*, pp. 231–33.

44.   It is unclear whether this piece of material comes from Q or a second source employed by Luke. See Bock, *Luke 9:51-24:53*, pp. 1130–31, 1143.

Mt. 12.39-40//Lk. 11.29-30

This Q saying will certainly be rejected by any who are sceptical of the scenario involving Jesus predicting his own death and resurrection.[45] But this is a well attested dominical teaching in the earliest strata of the tradition. It appears here in Q, and repeatedly in Mark (8.31; 9.9; 9.31; 10.34; 15.29). It is unlikely that the early church would attribute to Jesus the specific claim that he would spend 'three days and three nights in the heart of the earth' unless this memory was very firmly rooted in the tradition, as this is difficult to harmonize with the actual period of time Jesus spent in the tomb.[46]

Mt. 13.37, 41

Casey rejects the authenticity of these sayings because they treat 'son of man' as a title, whereas in Aramaic אנשׁא בר was simply 'a normal word for man', and thus could not have served as a title to designate Jesus specifically.[47] But as we have seen, the evidence for this bald assertion is lacking in Middle Aramaic.[48]

Mk 13.26 and 14.62

Casey rejects Mk 13.26 on two grounds: (1) The setting for the saying includes the anachronistic expectation of the Gentile mission, which 'does not have any *Sitz im Leben* in the teaching of Jesus'. (2) The saying is dependent on Dan. 7.13 and uses 'son of man' as a title for Jesus.[49] Given the likelihood that Jesus saw 'the kingdom of God' as somehow dawning on earth in connection

---

45. See now the thorough study of Scot McKnight, *Jesus and His Death* (Waco: Baylor University Press, 2005).

46. Luke edits his source to remove the chronological difficulty. The reference to 'three days and three nights' is not due to typical features of Jewish reckoning (a convention standing for any parts of a three-day period), but the specific duration mentioned in Jon. 2.1.

47. Casey, *Solution*, p. 234.

48. Casey goes on to discuss Mt. 16.13, 27-28; 19.28 (*Solution*, pp. 235–38). We will not discuss these verses, as they may well be examples of Matthean editorial glosses. The same can be said for Lk. 6.22 (p. 239). Lk. 19.10 is rejected by Casey because of the familiar claim that אנשׁא בר 'would not have sufficient referring power to make clear the reference to Jesus' (p. 241). Though this may well be a Lukan gloss (with 'son of man' being now a common title for Jesus), Casey's claim itself lacks clear evidence, and is insufficient to call into question the basic authenticity of the saying.

49. See Casey, *Solution*, p. 242.

with his ministry,[50] it is not at all clear why Jesus would not have expected the 'good news' of that arrival to be proclaimed to the Gentiles.[51] As for the claim that the expression 'son of man' could not have been derived from Dan. 7.13 and used as a title for God's agent of eschatological rule, we have already seen this claim to be without foundation.

Casey's rejection of Mk 14.62 is based on similar grounds: (1) The saying is dependent on Dan. 7.13 and uses 'son of man' as a title for Jesus (supposedly impossible in Aramaic). (2) The Greek term Χριστός, like its Aramaic equivalent (א)מְשִׁיחָ, 'had not yet crystallized into a title'. (3) The Blessed is 'not attested' as a circumlocution for God. (4) Jesus said nothing which would have justified the charge of blasphemy attributed to him in Mark's story. (5) The synoptic gospels always have Jesus refer to the second coming through allusion to Dan. 7.13. But it was 'not characteristic' of Jesus to deal with topics in such 'rigidly scriptural terms'. (6) Since the resurrection and the second coming are not combined in the synoptic sayings material (though they are both forms of vindication), 'this implies a separate origin for these two groups of sayings' (with the second coming sayings being the creations of the church).[52]

In reply, we might suggest: (1) Casey's claim about the linguistic range of בַּר אֱנָשׁ is lacking in hard evidence. (2) The term 'Christ' or 'Messiah' draws from a rich Old Testament background, and is used as a vehicle to convey messianic expectation in the Dead Sea Scrolls, the *Psalms of Solomon*, and *1 Enoch*.[53] (3) The title 'the Blessed' is attested in *1 Enoch* and the Mishnah.[54] 4) Jesus' expectation that he would soon be seated on God's own throne and return with heavenly authority *would* have been perceived as a blasphemous claim.[55] (5) It is absurd to argue that sayings which are overly dependent on biblical quotations could not go back to the historical Jesus. (6) It is far more

---

50. See C. C. Caragounis, 'Kingdom of God/Heaven', in *DJG*, pp. 417–30 and Dennis C. Duling, 'Kingdom of God, Kingdom of Heaven', in *The Anchor Bible Dictionary* (ed. David Noel Freedman; 6 vols; New York: Doubleday, 1992), vol. 4, pp. 62–65.

51. See Scot McKnight, 'Gentiles', in *DJG*, pp. 259–61 and now Michael F. Bird, *Jesus and the Origins of the Gentile Mission* (LNTS, 331; London: T&T Clark, 2006).

52. See Casey, *Solution*, pp. 243–44.

53. See Larry W. Hurtado, 'Christ', in *DJG*, pp. 106–107.

54. See Darrell L. Bock, *Jesus According to Scripture* (Grand Rapids: Baker, 2002), p. 373.

55. See Bock, *Jesus According to Scripture*, pp. 374–75.

likely that the resurrection and the second coming are not combined in the sayings material, simply because of the interval separating the two events.

Ability to explain the son of man sayings

A further problem with Casey's proposal lies in the explanation he offers for what he regards as authentic 'son of man' sayings.[56] Because of Casey's commitment to the generic meaning of the expression, he is forced to adopt somewhat novel interpretations of the meaning of such utterances.[57]

For example, Mk 10.45 becomes a general maxim for the sake of the disciples that, 'the purpose of life is service' (p. 132). Mk 14.21 becomes a general statement condemning traitors (p. 135). Mt. 11.19//Lk. 7.34 becomes an assertion that people must eat and drink in order to live (p. 137). Mt. 12.32// Lk. 12.10 (cf. Mk 3.28-29) is taken as stemming from an original comparison between the consequences of speaking against men, versus speaking against the Spirit of God (p. 140). Mk 2.10 is reduced to an original assertion that God has given some people the power to heal psychosomatic illnesses (p. 165). Mt. 8.19-20//Lk. 9.57-58 is understood as a comment upon the difficult life of those who accept a migratory ministry (pp. 177–78). Lk. 12.8-9//Mt. 10.32-33 and Mk 8.38 originate as a statement about the role of the heavenly court (which will include humans) in the final judgement (p. 185). Lk. 22.48 is a reflection upon the human experience of betrayal (p. 198). Mk 8.31 is reduced to the truism that all men must eventually die, but will be raised at the general resurrection (pp. 202–203, 205–206).

For the most part, the incredible glosses Casey puts upon such sayings stand as their own refutation. Why would the early church have bothered to preserve such mundane observations by their founder? Are we really to believe that the historical Jesus simply went about espousing general maxims about the human condition? How then did his message occasion so much controversy and subsequent religious transformation in the lives of his followers? Was Jesus really so utterly unwilling to make statements exclusively about himself, his divine vocation and his unique significance in God's plan? Why then did Casey's modest Jesus incur the wrath of the religious and political establishment? And

---

56. See Casey, *Solution*, pp. 116–211.

57. We will leave aside any discussion here of Mk 2.27-28 and 9.11-13, where Casey's proposal has some measure of plausibility. See Casey, *Solution*, pp. 121–25, 125–31.

why was he crucified as a blasphemer and threat to Roman power in Palestine? And how much does Casey's sanitized version of the authentic words of Jesus reflect his own low Christology and anti-orthodox theological agenda?[58]

Apocalyptic evidence

Casey is adamant that there is no precedent in first-century Judaism for the messianic interpretation of Dan. 7.13 which the early church invented. This leads him to deny, not only a messianic interpretation of Dan. 7.13, but also any appropriation of Daniel 7 to that end in *1 Enoch* 37-71, *4 Ezra* 13, and *Ezekiel the Tragedian* 68-89. His arguments, however, are open to question on several points.

1 Enoch

Casey argues that the usages of the relevant terminology for 'son of man' in the Similitudes of Enoch do not reflect any allusions to a messianic title drawn from Daniel 7,[59] but simply reflect normal Aramaic terminology for 'man', referring throughout the document to the person of Enoch himself.[60] But his whole explanation is built on a weak foundation. Even if we agree with Casey that Enoch is the 'son of man' throughout the Similitudes, it has no bearing on the relevant connection to Daniel 7.[61]

The first reference to the 'son of man' in this section (*1 Enoch* 46.1-4) is quite plainly drawing from the imagery in Daniel's vision.[62] Casey would then have us believe that all subsequent references to a 'son of man' within

---

58.   See Maurice Casey, *From Jewish Prophet to Gentile God* (Louisville: Westminster/ John Knox, 1991).

59.   On the date of chapters 37-71 see James H. Charlesworth, 'Can We Discern the Composition Date of the Parables of Enoch?', in *Enoch and the Messiah Son of Man: Revisiting the Book of Parables*, (ed. Gabriele Boccaccini; Grand Rapids: Eerdmans, 2007), pp. 450–68. Charlesworth suggests: 'If the Gospels preserve echoes of Jesus' own words, and at times accurately preserve them, then 'the Son of Man' is most likely an expression known to some Galilean Jews prior to Jesus' ministry in Galilee' (p. 465). Cf. Leslie W. Walck, 'The Son of Man in the Parables of Enoch and the Gospels', in *Messiah Son of Man*, pp. 299–337.

60.   See Casey, *Solution*, pp. 91–111.

61.   As it would simply mean that the text identifies Enoch (as opposed to Jesus or some other person) as the earthly manifestation of the elect, pre-existent agent of God's revelation and judgement (i.e. the Messiah). See the discussion of Sabino Chialà, 'The Son of Man: The Evolution of an Expression', in *Messiah Son of Man*, pp. 153–78 (esp. pp. 159–63).

62.   These connections are dismissed by Casey as mere 'reminiscences' (*Solution*, p. 111).

the text (involving three different Ethiopic expressions),[63] are simply alluding to the 'man' described in chapter 46, with no attempt to attribute a messianic interpretation to Daniel 7 through that language.[64] It strains credulity, in light of the Danielic allusions within 46.1-4, to think that the messianic figure who appears would be repeatedly described as a '*son of man*' throughout the Similitudes (46.2, 3, 4; 48.2; 62.5; 62.7, 9, 14; 63.11; 69.27; 69.29; 70.1; 71.14; 71.17), with no awareness or intentional development of the terminology used in the very biblical text *from which the original description of the 'son of man' was drawn*.[65]

4 Ezra

Casey's discussion of *4 Ezra* 13 is very short (p. 112). He basically argues that the original Hebrew wording of the passage probably did not use the term 'son of man', but simply 'man' (reflected in the word *homo* found in the Latin version). But regardless of the original language and terminology (whether Hebrew or Aramaic), it is clear that the imagery and eschatological expectation conveyed in 13.1-13 is drawn out of Daniel 7, and applied to a specific messianic figure (13.21-56). This is all that is necessary to assert in order to demonstrate that the passage bears witness to an appropriation of Daniel 7 which has some bearing on the son of man concept as a vehicle for messianic expectation in the first century CE.[66]

Ezekiel the Tragedian 68-89

Casey dismisses this passage in a short paragraph (p. 114), arguing that the date of the text is uncertain (hence it may not reflect the influence of Daniel 7 at all).

---

63.   There are differences among Ethiopic scholars as to the degree to which the three expressions should be viewed as interchangeable translation variations, or rather distinct linguistic expressions with distinguishable ranges of meaning. Cf. Caragounis, *The Son of Man*, p. 106, n. 115.

64.   On the inadequacy of this line of thought, see the detailed refutation of Caragounis, *The Son of Man*, pp. 104–11.

65.   See further Helge S. Kvanig, 'The Son of Man in the Parables of Enoch', in *Messiah Son of Man*, pp. 179–215; John J. Collins, 'Enoch and the Son of Man: A Response to Sabino Chialà and Helge Kvanig', in *Messiah Son of Man*, pp. 216–27; and Klaus Koch, 'Questions regarding the So-Called Son of Man in the Parables of Enoch: A Response to Sabino Chialà and Helge Kvanig', in *Messiah Son of Man*, pp. 228–37.

66.   See also Chialà, 'The Son of Man: The Evolution of an Expression', pp. 171–73.

The text uses the term φῶς for 'man', and the 'man' is God. The term 'throne' is only metaphorical. And 'son of man' does not appear in the passage. Casey's arguments seem to miss the point rather badly. First of all, if the text predates Daniel, it merely sheds light on the meaning of Dan. 7.13, making it all the more likely that it envisions a specific human being (like Moses) being exalted to a place of divine rule over all things. If it post-dates Daniel, then it shows how Daniel 7 was understood from a very early period (second century BCE). Second, the fact that the 'man' is God merely strengthens the connection with Daniel 7 (cf. 7.9). Third, to insist that the throne is a metaphor for participation in the divine sovereignty certainly does not help Casey, since it would simply tell us something about the extent to which God is willing to share his rule with certain human beings (including the Messiah). Fourth, the term 'son of man' simply does not have to appear in order for the passage to speak to the ways in which Daniel 7 was interpreted messianically and appropriated within Judaism.

Speculative Aramaic reconstructions

One final criticism which can be raised relates to Casey's method.[67] Casey's project involves attempting to 'reconstruct' the original Aramaic lying behind the 'son of man' sayings in the Greek gospels. Those sayings which cannot be 'satisfactorily reconstructed' (p. 119) into a plausible Aramaic original are to be viewed as of dubious authenticity. Casey acknowledges that the process must also take into account idiomatic expressions and the 'deliberate editing' (p. 120) of the gospel writers.

All of this is highly suspect. Simply because the Greek phrase ὁ υἱος τοῦ ἀνθρώπου lends itself to the supposition of a literal Aramaic expression in אנש בר is no basis to presume that recoverable, literal Aramaic expressions must underlie all of the authentic words of Jesus in the Greek gospels. The fact is that we have very little idea of what Aramaic utterances came out of the mouth of Jesus, short of those places where the gospel writers point to them.[68] The authors of the gospels made use of numerous oral and written sources, which may have varied in their degree of literalness and accuracy in translating the words of Jesus into Greek. The matter is complicated by the likelihood that

---

67. Casey offers an overview of his method in *Solution*, pp. 119–21.
68. See M. O. Wise, 'Languages of Palestine', in *DJG*, pp. 441–43.

Jesus on occasion conversed in Hebrew and possibly Greek.[69] Furthermore, the attempt to distinguish between the editorial glosses of the gospel writers and the actual words of Jesus, when working with what must often be translated paraphrases of the original sayings, can never be more than a tentative project. It is certainly not the stuff out of which one can propose to given any definitive 'solution' to the son of man 'problem'.

69. See Wise, 'Languages of Palestine', p. 442.

RE-SOLVING THE SON OF MAN 'PROBLEM' IN ARAMAIC

David Shepherd

Maurice Casey is well-known for arguing that the singular emphatic form בר (א)נשא should be reconstructed as a normal or ordinary way of generically referring to a man in the Aramaic of Jesus' time. There are some, however, who find Casey's evidence and arguments less than compelling, particularly given the absence of the singular emphatic expression in Middle Aramaic.[1] In recent publications Casey has continued to maintain his position.[2]

While it is clear that the singular absolute (*11QarJob* 9.9; 26.3; *1QapGen* 21.13) plural absolute (*1QapGen* 19.15) and plural emphatic forms (*11QarJob* [13.9]; 28.2; *4QenAst* 23; *1QapGen* 6.8-9) of this expression do occur in Middle Aramaic texts from Qumran, it seems equally obvious that the absence of the singular emphatic form (i.e. precisely the form required to explain the Greek) from any Middle Aramaic texts significantly undermines Casey's argument that the expression was a common or idiomatic way of generically referring to a man in the Aramaic of Jesus' time.

While the preceding chapter has clarified some ongoing points of disagreement between Casey and the position argued by Paul Owen and me, situating these points against the backdrop of the wider discussion, the following brief

---

1. See my earlier essay with Paul Owen, 'Speaking Up for Qumran, Dalman and the Son of Man: Was *Bar Enasha* a Common Term for "Man" in the Time of Jesus?' *JSNT* 81 (2001), pp. 81–122 as well as the preceding chapter in this volume.

2. Maurice Casey, 'Aramaic Idiom and the Son of Man Problem: A Response to Owen and Shepherd', *JSNT* 25 (2002), pp. 3–32 and *The Solution to the 'Son of Man' Problem* (London: T&T Clark, 2007).

study is a constructive attempt to extend the search for the singular emphatic form of נשא(א) בר in relevant phases of the Aramaic language.

Aware of the absence in Middle Aramaic of the precise form of the expression his argument requires, Casey continues, in his most recent publication, to insist on resorting to later texts in his quest for the singular emphatic נשא(א) בר, and he does so on at least three grounds.

First, Casey continues to argue that Aramaic is a stable language by drawing our attention to a selection of lexical and morphological features drawn from various phases of the history of the language.[3] The intended relevance of his discussion becomes clear when he cites a variety of words referring to herbs which do not happen to occur in extant Middle Aramaic texts but must have existed in that phase of the language in order to explain the Aramaic background of Mt. 23.23 and Lk. 11.42. In the same way, Casey argues, the Greek articular form of the expression in the Gospels requires the presence of נשא(א)(א) בר, which he insists is 'attested in earlier Aramaic'.[4] Again, however, it needs to be clarified that what is attested in Qumran Aramaic is the singular absolute and the plural emphatic and absolute forms of the expression. Unfortunately, Casey's difficulty is that the one form of this expression which is required to explain the Greek articular form of the expression – the singular emphatic form נשא(א) בר – is the one and only form of the expression which is manifestly not attested in Middle Aramaic. Obviously, the singular emphatic form of the expression need not have been an ordinary or common way of referring to 'a son of man' in the Aramaic of Jesus' time in order to explain the Greek articular title 'the son of man'. Indeed, as has been clarified in the preceding chapter, there are several other more plausible explanations for Jesus' use of the singular emphatic נשא(א) בר given that this use was apparently anything but ordinary for his fellow speakers of Aramaic.

Second, Casey presents evidence to suggest that the emphatic state was optional for some kinds of expressions in various phases of the history of the Aramaic language.[5] Unremarkably, he finds that the Qumran Aramaic version of Job from Cave 11 yields a host of examples of nouns in both the absolute and emphatic states in which these states do not appear to mark any discernible

---

3. Casey, *Solution*, pp. 56–57.
4. Casey, *Solution*, p. 59.
5. Casey, *Solution*, p. 60.

difference in definiteness. What this suggests to Casey is that in generic and some other expressions, the use of either state was optional and that it is 'therefore natural to find that בר (א)נש(א) may be used in either state, since it is a generic expression'. Again, however, if it is indeed natural to find that the expression can be used in either state, it seems odd that while the plural does appear in either state in Middle Aramaic texts, the singular only appears in the absolute state, not in the emphatic state required to explain the articular form of the Greek expression. That the states are in some sense 'optional' for some words/expressions in Middle Aramaic merely highlights the lack of evidence that בר (א)נש(א) is one of these such expressions.

Finally, well aware of the absence of the singular emphatic form of the expression in Aramaic texts originating from a Palestinian provenance around the time of Jesus' time, Casey resorts to later texts for examples of the form his argument requires by insisting that:

> Qumran Aramaic can safely be used in the reconstruction of the sayings of Jesus. It does not, however, go far enough, for the Dead Sea Scrolls do not contain enough Aramaic to form a language. If therefore we confine ourselves to them, we do not have enough Aramaic to reconstruct the whole language of anyone. (p. 57)

Casey is quite correct to suggest that the Scrolls do not contain enough Aramaic to form a language. Indeed, to rely on Qumran Aramaic in isolation to assess how normal the singular emphatic form of בר (א)נש(א) was in the Aramaic of Jesus' time would not only be unwise, it would also be unnecessary. The Qumran corpus is only one of several corpora which together comprise the phase of the language known as Middle Aramaic (200 BCE–200 CE).[6]

If the absence of the singular emphatic form of the expression from the Qumran corpus is indeed, as Casey suggests, an accident of preservation (or lack thereof), and if it was indeed a normal or ordinary way of referring to 'a man' at the time of Jesus, it seems reasonable that there should be at least

---

6. For an authoritative list of corpora belonging to Middle Aramaic, see S. Kaufman, 'Aramaic' in R. Hetzron (ed.), *The Semitic Languages* (New York: Routledge, 1997), p. 116.

some evidence for it in the not-insignificant number of Middle Aramaic texts originating in Palestine. It is, therefore, to these texts which we now turn.[7]

While the Jewish communities in the East later played an important part in the preservation and transmission of Targum Onkelos' translation of the Pentateuch and Targum Jonathan's version of the Prophets, there is wide agreement among Aramaists that the consonantal texts of both belong to the Middle Aramaic phase of the language, having originated prior to 200 CE.[8] While the question of provenance has also been long debated, few are able to escape the arguments of Nöldeke, Berliner, Dalman, Kutscher, Greenfield and Tal that Onkelos and Jonathan have their origins in Palestine.[9]

In view, therefore, of their appropriateness in terms of period and provenance, and because of the amount of textual material they offer for our purposes, what do Onkelos and Jonathan tell us about the use of בַּר (אֱ)נָשָׁא?

---

7.   The primary texts cited in the following discussion may be accessed online through the Comprehensive Aramaic Lexicon project (http://cal1.cn.huc.edu/).

8.   So, for instance, E. M. Cook, 'A New Perspective on the Language of Onqelos and Jonathan', in M. McNamara and D. R. G. Beattie (eds), *The Aramaic Bible* (JSOTSup, 166; Sheffield Academic Press: Sheffield, 1994), p. 150 on the basis of the existence of variant reading traditions from Nehardea which ceased to exist in 256 CE. For the early date see also S. Kaufman, 'Aramaic', pp. 115–29; Moshe H. Goshen-Gottstein, 'The Language of Targum Onqelos and Literary Diglossia in Aramaic', *Eretz-Israel* 14 (Hebrew; H. L. Ginsberg Volume; ed. Menahem Haran; Jerusalem: The Israelite Exploration Society in cooperation with The Jewish Theological Seminary of America, 1978), p. 187, and most recently Douglas Gropp, 'The Linguistic Position of Onkelos and Jonathan Aramaic', paper presented at the Meeting of the International Organization for Targum Studies in Ljubljana, 2006.

9.   *Contra*, for example, Geiger, Ginsberg, Rosenthal, Epstein and Kahle. See Goshen-Gottstein's review of the discussion in 'The Language of Targum Onkelos and the Model of Literary Diglossia in Aramaic', *JNES* 37 (1978) pp. 169–79 and cautious preference for a western origin. While E. M. Cook's critique ('A New Perspective') has helpfully sharpened the debate, see W. Smelik, *The Targum of Judges* (Leiden: Brill, 1995), pp. 20–21 for warranted reservations regarding Cook's position, partly on the basis of the clearly 'western' use of the *nota accusativi*, a feature which encourages Gropp 'Linguistic Position' to favour a Palestinian origin.

Targum Onkelos *to the Torah and* Targum Jonathan *to the Prophets*

Targum Onkelos *to the Torah*[10]

In Gen. 11.5, where the Hebrew text offers a definite form of the expression (בני האדם) 'the sons of mankind', Onkelos predictably supplies its Aramaic plural emphatic equivalent (בני אנשא) and offers the same in rendering an undetermined plural form (בני אדם) 'sons of man/Adam' where it appears in Deut. 32.8. On two other occasions, Onkelos also supplies the plural emphatic form in order to make explicit a subject which is merely implied or inflected in the Hebrew.[11] In Gen. 3.20, the same plural emphatic form (בני אנשא) is reasonably supplied as a substitute for Hebrew חי 'the living'.[12] Even less surprisingly, this same plural emphatic form is offered when the translator is confronted with definite (האדם [Gen. 6.1]) and indefinite (אנוש [Deut. 32.26]) words for 'mankind/humanity'. Finally, in Num. 23.19, the same plural emphatic form (בני אנשא) is used to render not only (איש ['a man']) in the first half of the verse, but also the Hebrew singular form of our expression (בן אדם ['a son of man']) in the second half.

On the evidence furnished by Onkelos, while the plural emphatic form of our expression (בני אנשא) is clearly a natural (or at least acceptable) way for the Aramaic translator to render a variety of related Hebrew expressions, it is striking that the singular form in either the absolute (בר (א)נש) *or* emphatic state (בר (א)נשא) is entirely absent from Onkelos – this absence made all the more conspicuous by the opportunity presented in Num. 23.19b to translate the singular form of the expression in the Hebrew (בן אדם) with what might seem to be its 'natural' equivalent (בר (א)נש). Indeed, that this latter form is not offered by Onkelos in its translation of Num. 23.19 or at *any* point in its translation of the first five books of the Hebrew Bible suggests that, so far as Onkelos is concerned, בר (א)נש/א (in whatever state) is not only an unnatural way to refer to 'a man', but in fact either unknown or unacceptable.

---

10.   The CAL text of Onkelos consists of the Bar Ilan text along with relevant variants from the base text and critical apparatus of Sperber.

11.   Gen. 4.26 בני אנשא (subject implicit in Heb.); Gen. 48.16 בני אנשא (subject implicit in Heb.).

12.   A more interpretive substitution is found in Num. 24.17 where the plural emphatic (בני אנשא) takes the place of Hebrew (בני־שת) 'the sons of Seth'.

Targum Jonathan to the Prophets[13]

The widespread conclusion reached by others that the linguistic features and translational approach of *Tg-Onkelos* are virtually identical to those of *Tg-Jonathan* is borne out by an examination of its use of our expression.[14] As we have seen in Onkelos, Jonathan predictably provides the Aramaic plural emphatic (בְּנֵי אֱנָשָׁא) 'the sons of man' to render both the analogous plural indefinite (בְּנֵי אָדָם, 'sons of man')[15] and definite (בְּנֵי הָאָדָם. 'the sons of man')[16] forms of the Hebrew expression. Also like Onkelos, the plural emphatic is used to translate both אֱנוֹשׁ[17] and אָדָם (in its definite[18] and indefinite[19] forms). In addition, but also unsurprisingly, the translator of *Tg-Jonathan* supplies this same plural emphatic form to render Hebrew אִישׁ (man)[20] and אֲנָשִׁים (men).[21] The 'naturalness' of *Tg-Jonathan*'s rendering of the above Hebrew terms and forms with the Aramaic plural emphatic (בְּנֵי אֱנָשָׁא) 'the sons of man' is supported by *Tg-Jonathan*'s provision of the latter even when there are fewer (or indeed, no) obvious prompts in the Hebrew text.[22]

More interestingly, whereas בֶּן אָדָם 'a son of man' in Num. 23.19 is, as we have seen, rendered by Onkelos with its own 'natural' plural equivalent (בְּנֵי אֱנָשָׁא) 'the sons of man', *Tg-Jonathan* prefers to render the Hebrew singular indefinite בֶּן אָדָם in Isaiah and Jeremiah with its own singular absolute equivalent (בַּר אֱנָשׁ) 'a son of man' as we can see from Jer. 49.18:[23]

13.   The CAL text of Jonathan is based on the Bar Ilan text (Sperber's J) along with variants from the latter's main text and critical apparatus (excluding tosefta variants) and the long tosefta annotation in Cod. Reuchlin as per Sperber.

14.   The differences which do exist appear to be lexical rather than morphological or syntactical. See A. Tal, *The Language of the Targum of the Former Prophets and its Position within the Aramaic Dialects* (Hebrew; Tel-Aviv: Tel-Aviv University, 1975), pp. 202–13, followed by W. Smelik, *Targum of Judges*, p. 15 and Gropp, 'Linguistic Position'.

15.   2 Sam. 7.14; Isa. 52.14; Jer. 32.19; Ezek. 31.14; Joel 1.12.

16.   1 Sam. 26.19; 1 Kgs 8.39.

17.   Isa. 33.8 and 51.7.

18.   הָאָדָם: Judg. 16.7, 11; 1 Sam. 16.7 (2×); 2 Sam. 7.19; Isa. 2.20, 6.12; Jer. 33.5, 47.2.

19.   אָדָם: 1 Sam. 24.9 [10]; 2 Sam. 23.3 (בָאָדָם); Isa. 13.12, 29.21, 44.11, 47.3, Jer. 32.20 (בָאָדָם), 49.15 (בָאָדָם); Zeph. 1.17 (לָאָדָם); Zech 9.1.

20.   Zech. 10.1.

21.   Judg. 9.9; 1 Sam. 2.26.

22.   1 Sam. 1.11, 2.8; 1 Kgs 8.27; 2 Kgs 10.27; Isa. 14.12, 24.21, 45.18, 65.4; Hab. 3.4; Zech. 4.10.

23.   See also Jer. 49.33, 50.40, 51.43.

MT   לא־ישב שם איש ולא־יגור בה בן־אדם

Tg-Jonathan   לא־יתיב תמן אנש ולא יתותב בה בר אנש

KJV . . . no man shall abide there, neither shall a son of man dwell in it.

Evidently, on these occasions, the translator's literalism (i.e. desire to render a singular with a singular) discourages him from supplying the plural emphatic form Jonathan and Onkelos normally provide elsewhere.[24]

While the absolute singular forms provided by *Tg-Jonathan* here still offer us no evidence for the use of the singular emphatic form which is required to explain the articular form of the Greek expression, *Tg-Jonathan*'s rendering of Isa. 51.12[25] and 56.2 (see below) might seem, at first glance, to offer some evidence of the use of the singular emphatic:

MT   אשרי אנוש יעשה־זאת ובן־אדם יחזיק בה

Tg-Jonathan   טובי אנשא דיעביד דא ובר אנשא דיתקף בה

RSV Blessed is the man who does this, and the son of man who holds it fast . . .

While the elusive singular emphatic (בר אנשא) does appear here and in 51.12, comparison with the example from Jer. 49.18 above explains why. The reason that the singular emphatic appears in 56.2 is that Hebrew אנוש and בן אדם function as the subjects of relative clauses whose definiteness is implied. Just as the RSV is obliged to supply the article ('*the* son of man') to express this in English, so too *Tg-Jonathan* supplies the emphatic form (בר אנשא) 'the son of man' in Aramaic. Far from suggesting that the singular emphatic form בר אנשא 'the son of man' was a natural way for Onkelos and Jonathan to refer to 'a man', all that such examples suggest is that the singular emphatic

---

24. Even more interesting is the case of Mic. 5.6 where for the comparable A-B pairing of לאיש/לבני אדם *Tg-Jonathan* actually supplies the singular אנש לאנש/לבר rather than the plural as might be expected. While such behaviour might be attributed by some to inconsistent translating practise or a different translator altogether, the change likely stems from the *Tg-Jonathan*'s desire to harmonize its rendering of the plural form (בני אדם) in v.6b with the singular form in 5.6a (איש).

25. MT אנכי אנכי הוא מנחמכם מי־את ותיראי מאנוש ימות ומבן־אדם חציר ינתן *Tg-Jonathan.*

אנא אנא הוא מנחמכון ממן אתון דהלין דמאית ומבר אנשא דכעסבא חשיב

was an acceptable way for an Aramaic speaker to specify a particular son of man (in this case, a son of man who 'holds it [justice/righteousness v.1] fast').

Summary of Onkelos and Jonathan Aramaic

While further analysis of the Onkelos and Jonathan Aramaic corpus would be required to determine what is statistically the most common means of referring to 'a man', the above investigation has at least served to establish that the singular expression אנשׁ(א) בר is not a 'common' or 'normal' way to refer to 'a man' in the Aramaic of Onkelos and Jonathan. Indeed, one can only speculate as to the considerations (socio-linguistic, religious or otherwise) which have motivated Onkelos to supply the plural emphatic Aramaic form to render Hebrew בן אדם, (Num. 23.19) rather than the absolute singular form, בר (א)נשׁ.

With regard to *Tg-Jonathan*, while the absolute singular form still appears far less frequently than its plural emphatic counterpart, בר (א)נשׁ does at least appear on seven occasions, allowing us to draw the safe but unremarkable conclusion that it is a 'natural' rendering of its Hebrew indefinite singular equivalent בן אדם, where the latter appears in the Hebrew text of the Prophets. While the singular emphatic does appear twice, it is clear that these appearances do not in any way support the notion that בר (א)נשׁא was anything like a natural or ordinary term for referring to 'a man' in the Aramaic of Onkelos and Jonathan.

Other Middle Aramaic corpora

Supplementing Onkelos and Jonathan is a wide range of original manuscript archival texts and epigraphic texts in Aramaic which have been found in and around Palestine (or closely associated with it) and are to be dated prior to 200 CE. Obviously, these texts provide a quite different literary flavour from Onkelos and Jonathan, reflecting the range of commercial transactions and personal correspondence found at Muraba'at, Nahal Hever and other locales. If the singular emphatic בר (א)נשׁא was indeed an ordinary or natural way to refer to 'a man' in first-century Palestine, one might suspect to find some evidence of it in texts such as these.

In the epigraphic texts, the plural emphatic form (בני אנשׁא) 'the sons of man' does appear on, for instance, amulets from Horvat Marish[26] and else-where[27] and on a manuscript preserved in a Geniza.[28] The singular absolute ברנש appears on a silver amulet bearing Greek and Aramaic[29] and בן גבר is found on a mosaic at Ein Gedi.[30]

Once again, however, this corpus provides no evidence that the singular emphatic form of our expression was a natural way to refer to 'a man', particu-larly given that this was apparently done by means of אנש.[31]

Likewise in the archival manuscripts, אנש is used on more than one occasion to refer to 'a man', as we can see from one of Bar Kosiba's letters:[32]

שמעון בר כובסה ליהונן ולמשבלא[ ] כול אנש מתקוע ומתל ארזין

'Simon son of Kosiba to Johanan and Masballah [ ] every man from Tekoa and Tel Arza'

In a divorce writ found at Murabba'at, we find גבר being used in a comparable way:[33]

למהי אנתא לכול גבר יהודי די תצבין

To be a wife to any man of the Jews who desires . . .

---

26.   J. Naveh and S. Shaked, *Magic Spells and Formulae: Aramaic Incantations of Late Antiquity* (Jerusalem: Magnes Press, 1993), amulet 13, column 1, line 14 (ובני אנשה).

27.   Naveh and Shaked, *Magic Spells and Formulae*, amulet 26, line 13.

28.   Joseph Naveh, 'A Good Subduing, There is None Like It', *Tarbiz* 54 (1984–85), pp. 367–82 (378–79). T-S K1.143 magic book (lines 8, 11). (CAL reference: 52701010)

29.   R. Kotansky, J. Naveh and S. Shaked, 'A Greek-Aramaic Silver Amulet from Egypt in the Ashmolean Museum', *Le Museón* 105 (1992), pp. 5–25 (line 16).

30.   J. Naveh, *On Stone and Mosaic: The Aramaic and Hebrew Inscriptions from Ancient Synagogues* (Hebrew; Jerusalem: Israel Exploration Society & Carta, 1978), text 70, line 9.

31.   See for instance, J. Fitzmyer and D. Harrington, *Manual of Palestinian Aramaic Texts* (Rome: Pontifical Institute, 2002) (hereafter, *MPAT*), text 69 (Ossuary Jebel Xallet et-Turi) line 1; L. Y. Rahmani, *A Catalogue of Jewish Ossuaries in the Collections of the State of Israel* (Jerusalem: The Israel Antiquities Authority and The Israel Academy of Sciences and Humanities, 1994), text 455, line 1 (pp. 178–79).

32.   *MPAT* 59 (5/6 HevEp 14, line 2).

33.   *MPAT* 40 (MUR 19 ar, lines 6 and 19).

Again, however we find no evidence of ‏בר (א)נשא‎ in either the absolute or emphatic state.

Finally, the only evidence from Megillat Ta'anit suggests that in the Aramaic of this text too, ‏אנש‎ rather than ‏בר (א)נש/א‎ in any form, is the natural way to refer to a man.[34]

Summary of Middle Aramaic found in other corpora

The solitary occurrence of the singular absolute expression ‏בר נש‎ in the Aramaic of these corpora (see above) and the apparent absence of the singular emphatic expression ‏בר (א)נשא‎ weighs heavily against the suggestion that the latter was a normal or ordinary way to refer to 'a man' as Casey suggests.

Taken as a whole, the evidence from Onkelos and Jonathan and other relevant corpora strikingly confirms the picture offered by the Qumran Aramaic. While the Aramaic of Palestine in the Middle Aramaic period had a range of ways of referring to 'a man', the only two occurrences of the singular emphatic forms of the expression appear in a context in which a particular son of man is being referenced (see above).

Given that the singular emphatic form would eventually appear in later phases of Aramaic (cited by Casey), how may we explain the striking absence of it in Aramaic of this provenance in this particular period (200 BCE to 200 CE)?

Curiously, one clue may come not from the Aramaic, but rather its more famous Semitic sister tongue, Hebrew, of this same period.[35] Indeed the analysis of the Aramaic above is strikingly paralleled by the situation in Rabbinic Hebrew in which the plural form (‏בני אדם‎) is found frequently in the Mishnah and the midrashim of the Tannaim as a way of referring to humanity.[36] But, as Fernández points out:

> the singular form, ‏בן אדם‎, is hardly used at all: it never appears in the Mishnah, not even in quotations, or in Sifra; it is found just once in *Sifre to Numbers* [103.4 (H102)] in a quotation of Ezekiel 16:2, five times in [the] Mek[ilta] always in

---

34. Vered Noam, *Megillat Ta'anit* (Jerusalem: Ben-Zvi Press, 2003), pp. 43–48 (line 38).
35. A. Sáenz-Badillos, *A History of the Hebrew Language* (trans. J. Elwolde; Cambridge: Cambridge University Press, 1993), p. 171; M. P. Fernández, *An Introductory Grammar of Rabbinic Hebrew* (trans. J. Elwolde; Leiden: Brill, 1999), pp. 1–2.
36. Fernández, *Rabbinic Hebrew*, p. 70.

quotations (Isaiah 56:2, Ezek 2:1, 17:2, 26:2, 28:2) and eight times in *Sifre to Deuteronomy* of which six are quotations (Ezek. 8:12, 17:2, 24:1-2, 33:7, 24, 39:17; 44:5). Thus in the whole of the Mishnah and the tannaitic midrashim, there are just two original passages in which בן אדם is employed.[37]

Given that the Aramaic influence on Rabbinic Hebrew has been widely observed,[38] it is perhaps not surprising that they share a similar aversion to the singular form of our expression and a virtual rejection of it in its definite (Heb.)/emphatic (Aram.) state. While few scholars these days argue that Jesus spoke Hebrew rather than Aramaic, the lack of this expression in either Semitic language in the first centuries of the Common Era deprives Casey of any substantial basis for the suggestion that the Greek was a mistranslation of such an expression. In the light of such a lack, the articular form of the Greek expression found on the lips of Jesus in the New Testament is best explained as a faithful translation of his use of the singular emphatic בר (א)נשא 'the son of man'. Indeed, if the Palestinian Talmud's memory of the tannaitic period is to be trusted, it was in some measure the titular use of this expression which would ensure that it would remain as 'extra-ordinary' in the years after Jesus' use of it, as it was before:

אמר רבי אבהו אם יאמר לך אדם אל אני מכזב הוא בן אדם אני סופו לתהות בה

Rabbi Abbahu said: 'If a man says to you "I am God", he is a liar; "I am a (the) son of man", he will regret it/it will be the end of him' (*y. Taanit*, ii, 65b).

Of course, for the moment, explanations such as the one offered above – which might account for the absence of the singular emphatic בר (א)נשא 'the son of man' in relevant phases/dialects of Aramaic – must remain within the realm of the hypothetical. On the other hand, unless or until further evidence is forthcoming, the hypothesis that this expression was either an ordinary or a common way of generically referring to 'a man' in the Aramaic of Jesus' time seems utterly bereft of relevant evidence.

37. Fernández, *Rabbinic Hebrew*, p. 71.
38. Fernández, *Rabbinic Hebrew*, pp. 5–6. See Saenz-Badillos, *History of the Hebrew Language*, pp. 162–64 for discussion of Kutscher's and Fellman's corrections of the excesses of Segal.

EXPRESSING DEFINITENESS IN ARAMAIC: A RESPONSE TO
CASEY'S THEORY CONCERNING THE SON OF MAN SAYINGS

P. J. Williams

Introduction

I present here a response to select aspects of Professor Maurice Casey's comprehensive explanation of the 'Son of Man' problem.[1] One of the elements in
Casey's 'solution' is the contention that there was a substantial change in sense
from what was originally intended by the Aramaic 'son of man' phrase and
the later sense in which ὁ υἱὸς τοῦ ἀνθρώπου was taken. In this contention
Casey's work displays affinities to that of other scholars, such as Vermes and
Lindars. However, since Casey has been the most prolific and persistent writer
arguing for such a change in sense, his approach merits a separate treatment.

The fullest expression of Casey's explanation comes in his 2007 monograph *The Solution to the 'Son of Man' Problem*. However, where ideas in that
monograph have been anticipated in Casey's earlier publications I will seek to
go to the earlier statements that he has made, provided that the approach in the
later monograph does not differ.[2] There will be various aspects of the recent
monograph and of Casey's general approach that I will not be addressing, in
particular his theories about the development of the sayings within the Greek
gospel tradition. My focus will rather be on Aramaic stages of the sayings
tradition and the transfer of sayings into Greek.

---

1. Maurice Casey, *The Solution to the 'Son of Man' Problem* (LNTS, 343; London: T&T
Clark, 2007).
2. A bibliography of Casey's writings on the Son of Man question is found in Casey,
Solution, pp. 327–28.

Casey's argument

The Son of Man question has been a continuous theme during Casey's career. He published three articles on the question in 1976 and completed his doctorate on the Son of Man in Daniel 7 the following year.[3] Since then he has published at least eight further articles on the question, two monographs on the gospel traditions in Aramaic,[4] one on the development of New Testament Christology,[5] and, of course, the 2007 monograph bringing together his ideas. There has been a considerable degree of consistency over the years in Casey's position on the development of the Son of Man sayings, though he has made a number of refinements in his approach to Aramaic sources and to questions of detail as well as to his understanding of the development of particular sayings. However, many of the pivotal points in his argument in his most recent monograph were already in his published doctoral work or even in a brief article entitled 'The Son of Man Problem', published in 1976.[6]

Casey's work takes its cue from the seminal article, published in 1967 by Geza Vermes, 'The Use of בר נש/בר נשא in Jewish Aramaic'.[7] Here Vermes argued that בר נש or בר נשא could mean 'I'.[8] This had previously been stated, but without the provision of examples. Vermes used examples from Palestinian Aramaic postdating the New Testament (e.g. Talmud and midrash) using the form בר נש or בר נשא to argue that the phrase 'son of man' could be a circumlocution for 'I'. Care is needed here, for instance when Vermes argues that one example makes it 'justifiable to assume that the speaker has in mind not some random member of the human race, but one particular person, and that that person cannot but be himself'.[9] To argue that an author may have the first

---

3.   Published as Maurice Casey, *Son of Man: The Interpretation and Influence of Daniel 7* (London: SPCK, 1980).

4.   *Aramaic Sources of Mark's Gospel* (SNTSMS, 102; Cambridge: Cambridge University Press, 1998); *An Aramaic Approach to Q: Sources for the Gospels of Matthew and Luke* (SNTSMS, 122; Cambridge: Cambridge University Press, 2002).

5.   *From Jewish Prophet to Gentile God: The Origins and Development of New Testament Christology* (Louisville, KY: Westminster/John Knox, 1991).

6.   'The Son of Man Problem', *ZNW* 67 (1976), pp. 147–54.

7.   Appendix E, Matthew Black, *An Aramaic Approach to the Gospels and Acts* (Oxford: Oxford University Press, 3rd edn, 1967), pp. 310–30.

8.   Vermes, 'Use', p. 323. Note the use of the phrase 'means "I"' followed by 'reference to' on p. 323.

9.   Vermes, 'Use', p. 326.

person in mind is different from arguing that a phrase 'means' the same as the first person pronoun. The implied reference might be something pragmatically indicated rather than belonging to the semantics of the phrase itself. Vermes did not show that the phrase *meant* 'I'. Casey and Lindars developed and adapted Vermes' approach, using some of the same textual examples. Lindars took it to mean 'A man in my position';[10] Casey took it to mean 'a man' (generally) but to contain an implicit reference to the speaker. Casey's argument includes the following ideas:

1. The phrase *bar enash(a)* was a normal word for 'man' in Aramaic.
2. Since *bar enash(a)* was a normal phrase for 'man', the gospels and the Similitudes of Enoch originally referred to 'a man' not a specific title 'The Son of Man'.
3. At the time of Jesus, Aramaic did not consistently use the definite (or emphatic) state and the indefinite (or absolute) state with a difference in meaning.
4. *Bar enash(a)* when used by Jesus had a general reference to people and can be translated 'a man' and yet Jesus could use it with particular application to himself.
5. Bilingual translators did a good job of translating this phrase into Greek using ὁ υἱὸς τοῦ ἀνθρώπου, using the first article as a 'generic' one.[11] Since they knew Aramaic they knew that this was a general (indefinite) phrase.
6. The translators knew that Jesus applied this term to himself and so rendered the phrase by ὁ υἱὸς τοῦ ἀνθρώπου in cases where they knew it applied to Jesus and by other terms when it referred to others.
7. However, monoglot Greek speakers *misconstrued* the phrase ὁ υἱὸς τοῦ ἀνθρώπου to be a definite title.

I will take up parts of Casey's argument in his own words:

> Moule declared that behind the Greek 'must be some Aramaic expression that
> meant, unequivocally, not just "Son of Man" but "*the* son of Man" or "*that* Son of

---

10.   Barnabas Lindars SSF, *Jesus Son of Man: A Fresh Examination of the Son of Man Sayings in the Gospels* (London: SPCK, 1983).
11.   In fact their translation was 'virtually inevitable' (Casey, *Solution*, p. 37).

Man'", and that this phrase was thus demonstrative because it expressly referred to Daniel's 'Son of Man'. Moule was not, however, able to produce a satisfactory expression. The definite state, בַּ(א) נַשָׁא, is not sufficient to do this, for two reasons. One is that it does not tell us which son of man is referred to. Given that it was a normal term for 'man', reference to Dan. 7.13 requires sufficient contextual indicators, which are absent from most Gospel sayings. The second point is that the force of the definite state was declining.[12]

Or again:

> The Aramaic term *bar nash(a)*, "son of man", was a normal term for "man": further, it now seems clear that it was not also a title in the Judaism of the time of Jesus. The mere fact that it was a normal term for man means that sentences containing *bar nash(a)* would not have sufficient referring power to denote a single individual, unless the context made this reference clear. This means that *bar nash(a)* was a generally unlikely term for an author or a social group to select for use as a major title.[13]

The assumption in both these quotations is that it is difficult for a word to be simultaneously 'normal' and a messianic title, though we should note that Horbury has proposed that no less common a word than ἄνθρωπος was recognized as a messianic title.[14] Thus, not all judge commonness to be an adequate ground to reject a term as a title. A further claim of Casey is that such a term would not generally have sufficient 'referring power' to denote an individual. This is presumably based on the assumption that Aramaic of the period could not mark definiteness. This assumption is implicit throughout Casey's work, as shown by the importance for him of stressing that the definite state was losing its force. However, it is difficult to find an explicit statement by him about definiteness in general in Aramaic. The nearest I have come to is the following citation in which he gives the lack of definite article as a secondary

---

    12.   Casey, 'Method in Our Madness, and Madness in Their Methods: Some Approaches to the Son of Man Problem in Recent Scholarship', *JSNT* 42 (1991), pp. 17–43 (40–41).
    13.   Casey, *From Jewish Prophet to Gentile God*, p. 47.
    14.   W. Horbury, 'The Messianic Associations of "the Son of Man"', *JTS* n.s. 36 (1985), pp. 34–55 (49).

reason alongside the fact that the term 'son of man' was common to argue that it was not a title:

> Black devotes a large part of his article to discussing the possibility that 'son of man' was a title in Judaism at the time of Jesus. Firstly, it seems very probable that the force of the emphatic state in Aramaic, the approximate equivalent of the English definite article, was declining in our period, though we do not know how far this had gone when the Similitudes of Enoch were written. It is therefore important that this is not the main point. Languages without definite articles can have titles. Accurate communication requires that the situational and linguistic context conveys what we would perceive as a titular usage in a different way. The fundamental point is that the Aramaic *barnash(a)* is generally agreed to have been a normal term for 'man'.[15]

By saying that the lack of a definite article was not the 'main point' he admits that he is using it as a subsidiary point. Clearly also in the exchange with Owen and Shepherd, the question of the definiteness of the phrase is important;[16] if Casey cannot maintain a general application for the son of man sayings then his interpretation falls.

In what follows I will illustrate a few points in which I take issue with Casey's approach. Obviously, at one level we both begin with the Greek text. If there were no Greek text there would be no discussion. However, Casey very quickly moves to his reconstructed Aramaic. As he says in relation to the Similitudes: 'it is the original text which is determinative for the author's meaning, not a hypothetical Greek intermediary translation nor the Latin terms which used to be conventional among classically trained scholars'.[17] Or again, 'hypothetical misunderstandings by Greek readers ignorant of semitic idiom

---

15. Casey, 'Aramaic Idiom and Son of Man Sayings', *ExpTim* 96 (1985), pp. 233–36 (233).

16. Paul Owen and David Shepherd, 'Speaking up for Qumran, Dalman and the Son of Man: Was *Bar Enasha* a Common Term for "Man" in the Time of Jesus?', *JSNT* 81 (2001), pp. 81–122; Maurice Casey, 'Aramaic Idiom and the Son of Man Problem: A Response to Owen and Shepherd', *JSNT* 25 (2002), pp. 3–32.

17. Casey, 'Aramaic Idiom and the Son of Man Sayings', pp. 233–34. Similarly, further on p. 234: 'Latin is irrelevant, Greek tells us no more than how uncomprehending readers of the possible mediating version in Greek might have understood the text . . .'.

cannot tell us what the author meant'.[18] But Casey's ideas of misconstrual by readers and interference in translators' minds are no less hypothetical. Casey thus moves too quickly to reconstructed Aramaic, without adequately considering all ways of explaining the text we actually have. I would agree with Tuckett who says, 'Thus, methodologically, one's first question should be about the meaning and intentions of those who recorded the words that now appear in the gospels.'[19]

Casey's method from the beginning has been to reconstruct Aramaic *behind* gospel sayings. Where such Aramaic can, according to him, be reconstructed then this is a reason for accepting authenticity. Where such Aramaic cannot, according to him, be reconstructed then this is an argument against authenticity.

From Greek back to Aramaic

It is almost a cliché to say that Jesus spoke Galilean Aramaic, though we should remember that even the idea of Galilean Aramaic is not in itself simple. Mt. 26.73 expresses the belief that a disciple of Jesus might be identified by his (presumably Galilean) speech, and in Mk 14.70 (A N Θ *al*) a group maintains that a Galilean could be identified by his speech, though it is unclear whether the chief distinguishing linguistic traits related to phonology, rhythm, lexical choice, idiom, morphology, syntax, or a combination of these. Moreover, it is likely that an itinerant preacher, like Jesus, who had frequently travelled to Judaea, would adapt his speech somewhat when in the presence of those from other localities. It is also likely that sayings transmitted within groups of disciples in Judaea in the early church did not always retain putative Galilean features. All of which is to say that even the linguistic nature of the form of Aramaic which Jesus spoke or of Aramaic sayings traditions is far from simple.

When we consider the question of the sources available to reconstruct the Aramaic of Jesus, we find that we are either faced with the small corpus of Aramaic among the Dead Sea Scrolls, inscriptions and contemporary documents, or we have to use sources from considerably later, including the Jerusalem Talmud, Palestinian Targums and Christian Palestinian Aramaic

---

18.   Casey, 'Aramaic Idiom and the Son of Man Sayings', p. 234.
19.   C. Tuckett, 'The Present Son of Man', *JSNT* 14 (1982), pp. 58–81 (58).

sources. Casey has been criticized for relying on Aramaic sources from after the time of Jesus to reconstruct the Aramaic of Jesus. In response to this Casey replies:

> I have shown elsewhere that we must use sources from after the time of Jesus, contrary to some scholars' dogmatic insistence that we should use earlier sources only. This is basically because there is not enough earlier Aramaic extant to form a language, and virtually none of it is from first-century Galilee.[20]

But there seems to be a possibility that is not considered by Casey, namely that scholars might not have enough relevant material of any kind to reconstruct sayings of Jesus with any confidence. There are all sorts of aspects of what has happened in the past which are effectively shut off for us from investigation by lack of literary evidence. What if the Aramaic sayings of Jesus were often in that situation? This might seem a pity, but our mere desire that there be sufficient evidence is not enough to generate evidence. Using problematic sources (such as Aramaic from centuries later) simply because we have no other evidence is not satisfactory.

However, Casey has a response. In several of his publications he insists on the stability of the Aramaic language in order to justify his use of later sources. He says,

> While it is clear that some changes such as the dropping of א at the beginning of אנש and the decline of the use of the absolute state of the noun did take place, it is equally clear that the basic vocabulary and structure of the language did not alter over a period of centuries. The semantic area of common words such as אב, אמר and קום continued to include all the basic uses attested in earlier Aramaic, and idiomatic features such as the construct state of the noun and the uses of participles as finite verbs are also found in many different dialects over a long period of time.[21]

---

20. Casey, 'The Aramaic Background of Mark 9:11: A Response to J. K. Aitken', *JTS* n.s. 55 (2004), pp. 92–102 (101).

21. Casey, 'General, Generic and Indefinite: The Use of the Term "Son of Man" in Aramaic Sources and in the Teaching of Jesus', *JSNT* 29 (1987), pp. 21–56 (23). A similar list can be found in Casey, 'Aramaic Idiom and the Son of Man Problem', p. 5, though four of the five terms he cites also occur in Hebrew.

However, on the basis of the arguments presented in this quotation, it would be equally possible to claim that Modern Hebrew could be used as a reliable source for the language of Jesus since it possesses אמר, אב, and קום in approximately the right senses, uses the construct state and uses participles to express the present tense.

Casey's argument is not merely problematic with respect to the Aramaic which he actually reconstructs, but also with respect to the Aramaic he does not reconstruct. Negative evidence is difficult to evaluate, but if we begin by asking, on the basis of our positive evidence, how much of all the evidence that has existed we actually have, we are starting from a legitimate point. It seems that the extant first-century Aramaic represents a small fraction of the Aramaic that once existed. We therefore need to exercise extreme caution in making claims such as that Aramaic could have or could not have said a certain thing. And yet Casey uses whether he can reconstruct a saying in Aramaic as one of his foremost criteria for whether or not a saying is authentic.[22]

From Aramaic into Greek

Casey's theory of the translation of Aramaic into Greek is that the phrase was properly translated, but then misconstrued – not mistranslated. The bilingual speakers of Aramaic and Greek intended the phrase ὁ υἱὸς τοῦ ἀνθρώπου in a different sense from how it was understood by monoglot Greek speakers. At the same time the reason for the use of the first article by the bilingual speakers was 'interference' from Greek. In a fascinating passage Casey even allows for the possibility that Jesus might have approved of the Greek expression ὁ υἱὸς τοῦ ἀνθρώπου himself. He says: 'A bilingual Jesus might have accepted this translation [ὁ υἱὸς τοῦ ἀνθρώπου]. A Jesus who taught in Greek, however, would surely have expressed himself quite differently.'[23]

If Casey is prepared to envisage a bilingual Jesus, this raises a question as to why so much emphasis is put by him on the Aramaic. He may, of course,

---

22.   In a similar way, Richard Bauckham, 'The Son of Man: "A Man in My Position" or "Someone"?', *JSNT* 23 (1985), pp. 23–33 (23–24), notes how Lindars uses conformity with the idiom he has reconstructed as a criterion of 'dominical authenticity'.

23.   Casey, 'Idiom and Translation: Some Aspects of the Son of Man Problem', *NTS* 41 (1995), pp. 164–82 (178).

merely be entertaining the possibility for the sake of argument, but there is a serious possibility that, even if Jesus did not teach in Greek, his sayings were discussed in Greek in his hearing contemporaneously. If so, the translation ὁ υἱὸς τοῦ ἀνθρώπου may be almost authorized by Jesus. This in itself would be a reason to put the emphasis on the Greek. Likewise, we would be wise not to put too much stress on the Aramaic if, as Barr and Emerton maintain, Hebrew was also widely used.[24]

But suppose we knew that Jesus taught only in Aramaic, would this not give us ground to begin with the Aramaic? As Casey says,

> [i]f Jesus spoke Aramaic, it should be possible to see more clearly what he meant
> in Aramaic, rather than in translation Greek. In principle, sayings which cannot be
> reconstructed in feasible Aramaic cannot be authentic sayings of Jesus, though this
> criterion must be handled with care, because severe problems can be caused both
> by free translation and by the meagre remains of Aramaic from the time of Jesus.[25]

I would wish to qualify this statement: if both the Aramaic and Greek were extant, it would obviously be possible to see the intention more clearly in the original than in the translation. However, it is not evident to me that the same can be said when comparing a reconstructed original with an extant translation.

We proceed now to consider how to reconstruct the *Vorlage*. To quote Casey: 'Reconstruction of a *Vorlage* is possible only from a literal translation.'[26] I quite agree. The question is how we know that the translators did translate literally. Here Casey comes to his principal piece of evidence: 'Nothing gives clearer evidence of literal translation than ὁ υἱὸς τοῦ ἀνθρώπου. Neither this phrase, nor the anarthrous υἱὸς ἀνθρώπου, is found in natural Greek.'[27] Casey does cite other evidence, but, according to him, none is as strong as this. Yet, in claiming that υἱὸς ἀνθρώπου is also not natural Greek, he is presumably saying that the Greek phrases with and without the article would *both* be able

---

24.   Details in Randall Buth, 'A More Complete Semitic Background for בר־אנשא, "Son of Man"', in C. A. Evans and J. A. Sanders (eds), *The Function of Scripture in Early Jewish and Christian Tradition* (JSNTSup, 154; Sheffield; Sheffield Academic Press, 1998), pp. 181–86.

25.   Casey, 'Idiom and Translation', p. 179.

26.   Casey, 'Idiom and Translation', p. 171.

27.   Casey, 'Idiom and Translation', p. 173.

to be cited as evidence of literal translation, which in turn challenges Casey's view that *one* of the renderings can be used as evidence of literal translation. Moreover, if this is the strongest argument, some might perceive a degree of circularity in Casey's position. Even if we could establish that it was mean-ingful to use the word 'literal' of the translation of this phrase, this would not establish that the translation was *consistently* literal. A translation can be partially literal too. Nothing but a consistently literal translation will allow us to reconstruct its *Vorlage*.

But here I come to a deeper reservation about Casey's method. There is an extensive literature on the translation technique of biblical versions. Those undertaking research in this area have compared extant texts of the translation with extant texts in the source language. In this way, analysis of translation technique has been based on evidence that is to a certain degree known. Nevertheless, the procedure is complicated. There is often legitimate schol-arly disagreement as to which source text gave rise to the text in the receptor language. To cite the most significant parallel to the situation Casey envisages: there is often dispute as to which Hebrew text stands behind a translation of the Greek Old Testament. If this happens where texts in the source language are extant and we have a considerable body of comparative material, it is surely even harder to know anything about translation technique from Aramaic into Greek in the first century, from which we have no firm illustrations of transla-tion technique based on knowledge of texts in both source and target languages and our best information is provided by the way parts of Ezra and Daniel were rendered into Greek. The method of using such a little known area as the *foundation* for study, as Casey does, is problematic.

We come then to more specific questions of how the translation that Casey proposes occurred. He proposes that more than one translator, specifically the translators of the Aramaic sayings material in Mark and the Aramaic material in Q, chose to represent cases of *bar enash(a)* by ὁ υἱὸς τοῦ ἀνθρώπου when it contained application to Jesus, but not otherwise.[28] I have three objections to this supposition:

---

28. Casey, *Solution*, pp. 253–54. Casey seeks to account for the uniformity in an ad hoc manner on p. 265.

1. Translators of this period were not consistent unless they chose to be consistent (as occurred to some degree with the *kaige* translations); consistency does not occur naturally without effort.
2. The process of differential translation, whereby translators rendered the same phrase in two different ways, lacks adequate parallels from ancient translations.
3. To suppose that the *same* striking differential translation method occurred in two translations independently with no sign of alternatives presupposes an implausible coincidence.

As for the specific mechanism he proposes which triggers the translation, he speaks of 'interference'. I note here that if the translators were genuinely bilingual, then interference from Greek to Aramaic was just as likely as interference the other way round. But if we suppose that there was interference from Aramaic to Greek, what would this look like? Here I will quote Casey:

> A particularly important distorting factor is the double level of interference present when bilingual people translate texts. Bilingual people generally experience interference between the languages which they use. This is increased when they translate from one language into another, because the features of the host language are present before them to cause the interference. Neubert has noted the problems which arise when monoglot users of the target language do not share the presuppositions of the language community in which the text was written. These problems should not be confused with mistakes. . . . Perhaps the most famous cultural shift in our field is the regular translation of תורה with νόμος.[29]

This seems to be correct as far as interference goes. However, 'generally experience interference' allows for a range of possibilities and it would be appropriate to suggest that it could more helpfully be stated that bilinguals *sometimes* experience *some* interference. The question then arises as to how likely it is that interference has occurred in any given instance, but Casey supplies no indications of frequency. If it is not a frequently occurring phenomenon, or one that is frequently detectable, why should we prefer an explanation invoking

---

29. Casey, 'Idiom and Translation', p. 175.

it in any particular instance? I would maintain that an explanation involving interference should only be preferred if all comparable explanations without positing it are shown to fail. The positing of a relatively infrequent occurrence should thus only occur if it is not possible to explain the text in the receptor language without interference.

Expressing definiteness in Aramaic

Back in 1967, Vermes said, 'It might seem from the vast mass of "son of man" literature that the linguistic aspect has been explored in such depth that nothing new can possibly emerge; but this is not so.'[30] If I am not mistaken, there continue to remain open significant avenues for linguistic research upon this question. Arguably there has been myopia concerning the sorts of linguistic questions that have been addressed in debates about the Son of Man. More particularly, debate has often assumed that the question of whether or not the phrase as used by Jesus was definite or indefinite can only be settled by investigating whether the Aramaic definite state (originally, a sort of post-positive definite article) had continuing force at the time of Jesus. This is a significant question, and I think there is much to be said for the view that it retained considerable force in Western Aramaic.[31] Even if the Aramaic definite state was breaking down, this does not mean that it was breaking down at the same rate and in the same way for all nouns simultaneously. But even if I were to concede the unlikely position that the definite state had no force that still would not lead me to the view that definiteness was not expressed. In fact, Aramaic had numerous ways of indicating whether or not an entity was definite. Moule intuitively sensed this, but could not provide specific relevant evidence:

> It has been asserted (though the assertion has not gone unchallenged) that in Palestinian Aramaic of this period *bar naš* and *bar naša* [sic] were indistinguishable in meaning, so that an unambiguous definite – 'the Son of Man' – could not have been expressed. But it is hard to conceive that it would have been beyond the

---

30. Vermes, 'Use', p. 311.
31. Casey, 'Aramaic Idiom and the Son of Man Problem', p. 6, uses ad hoc arguments to seek to deny the significance of the distinction between Eastern and Western Aramaic which is generally made by scholars.

capacity of the language to indicate an unambiguously definite or deictic sense by
some means or other – perhaps by a periphrasis.[32]

Quite apart from the definite state, there are many ways in which relevant
dialects of Aramaic could mark definiteness. These are often at the discourse
level or at the level of the sentence rather than the phrase. This should not be
a problem since, after all, Casey has often extolled the virtue of reconstructing
whole sentences or paragraphs in Aramaic,[33] and has even spoken of the 'dire
effects . . . of treating sentences "in isolation"'.[34] One demonstrative pronoun
accompanying a specific phrase early on in a discourse may well help that
phrase to be understood as definite through the following discourse. But we can
also look at other clues at the phrase level. To begin with the first example we
can take the direct object marker. In Hebrew there is a significant correlation
between the object marker אֵת and definiteness. Aramaic dialects have their
own equivalents, לְ and יָת. In Biblical Aramaic לְ marks a definite pronominal
object and it seems probable that לְ or יָת would have been used by Jesus at least
before some definite common nouns.[35] If Jesus used the phrase 'son of man'
with any frequency in his teaching then it would be bound to occur in some
object constructions and thereby indicate to Aramaic speakers whether or not
it was definite. In fact, the 'son of man' sayings in the gospels are sometimes
found to have the 'son of man' in object position. Verbs used include 'see'
(Mk 13.26; 14.62; Mt. 16.28; 26.64; Lk. 21.27)[36] or 'betray' (Lk. 22.48). It
might be objected that some of these sayings are not authentic, but we must
remember that in the work of Casey (and Lindars for that matter) the limits
of what is authentic have been set by their own understanding of the Aramaic
idiom. Even if one were to dispute the authenticity of all of these sayings, the
overwhelming balance of probability rests with the view that Jesus would

32. C. F. D. Moule, '"The Son of Man": Some of the Facts', *NTS* 41 (1995), pp. 277–79
(278). For a consideration of possible ways of marking determination see James Barr,
'"Determination" and the Definite Article in Hebrew', *JSS* 34 (1989), pp. 307–35.
33. Casey, *Solution*, p. 19.
34. Casey, *Solution*, p. 41.
35. Cf. E. Y. Kutscher, 'The Language of the Genesis Apocryphon' in Kutscher, *Hebrew
and Aramaic Studies* (Jerusalem: Magnes, 1977), pp. 20–21; G. Dalman, *Grammatik des
Jüdisch-Palästinischen Aramäisch* (Leipzig: J. C. Hinrichs, 2nd edn, 1905), p. 110.
36. Casey, 'Idiom and Translation', p. 167, even cites a Syriac text using the object marker
l after the word 'see' in conjunction with a definite 'son of man'.

sometimes have had cause to utter the phrase in question as an object in a sentence, and listeners would have known thereby whether or not he intended it to be understood as definite. An Aramaic example using the word 'see' is from 4Q214b 2, which reads חזית לאברה[ם] 'I saw Abraha[m]'. Another possible example of this from later Aramaic would be the example cited from Genesis Rabbah 38.13 by Vermes:[37]

נסגוד לבר נשא דסביל רוחא

'Let us worship the man who bears the wind/spirit'.

The object marker is used and the phrase 'son of man' is understood as definite. Note also the relative clause which we will comment on shortly.

A further way of marking definiteness would involve an anticipatory object suffix on the verb followed by an object marker as in אשכחה לחנוך '[he found + him] [object marker + Enoch]' (*1QapGen* ar 2.4.23).

There are other ways whereby definiteness could have been indicated. With each of these we are hampered by our lack of knowledge of the details of the precise form of language Jesus spoke. It is difficult therefore to be sure which constructions may have been used by Jesus and which not, and also difficult to know whether, even if a construction was used by Jesus, it was brought into connection with the phrase 'son of man'. However, together they indicate the many ways in which definiteness may have been indicated.

1. Repetition of a noun within a discourse may indicate that later occurrences within the discourse are identifiable and thus definite.
2. If an indefinite noun is introduced in a narrative and then referred to by use of a pronoun, a subsequent use of the full noun within a narrative may be judged to be definite.
3. Some nouns, such as proper nouns, may be inherently definite.
4. A preceding genitive phrase may use an anticipatory suffix and thereby indicate that what follows is definite. It is conceivable that this could have occurred with phrases such as 'the parousia of the son of man' (Mt. 24.27,

---

37. Vermes, 'Use', p. 324.

37, 39) or 'the sign of the son of man' (Mt. 24.30), or 'the days of the son of man' (Lk. 17.22, 26). A relevant example of this is the famous ברה די אל in 4Q246 2.1.[38]

5. A preceding prepositional phrase may be repeated with use of an anticipatory suffix and thereby indicate that what follows is definite. A possible example of this could be 'because of the son of man' (Lk. 6.22); 'before the son of man' (Lk. 21.36).

6. A demonstrative pronoun may be used and one use within a discourse may indicate that the noun is definite on occasions when the demonstrative is not used.

7. A restrictive relative clause may indicate definiteness by narrowing interpretative possibilities in such a way that the phrase 'son of man', whether governing the clause or contained within it, may be presumed to indicate a definite entity. For instance, Lk. 17.30 speaks of 'the day on which X is revealed', where X is the 'son of man' phrase. In some languages, including Greek and Hebrew, the definite article can precede a participle to form what is in effect a relative clause, thereby indicating the close relationship between the definite article and relative clauses.

8. Words can be definite due to cultural assumptions. For instance, in a Jewish monotheistic culture, a Jewish Aramaic speaker using the word אלהא will necessarily be understood to be speaking of a particular identifiable and therefore definite deity. Thus a vital question relative to the definiteness of the phrase son of man is whether there was a defined concept of a Son of Man. Casey begins with the language, finds no explicit linguistic evidence for a defined concept, and then reads all occurrences in the light of that. I am of the persuasion that the linguistic evidence is compatible with the idea of a defined concept, if that concept could be established in pre-Christian sources on other grounds.

In order to conclude that definiteness would have been known by hearers of Jesus, none of my particular examples needs to be authentic logia. The point can be established that if the phrase 'son of man' was indeed used by Jesus it

---

38. Comparison with other Aramaic makes it highly unlikely that the first member of this construction is in the emphatic state. See also 4Q212 5.21.

is unlikely that his hearers were always unaware of whether it was definite or indefinite. I do not wish here, however, to drive too firm a distinction between these two categories and thereby preclude the possibility that any of Jesus' sayings were ambiguous when taken by themselves. I am rather suggesting that discussion of 'son of man' sayings needs to begin from the acknowledgement that if Jesus, or anyone else, wanted a reference to a 'son of man' to be understood as definite he would be quite capable of indicating this, whether or not there was a definite concept of a son of man prior to his time.[39]

In addition to syntactic ways in which definiteness might be indicated, we may also note specific texts in which some indication of definiteness would be required. I refer here to Mk 2.28 and parallels. In Greek we have ὥστε κύριός ἐστιν ὁ υἱὸς τοῦ ἀνθρώπου καὶ τοῦ σαββάτου. What we notice about the word order is that the predicate (or part of it) precedes the subject. The main nominal element of the predicate is κύριος 'Lord', which is anarthrous precisely because it is the predicate.[40] It is because it is anarthrous in Greek that we know it says that 'the son of man is master' rather than 'the master is the son of man'. A similar thing may be said in general terms in Northwest Semitic languages. The word order when we are not dealing with finite verbs tends to be subject–predicate ('I am he' rather than 'He am I'). If one simply joins two nouns together in a predication and neither has any way of indicating that it is definite or indefinite, the former of the two will be understood to be the subject. Now if the saying in Mk 2.28 is genuine, as Casey maintains, and has preserved the word order of the original as regards subject and predicate, as Casey also maintains,[41] how would we know that the 'son of man' phrase is the subject and not the predicate if the 'son of man' phrase were not understood to be definite? Casey may avoid some of the force of this argument by translating the noun κύριος using a word that is more adjective than noun, namely שׁליט, but this

---

39. C. F. D. Moule, 'Neglected Features in the Problem of "the Son of Man"', in J. Gnilka (ed.), *Neues Testament und Kirche* (Festschrift R. Schnackenburg; Herder: Freiburg, 1974), p. 421, allows for the unlikely possibility that Jesus might have used the phrase *brh dgbr'* which is found in the Old Syriac Gospels.

40. '. . . definite predicate nouns which precede the verb usually lack the article . . .' in E. C. Colwell, 'A Definite Rule for the Use of the Article in the Greek New Testament', *JBL* 52 (1933), pp. 12–21 (20).

41. In *Aramaic Sources*, p. 138, Casey reconstructs the Aramaic of Mk 2.28 as follows: שׁליט נא הוא נשׁ בר אף בשׁבתא.

merely creates an unlikely word order in his reconstructed Aramaic. Here Casey's explanation that 'interference' in the mind of a bilingual translator has been responsible for the translation encounters serious difficulty. If the bilingual translator was in any way competent, he had to know that with the article ὁ υἱὸς τοῦ ἀνθρώπου in Greek had to be the subject. The easiest explanation for this was that he understood the phrase 'son of man' in the Aramaic to be subject and to be definite.

Thus there are a number of signs that definiteness was indicated within the text. In addition to this we may note that there were ways that a text might formally mark *indefiniteness*, for instance by using the numeral 'one' in a quasi-articular way. It could be that the consistent absence of any markers of indefiniteness could increase the sense of ancient recipients of a text that an entity was definite.

Conclusion

I have paid disproportionate attention to the aspects of Casey's work that deal with original wording in Aramaic. Since this is the foundation of his analysis, serious questions about the foundation must affect what has been built on top of it. Though it is possible that, as Casey contends, there was no title of 'Son of Man', the phrase was indefinite and of general applicability, his account of the Aramaic origin of these sayings has been shown to be unnecessarily complex and there is room for analyses treating the phrase as definite. In particular, we need not posit a strong dichotomy between the Aramaic sayings as spoken by Jesus and the Greek words recorded in the gospels.

THE USE OF DANIEL 7 IN JESUS' TRIAL, WITH
IMPLICATIONS FOR HIS SELF-UNDERSTANDING

Darrell L. Bock

Jesus' potential use of the title Son of Man at his examination by the Jewish leadership is one of the more acute specific problems this scene generates. I have written a great deal already on this event and its background, but in this chapter I wish to concentrate specifically on the possibility that Jesus appealed to the Son of Man imagery and Daniel 7 during his examination.[1] In fact, this response was an important factor in that examination's determination to take Jesus on to Pilate and the crucifixion that was the result of his meeting with the Roman prefect. I cover this specific question in two steps: (1) the use of Ps. 110.1 and Daniel 7 together and (2) the Apocalyptic Son of Man as a category Jesus used.

The use of Ps. 110.1 and Dan. 7.13 together

This topic and the next one are closely bound. One could discuss them together, but the availability of these Old Testament (OT) images is still a separate discussion from Jesus' general use of the Son of Man title. So I will consider

---

1. See my *Blasphemy and Exaltation in Judaism and the Final Examination of Jesus* (WUNT, 2.106; Tübingen: Mohr Siebeck, 1998) for a look at all the background and conceptual issues tied to this event. I have followed this up with a more comprehensive look at this specific scene in 'Blasphemy and the Jewish Examination of Jesus', *BBR* 17.1 (2007), pp. 53–114. Yet another updated version forms one essay for a forthcoming WUNT volume yet to be titled on the historical Jesus edited by Robert Webb and me. The present essay seeks to get into yet more detail on the specific question of Jesus' use of the Son of Man imagery in this context.

issues tied to the question of the apocalyptic Son of Man separately. First, I discuss the use of Ps. 110.1, especially as it appears in Mark 12. Then I take up the question of Daniel 7 and the debate over the Son of Man.

In considering authenticity issues associated with the use of Ps. 110.1, our key text is Mk 12.35-37, because it sets the backdrop to the examination scene. In that passage, Jesus raised the question why David calls the Christ Lord, if he is supposed to be David's son.[2] If this passage raising the issue of what Messiah should be called is authentic, there is nothing unusual about its presence in the trial scene.

Now the major objection to the authenticity of this Mark 12 text and its use of Ps. 110.1 is its alleged dependence on the LXX to make its argument. It is claimed that the wordplay involving the title 'Lord' is only possible in the LXX, so this text must be a later Christological reflection of the post-Easter, Hellenistic Christian community.[3] Hahn also rejects any attempt to suggest how this text may have been read in Hebrew or Aramaic had there been an attempt to avoid pronunciation of the divine Name, a point raised by Dalman years ago.[4]

Two points need to be made here. The first point in response to Hahn is that one cannot exclude by mere declaration the possibility that the divine Name was not pronounced in an oral setting. It must be noted that it was common for biblical texts to be pronounced with a substitute for the divine Name, as also was the case for benedictions, with the exception of a few specified cases. One of the situations with benedictions is noted in *m. Sotah* 7.6. This text describes how the common priestly benediction of Num. 6.24-26 was given to the people. So here we have a scriptural text and a benediction. In the provinces, each

2. For a full treatment of Ps. 110.1 and its suitability to this setting, see my *Luke 9:51–24:53* (BECNT, 3b; Grand Rapids: Baker, 1996), pp. 1630–41.

3. This argument is clearly summarized by Ferdinand Hahn, *Christologische Hoheitstitel* (5th edn; Göttingen: Vandenhoeck & Ruprecht, 1995), pp. 112–15.

4. Dalman, *Die Worte Jesu*, p. 270. In the English version, the discussion of avoiding the divine name appears on pp. 182–83 and 194–98. In these sections he shows the kinds of things that were done at the time. On p. 182 he says, 'It may be accepted as certain that by the time of Jesus the divine name יהוה had long disappeared from popular use, and that in the public reading of Holy Scripture the word was replaced by אדני'. He also notes here how this was done in rendering the divine name into Aramaic as well by mixing vowels of אדני with the radicals of יהוה. He suggests that perhaps the phrase 'the name' may have been used. One of the things the rendering of κύριος in the LXX already indicates is that some type of practice making this kind of a move for the divine name already existed when this translation was made by Jews of the time.

verse was read by itself, and the crowd would respond with amen in each case, while at the temple it was read as a whole and treated together. But the more important consideration for us comes next when the issue of the pronunciation of the Name is treated. The text reads, 'in the temple they pronounced the Name as written, but in the provinces by a substituted word'. So it is no guarantee that the presence of the divine Name in Scripture meant that it would be read or spoken in public.

Another text is *m. Yoma* 6.2. This text records the confession of the high priest over the lamb for the nation's sins on the Day of Atonement. Included in the saying is the citation of Lev. 16.30. This verse includes a reference to the divine Name, which the high priest did read, and the crowd bowed and fell on their faces when 'the people which stood in the temple court heard the expressed Name come forth from the mouth of the high priest'. In addition, they responded to the confession and the use of the Name with a euphemism, 'Blessed be the name of the glory of his kingdom forever and ever'.[5]

These two texts show that using Scripture in the temple (or in public) did not guarantee the divine name was pronounced.

Still a third example appears at Qumran, though it is not consistent.[6] In the *Isaiah Scroll*, יהוה is occasionally altered to אד"ני, or the dual phrase (אד"ני יהוה) is reduced to only אד"ני (1QIsa glosses the Name in 28.16, 30.15, 65.13, by writing above it אדוני; and reduces it in 49.22, 2.4, 1.1).[7] In 1QIsa 50.5,

---

5. The command is also noted in exactly the same way in *m. Yoma* 3.8.

6. Stephen Byington, 'יהוה' and 'אד"ני', *JBL* 76 (1957), pp. 58–59.

7. *Contra* Siegfried Schulz ('Maranatha und Kyrios Jesus', *ZNW* 53 [1962], pp. 125–44 [133]), there is evidence of this type of change in early material. On pp. 132–33, he notes that a shortened form of the divine Name (יהו) appears in the Elephantine papyri of the fifth century BCE (ιαω), but he raises questions about how much can be drawn from this practice. However, the very presence of an alternate and *abbreviated* form of the Name shows that the Name is being treated with respect by not being reproduced exactly. The texts at Elephantine can be found in A. Cowley, *Aramaic Papyri of the Fifth Century B.C.* (Oxford: Clarendon Press, 1923). The passages where the Name appears are: 6.4, 6, 11; 22.1, 123; 25.6; 27.15; 30.6, 15, 24-27 (3×); 31.7, 24-25 (2×); 33.8; 38.1; 45.3-4; and 56.2. Care with regard to speaking the divine Name is also noted in Josephus, *Ant* 2.12.4 §§275–76; and in Philo, *Vit. Mos.* 2.114. For evidence of a substitution of the Name with Lord, one can note the LXX and the examples at Qumran; see Note 8. On the use of ιαω, see R. Ganschinietz, 'Iao', in *Paulys Real-Encyclopädie der classischen Altertumswissenschaft* (Stuttgart: Metzlersche, 1916), vol. 9, cols. 698–721; Menaham Stern, *Greek and Latin Authors on Jews and Judaism* (Jerusalem: Israel Academy of Sciences and Humanities, 1974), vol. 1, pp. 98, 171–72, 211–12, and vol. 2, pp. 140–41, 410–12, 673; and David Aune, 'Iao ('Ιαώ)', *RAC* 129, cols. 1–12.

it is replaced with אלוהים. The Name is omitted from 1QIsa 45.8, while in 1QIsa 52.5 and 59.21 it is omitted once when it appears twice in the MT. In 1QIsa 3.17, ואדוני appears for the Name, while 3.15 writes אדוני over the Name. In 1QIsa 40.7 and 42.6, a row of dots appears where the Name would be expected, while in 42.5 the term האלוהים appears instead of the Name. The same occurs in other texts from Qumran as well.[8] These changes show that some Jews were careful to avoid writing the divine Name in Scripture, which in turn would prevent its being pronounced as well. These examples show it is an open question whether the Name would have been pronounced or avoided.

What these examples mean is that it is not certain that even if Jesus cited Ps. 110.1 he would have spoken the divine Name as written, given the possible variations permitted within oral delivery. This raises doubts about whether Jesus pronounced the divine Name. It is quite possible that the divine Name was not pronounced, but a substitute was given, although the alternate option also exists. The minute such a substitution was made, the ambiguity would exist in Aramaic (אמר מריא למרא). In Hebrew, a substitution revolving around the reuse of אדני is also a possibility.

The second point in response to Hahn applies even if a substitution for the Name was *not* made, namely, that the problem introduced by Mark 12 text remains, though with slightly less of an edge. The issue raised by Mark 12 is not that the divine title Lord is used, but that David, an ancestor in a patriarchal society, calls a descendant his Lord.[9] This problem exists in the text in its Hebrew form as well. In the entire dispute over the later Christological significance emerging from this text, it has been forgotten that the dilemma

---

8.   Michael A. Knibb, *The Qumran Community* (Cambridge: Cambridge University Press, 1987), pp. 134, 170, 232–33, 250. He notes how the Name is written in old script in *1QpHab* vi 14, while in *1QS* VIII 14, the citation of Isa. 40.3 leaves only four dots where the name YHWH appeared. Interestingly, in *4QpPsa* ii 13 the reverse is the case, as YHWH appears where 'Lord' was present. J. A. Fitzmyer has criticized Schulz at this point in 'The Contribution of Qumran Aramaic to the Study of the New Testament', *NTS* 20 (1974), pp. 382–407 (386–91). He notes in *11QTgJob* the absolute use of Aramaic and comments on: (1) the construct chains Schulz mentioned in the Elephantine papyri at 30.15, (2) the use of אלהא for the tetragrammaton in *11QTgJob* 37.3, 38.2 (2×), 38.3, and 38.7, and (3) the rendering of שדי twice by מרא in *11QTgJob* 34.5, 7, as well as its likely presence in 36.8. In 34.6-7 he is confident it appears for the divine Name. For another probable absolute use of the term Lord (מרי), see also *1QapGen* 20.12-13.

9.   Jesus' argument appears to assume that David is the speaker of the utterance.

originally rotated around the honour that David gives to the proposed Messiah, who also is his descendant, a fact that is ironic in a culture that gives honour to the elder, not the younger.[10] Thus it is quite possible that the text in an unaltered Semitic form could raise the dilemma that Jesus points out in the text. Why would David call his descendant Lord? Might whatever significance is attached to being seated at God's right hand be the reason? Might that promise, then, call for reflection?

These two considerations (the possibility the Name was not pronounced and the tension of the elder respecting the younger) mean that Ps. 110.1 could be used as a way of probing the authority of the Messiah from the perspective of David as the one affirming the royal promise, according to Jewish tradition.[11] There is nothing here that requires a post-Easter reading of this passage.

But there is a final consideration as well that speaks for the authenticity of Jesus' use of Ps. 110.1 in Mark 12. It is the very ambiguity and Jewishness of the way Jesus makes his point. The playing down of the Davidic sonship of the messianic figure is counter to the normal post-Easter emphasis, as Acts 2.30-36, 13.23-39; Rom. 1.2-4; and Heb. 1.3-14 show. Those who see a post-Easter creation must deal with this question: would the later, post-Easter community have expressed its conviction about Jesus as Lord in a way that is so ambiguous and that at the same time gives an impression that the long-established and quite traditional Son of David title is insignificant?

The form of Jesus' query has long been noted to parallel the Jewish style of putting two statements in opposition to one another. The point is not to deny one or the other but to relate them to each other.[12] Jesus is simply affirming that David's calling Messiah Lord is more important than his being called Son of David. The query, which is unanswered in the Mark 12 context, serves to underscore the Messiah's authority and the ancestor's respect for his anticipated

10.   It should be noted that one rabbinic reading of Ps. 110.1 does regard Hezekiah as the figure mentioned here, but does not probe what that implies about the giving of such honour to a younger one. This Jewish view is noted by Justin Martyr, in *Dial.* 33 and 83.

11.   The one assumption that Jesus and his audience share about the psalm is that David is the speaker, a view that would fit the first-century setting. Given that the text is royal and that Israel lacks a king in Jesus' time, it is also likely that the text would be seen as applying to a king in a restored monarchy, a restoration that could easily conjure up messianic implications.

12.   David Daube, *The New Testament and Rabbinic Judaism* (London: University of London/Athlone, 1956), pp. 158–63.

great descendant. At a narrative level, the unanswered question looks for a resolution. The trial scene does that for Mark. The coming exaltation of the One to be crucified explains the passage, and the passage explains the significance of that exaltation. The development is subtle, coming in two stages somewhat detached from each other in the narrative flow.

Now this issue of Messiah's authority as an abstract theological topic is not a post-Easter question. It has been raised by the very nature of the Jerusalem events in which this dispute appears. An earlier query about Jesus' authority came after he cleansed the temple (Mk 11.27-33). Jesus' query here is an answer to the question the leadership posed to him earlier, but with a critical and reflective edge. If David, the one who received the promise, responds to Messiah as Lord, how should others (including you leaders!) view him? Jesus does not make an identification of himself with Messiah in Mark 12, but merely sets forth the question theoretically and leaves the conclusions to his listeners, as Mark does for his readers. Would a post-Easter creation be so subtle?

James Dunn, in treating the Messiah issue and Jesus' self-understanding, argues that Jesus rejected the messianic title and its linkage to the 'long-hoped-for David's royal son' with a qualified no.[13] We prefer to argue that the reply is a qualified yes. The category of David's son is at work, but its role is not as central as others wish to make it. The messianic role Jesus undertakes is more comprehensive in its authority than the Davidic son category suggests. This scene is like Peter's confession at Caesarea Philippi in representing a reprioritizing of how Christ is seen. At Peter's declaration, 'Christ' is affirmed as the better confession than 'prophet', but it lacks the note of suffering it must bear, so that Jesus urges silence for a time. With the query over Ps. 110.1 treated here, Jesus points out that the Messiah is David's Son, but far more importantly he is David's (i.e. his ancestor's!) Lord. In agreement with Dunn, I would argue that Jesus rejected the understanding of Christ as currently seen by many in Judaism, but in the end Jesus embraced the association, once it was related to other realities of his divinely anointed call. The events of the final week were helping to reveal the fresh points of association. Where Dunn argues that the early church 'emptied the title of its traditional content and filled it with new

---

13.   James D. G. Dunn, *Jesus Remembered* (Grand Rapids: Eerdmans, 2003), p. 652.

content provided by the law and the prophets and the psalms'[14] after Good
Friday, I contend it was Jesus who started them on this road to reconfiguration
by his acts as well as words like those present here. What gives the appearance
that this creative work was from the early church was that Jesus did not push
hard to express these points until the end of his ministry as he faced the events
that were disclosing what God was doing through him. So while Dunn sees
little of value tied to the title Christ for getting to Jesus' self-understanding,
I would contend it was a base from which he built in a gradual way to avoid
confusion. However, as we move into the decisive confrontation in Jerusalem,
Jesus pushes such acts and remarks more to the fore as he fills out the portrait
he sees himself representing.

In sum, the evidence of Mk 12.35-37 indicates that it is far more likely that
Ps. 110.1 goes back to a period when the issues surrounding Jesus' identity
were surfacing than to roots in a community that was openly confessing and
preaching him in the midst of dispute. As such, its claims to authenticity are
strong. This means that the roots of the well-attested NT use of Ps. 110.1 go
back, in all likelihood, to Jesus himself, and so this was a text he could use in
his defence later, particularly if he contemplated an eventual vindication by
God. But to show that Ps. 110.1 could be used by Jesus, or even was used by
him on one occasion, does not indicate that it was used as shown in Mk 14.62.
This requires consideration of the text that is paired with Daniel 7, along with
some reflection on the Son of Man concept that is also present in the examination scene.

So I turn to Daniel 7 as a way into the discussion about the Son of Man.
The question of the possibility of Jesus' use of Dan. 7.13-14 is closely tied to
the issue of the apocalyptic Son of Man. This question is examined now in
two steps. Here we consider the conceptual parallels that indicate that, during
the time of Jesus, there was speculation about an exalted figure like the Son
of Man in Judaism. If this is the case, it can be seriously questioned whether
such reflection would have taken place only in a post-Easter context. The next
section will consider the issue of the apocalyptic Son of Man and Jesus by

14.   James D. G. Dunn, *Jesus Remembered*, p. 653.

looking at the evidence of these sayings themselves, regardless of whether the evidence discussed in this section is deemed persuasive or not.[15]

It has been a hotly debated question whether one should speak of a Son of Man figure in Judaism, because (1) the expression in Daniel 7 is not a title but a description ('one like a son of man'), and (2) it has been argued that there is no clear evidence in early Jewish texts that such a figure was ever the subject of intense Jewish speculation.[16] More recently, the debate has been renewed in a more cautiously stated form. Whether there was a single Son of Man concept might be debated, but there certainly was speculation about an exalted figure whose roots lie in Daniel 7.[17]

The summary evidence involves a wide array of sources from Judaism of varying strength. For example, in *11QMelch* 2.18, there is reference to the bearer of good tidings, who is 'the messiah of the spirit of whom Dan[iel] spoke'. Now, the allusion in the context is probably to Dan. 9.25 because seven weeks are mentioned, but Horbury notes that this text was often associated with Daniel 2 and 7 in Jewish thinking, so the same figure may be in view.[18] *Ezekiel the Tragedian* contains a text where in a dream Moses gets to sit on God's throne. What is most important for the issue of conceptual association is that the throne of exaltation on which Moses sat was associated with the plural expression 'thrones', language from Dan. 7.9.

Other slightly later texts have even clearer points of contact. *1 Enoch* is filled with Son of Man references (46.2-4; 48.2; 62.5, 7, 9, 14; 63.11; 69.27, 29 [2×]; 70.1; 71.14, 17). His enthronement in 62.2-14 is clearly connected to Daniel 7,

---

15. This two-tiered division of the discussion reflects the way the issue is carefully discussed by Brown (*The Death of the Messiah* [New York: Doubleday, 1994], pp. 509–15).

16. Ragnar Leivestad, 'Exit the Apocalyptic Son of Man', *NTS* 18 (1971–72), pp. 243–67. His argument is that only *1 Enoch* gives potential early Jewish evidence for such a title, that it is too late to count, that a title is not certain in the Similitudes, and that a title is not present in Daniel 7. One can certainly challenge Leivestad's view of the date of *1 Enoch*. Other points that he raises will be addressed shortly.

17. John J. Collins, 'The Son of Man in First-Century Judaism', *NTS* 38 (1992), pp. 448–66; and William Horbury, 'The Messianic Associations of "The Son of Man"', *JTS* 36 (1985), pp. 34–55.

18. Horbury, 'Messianic Associations', p. 42. Among the texts he notes are *Num. Rab.* 13.14 on Num. 7.13 and *Tan.*, Toledoth 20. (ed. Buber), with the second text including a reference to Isa. 52.7 as well.

with its reference to a seat on the 'throne of glory'.[19] *1 Enoch* 46.1 and 47.3 also seem to allude to Daniel 7, as do 63.11; 69.27, 29. The three variations in the way 'Son of Man' is referred to here do not alter the point that it is Daniel 7 that is the point of departure for the imagery here.[20] Finally, there is the image of the exalted figure in 4Q491, who also echoes themes of Daniel 7.[21] Every text discussed up to this point precedes or is contemporary to Jesus.

4 Ezra 13 is another, later text that also reflects speculation about the figure of Daniel. A rabbinic dispute attributed to the late first century involves Akiba's claim that the 'thrones' are reserved for God and David. It suggests an interesting regal, connection to Daniel 7 (*b. Hag.* 14a; *b. Sanh.* 38b).[22] Some have compared the Melchizedek figure to aspects of Son of Man speculation.[23] The variety of passages indicates that Daniel 7 imagery was a part of first-century Jewish eschatological and apocalyptic speculation, apart from the question of the presence of a defined Son of Man figure. This means that Daniel 7 was a text that was present in the theologically reflective thinking of those strands of eschatologically oriented Judaism and was quite available to Jesus once he

---

19.   On the disputed date of *1 Enoch*, see E. Isaac in *Old Testament Pseudepigrapha* (ed. J. H. Charlesworth; 2 vols; Garden City, NY: Doubleday, 1983–85), vol. 1, pp. 6–7, who argues for a first-century date; and Siebert Uhlig, *Jüdische Schriften aus hellenistisch-römischer Zeit: Das Äthiopische Henochbuch* (vol. 5/6; Gütersloh: Gütersloh Verlagshaus, 1984), pp. 574–75, who considers dates ranging from the end of the Hasmonean period into the first century and sees roots extending back into the first century BCE. A fresh discussion of the date debate appears in G. Boccaccini (ed.), *Enoch and the Messiah Son of Man: Revisiting the Book of the Parables.* (Grand Rapids: Eerdmans, 2007), pp. 415–96. A full review of the history of this discussion about dating the Parables of Enoch is found in my forthcoming, 'The Date of Enoch's Parables: A *Forschungsbericht*', in a yet to be titled book edited by James Charlesworth and me. It will argue for a late first century BCE or early first century CE date given the latest allusion in the material is to conflict with the Parthians in c.40 BCE (*1 Enoch* 56.6-8). It is probably a first-century text. On the differences between the Enoch imagery and Ps. 110.1–Daniel 7, see Hengel, *Studies in Early Christology*, (Edinburgh: T&T Clark, 1995), pp. 185–89. Enoch lacks explicit reference to the intimate right-hand imagery. However, it must be noted that Enoch's imagery otherwise is very close to these older texts. The issue in all of them is judging authority carried out as the exclusive representative of God from a heavenly throne. The throne and authority are associated directly with God.

20.   *Contra* Leivestad, 'Exit the Apocalyptic Son of Man', n. 105.

21.   Hengel, *Studies in Early Christology*, p. 202.

22.   These Talmudic texts were also discussed in my *Blasphemy and Exaltation*, pp. 145–54, under David with mention of *4 Ezra* in a separate subsection.

23.   P. J. Kobelski, *Melchizedek and Melchireša'* (CBQMS, 10; Washington, DC: Catholic Biblical Association, 1981), p. 136.

started thinking in eschatological-vindication terms. There is nothing here that requires a post-Easter scenario. So the availability of Daniel 7 for reflection about the end seems clear enough.

Only two questions remain with regard to the use of these texts. (1) Did Jesus speak of himself as the apocalyptic Son of Man? (2) Is the kind of stitching together of OT allusions such as the combination in Mk 14.62 possible for Jesus? It is to those questions I now turn, but it must be said before considering them that there is nothing in the evidence about the use and availability of Ps. 110.1 or Dan. 7.13 that demands that the usage here be seen as post-Easter. When Perrin wrote arguing that Mk 14.62 reflected a Christian pesher tradition, he did not note any of the Jewish texts alluding to Daniel 7 texts already cited, a collection of passages showing how alive these ideas were in the first century.[24] Little has changed since Perrin wrote for many commentators of Mark, who think Mark has given us only a carefully crafted narrative that has historical verisimilitude. Boring says it like this: 'However, such historical verisimilitude is almost incidental to Mark's purpose, and should not divert attention from the primary meaning at the Markan level of the text.'[25] Boring sees this as Jesus' climactic claim that he is the Christ, pointing to an affirmation of what he regards as a later Christian confession placed into Jesus' mouth, as Jesus definitively dissolves the messianic secret by his answer (although all the acts Jesus has performed in this last week have already done as much). Later Boring says, 'Thus the reason for Jesus' condemnation and death in Mark is not to be explained in political and juridical terms, but is a matter of Markan Christology and discipleship.'[26] The only question such views have is to ponder whether Jesus would have portrayed himself as the authoritative figure described in Daniel 7, whether Mark would be interested in such questions and

24. Norman Perrin, 'Mark XIV.62: The End Product of a Christian Pesher Tradition?' *NTS* 13 (1965–66), pp. 150–55.

25. Boring, *Mark* (Louisville: Westminster John Knox Press, 2006), p. 413.

26. Boring, *Mark*, p. 414. It is important to note that Boring later argues that Mark presents the blasphemy as 'an affront to God, the temple, and the Torah, which qualified as blasphemy in Jewish eyes, and his declaring himself to be the Christ could be represented to Pilate as claiming to be king' (pp. 414–15). This lofty claim is what I propose Mark is interested in showing as historically tied to Jesus. Earlier he called the scene rooted in a historical core and historically plausible (p. 410). So why is one forced to choose between history and Christological confession here? Surely, Jesus gave thought to who he was and why he was in this situation, including what in God's programme could help to explain what he was doing.

how such affirmations fit early Christian confession.[27] For the view which sees a post-Easter confession in play, the fact that these remarks fit into the church's confession, and the confession subsumes everything under the idea of the Son of Man, disqualifies the remark from being historical because that association is the work of the later church. But is it really clear, in light of the contemporary Jewish evidence already noted, that the Son of Man title is late and that one must see the Christ confession and the use of the Son of Man as confined to a post-Easter setting? Could Jesus not have formed these associations as an eschatological figure who preached the coming kingdom? This kind of either/ or thinking really does not pursue seriously the issue of whether there might be a real cause–effect between Jesus' teaching and the church's confession. It rejects the option of a both–and linking at work here that could go back to Jesus. Our reading seeks to challenge such a one-sided reading of Mark. This way of dividing eschatological hope, Son of Man and Jesus does not take seriously the historical possibilities and connections raised by the ancient evidence. We have already argued the case for Jesus' use of Ps. 110.1 above in discussing Mk 12.35-37, but what of the apocalyptic Son of Man?

27.   The respective answers to these questions for critical sceptics are: (1) that Jesus would not be so explicit or did not make such connections, (2) that Mark was not interested in such questions, and (3) that Mark was solely concerned with an affirmation of pastoral Christology for discipleship.

Jesus' use of the image of the apocalyptic Son of Man

The Son of Man title has been the object of intense debate for years and shows no signs of abating.[28] In this article, we can only treat where the discussion stands and develop the points most relevant to our concern.

Numerous issues surround the discussion, including an intense debate over whether the expression is representative of a title (like the form of its consistent NT use) or is an idiom. If it is an idiom, then it has been argued that the meaning is either a circumlocution for 'I' (Vermes) or an indirect expression with the force of 'some person' (Fitzmyer).[29] It seems that, for most students of the problem today, a formal title, or at least a unified Son of Man concept, did not yet exist in the early first century and that Fitzmyer has more evidence available for his view on the idiom. It is the idiomatic element in the Aramaic expression and the lack of a fixed concept in Judaism that allow any 'son of man' remark to be ambiguous unless it is tied to a specific passage or context. This means the term could be an effective vehicle as a cipher for Jesus that he could fill with content, defining it as he used it. One can argue, looking at the flow of Jesus' ministry as it appears in the Synoptics, that Jesus used the term ambiguously initially and drew out its force as he continued to use it, eventually associating it with Daniel 7.[30]

28. Representative of a host of recent monographs since 1980 are: A. J. B. Higgins, *The Son of Man in the Teaching of Jesus* (SNTSMS, 39; Cambridge: Cambridge University Press, 1980); Seyoon Kim, *The 'Son of Man' as the Son of God* (WUNT 30; Tübingen: Mohr Siebeck, 1983); Barnabas Lindars, *Jesus Son of Man* (Grand Rapids: Eerdmans, 1983); Chrys C. Caragounis, *The Son of Man: Vision and Interpretation* (WUNT, 38; Tübingen: Mohr Siebeck, 1986); Volker Hampel, *Menschensohn und historischer Jesus: Ein Rätselwort als Schlüssel zum messianischen Selbtsverständnis Jesu* (Neukirchen-Vluyn: Neukirchener Verlag, 1990); Anton Vögtle, *Die 'Gretchenfrage' des Menschensohn-Problems: Bilanz und Perspective* (QD, 152; Freiburg im Breisgau: Herder, 1994); D. Burkitt, *The Son of Man Debate: A History and Evaluation* (SNTSMS 107; Cambridge: Cambridge University Press, 1999).

29. I have already commented on this issue in a special excursus entitled 'The Son of Man in Aramaic and Luke (5:24)', in *Luke 1:1–9:50* (BECNT, 3a; Grand Rapids: Baker, 1994), pp. 924–30; and in 'The Son of Man in Luke 5:24', *BBR* 1 (1991), pp. 109–21. For Vermes' argument, see 'The Use of נש בר/נשא בר in Jewish Aramaic', *An Aramaic Approach to the Gospels and Acts* (3rd edn, by M. Black; Oxford: Clarendon Press, 1967), pp. 310–30. For J. Fitzmyer, 'Another View of the "Son of Man" Debate', *JSNT* 4 (1979), pp. 58–68; and *A Wandering Aramean: Collected Aramaic Essays* (SBLMS, 25; Missoula, MT: Scholars Press, 1979), pp. 143–61.

30. I have made this argument elsewhere already in 'The Son of Man in Aramaic and Luke (5:24)' in *BBR* 1 and in 'The Son of Man in Luke 5:24' in my *Luke* commentary.

But as was shown above, it is one thing to say that the Son of Man figure was not a given in Judaism and quite another to say that Daniel 7 was not the object of reflection in that period. Even if a fixed portrait and title did not exist, the outlines of such a figure were emerging and the context for his activity was being appealed to regularly in the midst of expressions of eschatological hope. These ideas were 'in the air' and thus were available for reflection *and* development.

So what is the evidence in the Gospels themselves concerning the apocalyptic Son of Man? The designation Son of Man appears 82 times in the Gospels and is a self-designation of Jesus in all but one case, where it reports a claim of Jesus (Jn 12.34).[31] When one sorts out the parallels, it looks as though 51 sayings are involved, of which 14 appear to come from Mark and ten from the sayings source, often called Q.[32] Of the four uses outside the Gospels, only one (Acts 7.56) has the full phrase with the definite article as it appears in the Gospels (Heb. 2.6; Rev. 1.13, 14.14). In other words, the term is very much one associated with Jesus' own speech. So in texts where the early church is clearly speaking, the term is rare, and the full form of the title almost never appears. The nature of its usage by Jesus and the oddity of the term as a Greek expression are the probable reasons that the expression appears in this limited way. Other titles such as Son of God, Messiah and Lord were more functional. Jeremias makes the following observation about the pattern of usage:

> How did it come about that at a very early stage the community avoided the title ὁ υἱὸς τοῦ ἀνθρώπου because it was liable to be misunderstood, did not use it in a single confession, yet at the same time handed it down in the sayings of Jesus, in the synoptic gospels virtually as the only title used by Jesus of himself? How is it that the instances of it increase, but the usage is still strictly limited to the sayings of Jesus? There can only be one answer; the title was rooted in the tradition of the sayings of Jesus right from the beginning; as a result, it was sacrosanct, and no-one dared eliminate it.[33]

---

31.   Mk 2.10 is sometimes seen as an editorial aside by Mark, but the syntax of the verse makes the case for this awkward and quite unlikely. The breakdown is 69 times in the Synoptics (Matt 30, Mark 14, Luke 25) and 13 times in John.

32.   Brown, *The Death of the Messiah*, p. 507.

33.   J. Jeremias, *New Testament Theology: The Proclamation of Jesus* (trans. John Bowden; New York: Scribner, 1971), p. 266.

These factors make a good case for seeing the expression as having roots in Jesus' own use. But such observations only defend the general use of the term. What can be said about the apocalyptic Son of Man sayings?

It is significant to note how well-attested the apocalyptic Son of Man is within the tradition:[34]

Mark: Mk 8.38
Mk 13.26
Mk 14.62

Q: Mt. 24.27 (like Lk. 17.24)
Mt. 24.37 (like Lk. 17.26)
Mt. 24.39 (like Lk. 17.30)
Lk. 12.8 (Mt. 10.32 lacks the title)

M: Mt. 10.23
Mt. 13.41
Mt. 19.28 (Lk. 22.30 lacks the title) [this could be Q]
Mt. 24.44
Mt. 25.31

L: Lk. 17.22

What the list clearly shows is that the apocalyptic Son of Man shows up in every level of the Synoptic Gospel tradition. If the criterion of multiple attestation means anything or has any useful purpose, the idea that Jesus spoke of himself in these terms should not be doubted. At the least a significant burden of proof is required to deny the term's authenticity and to explain the depth of the presence of this theme across the tradition. The text that a few of these sayings most naturally reflect is Dan. 7.13-14 (triple tradition: Mk 13.26 = Mt. 24.30 = Lk. 21.27; Mk 14.62 = Mt. 26.64 [though Lk. 22.69 lacks an allusion to Daniel 7]; M: Mt. 13.41; Mt. 19.28; Mt. 25.31; Q: possibly Lk. 12.8 [though

---

34. The following list is part of a longer apocalyptic Son of Man discussion in my *Luke 9:51–24:53*, pp. 1171–72.

the parallel in Matthew lacks the title, it does have a vindication-judgement setting]). Though the association with Daniel 7 is less widely attested, it is the only biblical text that supplies the elements for the texts that do treat vindication. Once the category of apocalyptic Son of Man is present, then a connection with Daniel 7 cannot be very far away.

The idea that this expression was solely the product of the early church faces two significant questions that bring a post-Easter church view into doubt. (1) Why was this title so massively retrojected, seemingly being placed on Jesus' lips in an exclusive way unlike any other major title, such as 'Lord', 'Son of God' and 'Messiah'? (2) If this title was fashioned by the early church and was created as the self-designation of Jesus, why has it left almost no trace in non-Gospel NT literature, unlike the other titles?[35] Martin Hengel may summarize all of this best when he says,

> I am simply unable to believe that the so-called earliest Palestinian community (that is, in reality, his closest disciples) made him the resurrected Son of Man after the appearances, and then quickly suppressed the cipher because it was unsuitable for mission proclamation, while at the same time being extremely careful to insure that in the gospels tradition only Jesus speaks of the Son of Man, never his disciples, just as the Messiah title was strictly held at a distance from him in the production of the dominical sayings. Radical critical exegetes seem to me to be too trusting here. In a similar context, A. Schlatter speaks of the 'conjecture that creates "history"'.[36]

35.   These two penetrating questions are raised by Brown (*The Death of the Messiah*, p. 507).

36.   Hengel, *Studies in Early Christology*, pp. 59–60. He cites A. Schlatter, *Der Zweifel an der Messianität Jesu*, p. 182. Later Hengel notes, 'It is in any case wrong to construct a thoroughgoing antithesis between the "(Son of) Man", and the "Messiah": both the Jewish and the early Christian sources forbid this. Jesus employs "(Son of) Man", an expression characterized both by Dan. 7.13, and ordinary, everyday use, precisely because it is a cipher, and not explicitly messianic. It becomes, then, paradoxically, the expression for the eschatological mystery connected with his mission and passion' (p. 60). Hengel's proposition assumes that the latest origin for the Son of Man tradition comes from the Jewish Christian context within the area of Palestine; it is a Semitic, not a Hellenistic tradition. The case for this conclusion is shown by Donald R. A. Hare, *The Son of Man Tradition* (Minneapolis: Fortress Press, 1990), pp. 231–35. It is the consistent and unusually awkward construction of the phrase ὁ υἱὸς τοῦ ἀνθπώπου in Greek that leads to this conclusion.

All of this makes it inherently much more likely that Jesus referred to himself as Son of Man in an apocalyptic sense than that the church was responsible for this identification, despite claims otherwise in studies on the Son of Man as recent as Burkett's survey of the Son of Man discussion in New Testament.[37] The evidence suggests that Dan. 7.13 was a significant feature of his thinking by the end of his ministry, because most of the explicit references to Daniel 7 appear as Jesus drew near to Jerusalem.

One other strand of evidence also makes a connection between king and Son of Man. The combination of Son of Man imagery and the imagery of a royal figure, the very combination appearing in Mk 14.62, also has traces in the NT and in Jewish tradition. In the NT the other such text is Mk 2.23-27, where the authority of David appears side by side with an appeal to the authority of the Son of Man, because the famous king is the prototype and justification for Jesus' exceptional activity with his disciples on the Sabbath.[38] In Judaism, it has been noted how the Danielic figure has elements of authority that other texts from the Jewish Scriptures attribute to the great expected king.[39] Bittner notes how the themes of rule, kingdom and power reflect the presentation of a regal figure, not a prophetic figure: 'Das Wortfeld von Herrschaft, Königtum, und Macht ist in der altorientalischen Königsvorstellung, wie sie sich in der davidischen Königstradition widerspiegelt, verwurzelt, hat aber mit

---

37. Delbert Burkett, *The Son of Man Debate: A History and Evaluation* (SNTSMS, 107; Cambridge: Cambridge University Press, 1999). Hengel's questions and perceptions challenge the conclusions of Burkett, who relies on Perrin's approach (pp. 53–56), while work in Second Temple Judaism on the Son of Man and the dating of *1 Enoch* raise questions about the significance of his claim of no unified Son of Man title or concept in pre-Christian Judaism (pp. 121–22). Burkett favours a first century CE date for *1 Enoch*. On this dating question, see above, n. 19. The key here is not whether such a unified view existed, but whether these concepts were extant and able to be utilized. Thus, Burkett's analysis gets us off the track for what may be required and relevant for Jesus to have appealed to such categories. He downplays the issue of the date of *1 Enoch*, but it is more significant than he allows.

38. This example is noted in Evans (*Jesus and His Contemporaries*, p. 452). One must be careful here. There is no direct reference to Daniel; only the title is present. Nonetheless, the issue of authority in a major area, the Law, leads one to see the usage as descriptive of a person with some form of judicial or discerning authority.

39. Wolfgang Bittner, 'Gott-Menschensohn-Davidssohn: Eine Untersuchungen zur Traditionsgeschichte von Daniel 7,13f.', *FZPhTh* 32 (1985), pp. 343–72 (357–64).

Prophetenberufungen nichts zu tun'.[40] He also notes that such authority, when it involves vindication or the subordination of the nations, points to the royal office (Mic. 5.3–4; Zech. 9.10; Pss. 2, 89). When the issue of duration surfaces, it is kingship that is present (2 Sam. 7.16, Isa. 9.5 [6–7]). The description of the king as Son and the closeness of the Son of Man to God is paralleled most closely by the image of the king as son (2 Sam. 7.14, Ps. 2.6, Isa. 9.5 [6–7]). As such, the parallels, all of which are a part of the Jewish Scripture and so were available to Jesus, suggest the possibility of making the association present in this text between Messiah and Son of Man. Thus, the old and famous attempt to separate kingdom from Son of Man will not work; it underplays the most natural set of associations.[41]

Another challenge to the use of these two texts together comes from James Dunn.[42] Dunn argues that Ps. 110.1 was not likely to have been originally present. So he sees Daniel 7 as original, the early church adding awkwardly the Ps. 110.1 reference, and then Luke resimplifying the reference by dropping the Daniel 7 allusion in this scene.[43] He goes on to suggest the possibility that Jesus did appeal to the representation in Daniel 7 as a way of declaring his own vindication, a move that he sees just as possible for Jesus as the early church. This was then heard as a self-claim of Jesus. Each of these suggestions, though possible, seems unduly complicated. The traditional historical sequence

40. Ibid., p. 358. Bittner's quotation observes that sonship language is associated with kingship in the ancient Near East and in Israel is associated with the Davidic House, not with the prophetic office.

41. This point about the connection between Son of Man and king (and thus kingdom) is our ultimate response to a view like Douglas Hare's, where Son of Man is an acceptable reference from Jesus as a modest self-reference but then cannot be used apocalyptically. This kind of either-or division seems to ignore the entire context of how Jesus presented his own authority as he discussed the approach of the kingdom. For Hare's view, see his *The Son of Man Tradition*, especially his conclusion on pp. 277–80.

42. James D. G. Dunn, *Jesus Remembered*, pp. 749–54.

43. Dunn claims an awkward syntax because Son of Man is interrupted by the 'at the right hand' reference. He sees this as pointing to an insertion and a shift from coming *to* the Ancient of Days to coming *from* him. Dunn fails to see that if one is going to combine these references and speak of judging the leaders one day, then the point of the clouds is not merely a vindication in exaltation, but a reception of authority that will one day be exercised on the earth. This point is correctly made by C. F. D. Moule, namely, that Jesus' vindication by God means that this Jewish examination is not the last, or even the key, examination about who he is. See *The Origin of Christology* (Cambridge: Cambridge University Press, 1977), p. 18.

requires three changes,[44] while the use of Daniel 7 requires a simple move from a vague allusion in an eschatological context in Daniel to a more direct reference to Jesus once there is a hope of vindication. The key problem is that Daniel 7 is never entirely absent from the citation, since the title that remains in Luke's version is from Daniel 7, which by the time of the gospels would have been seen as appealing to the rest of the Daniel 7 scenario. This retention of Son of Man does show Daniel 7 is rooted deeply in this particular saying's tradition. This is reinforced by the fact that Son of Man is Jesus' key self-designation. I have already argued above that the use of Ps. 110.1 also makes sense as a text Jesus used by the ambiguous way Jesus appeals to it in Mk 12.35-37. So both texts are available to Jesus. In my view, the 'right hand' reference points to near-term vindication, while Daniel 7 points to long-term vindication. Luke's lack of a use of the image of 'coming on the clouds' is simple to explain. To establish his point about immediate divine vindication, Jesus' allusion to the right hand of God makes the key point. It is all that is required. Even harder to see from Dunn's proposal is how a vague reference to the Son of Man would be seen as blasphemous, *unless* it was a reference to Jesus, not merely heard as such. Had Jesus merely desired to point to some vague future divine vindication outside of himself for his mission, he could have made such a point clearly enough. However, Jesus' own consistent use of Son of Man in the tradition is against such a vague association here.

Although I am challenging Dunn's reading, one other point needs to be made. Had Jesus used only one of these texts in his reply, then either one of them by itself could have generated the leadership's charge of blasphemy. Ps. 110.1 would have said Jesus had the right to share God's rule, presence, *and* glory in heaven, pointing in the direction of something Richard Bauckham has called monolotry.[45] Invoking Daniel 7 signalled that Jesus would execute a judgement (or, at least would reside in a position of vindication against the leadership) with an authority that used the imagery of a divine act in the riding of the clouds. So, although I am contending for Jesus' use of both texts, the

44.   The three-fold sequence is: no use of Ps. 110, then Ps. 110 added, and then Daniel 7 removed.

45.   Richard Bauckham, *God Crucified: Monotheism and Christology in the New Testament* (Grand Rapids: Eerdmans, 1998), pp. 13–16.

case for core historicity only requires one of these texts to generate the central charge of blasphemy.

A look at the nature of the use of Daniel 7 and Ps. 110 suggests that both texts were passages that Jesus was aware of and could have used. Each passage contributes to the argument Jesus made as presented in Mark, in ways that do not require later Christology. In terms of content, nothing in the use or argument from these passages prevents the allusions to them from having been made by him as depicted here. However, an argument from content alone does not make the full case.

A formal question remains. Is there evidence that Jesus may have combined OT texts in a way similar to that found in this passage? Objection is often made that Jesus does not combine texts from the Scripture in the way Mk 14.62 does.[46] Yet two texts point to the potential of Jesus' conceptually linking texts together like this, side by side. In Mk 7.6-10 = Mt. 15.4-9, Jesus ties together references to the honouring of parents and the honouring with lips (Isa. 29.13; Exod. 20.12 [Deut. 5.16]; Exod. 21.17 [Lev. 20.9]) in a way that recalls Jewish midrashic reflection. The concepts of 'honour' and 'father and mother' appear here. In a second text, Mt. 22.33-39 (like Mk 12.29-31), there is a linkage involving the concept of love (Deut. 6.4-5, Lev. 19.18), resulting in a text on the great commandments of love.[47] This kind of linkage was a very Jewish way to argue, rooted in the hermeneutical rules associated with Hillel. These texts touch on ethical themes often seen as reflective of Jesus' social emphases. They indicate in terms of their form of presentation that the style of linking two themes from the Scriptures together could be reflective of Jesus.[48] So, there is nothing in terms of content or form that prevents this kind of association of texts

46. So, for example, Hampel, *Menschensohn und historischer Jesus*, pp. 179–80. He argues that this form of the combination reflects the early church, as does the reference to a returning Son of Man. Against the second point, see above on apocalyptic Son of Man. In fact, this formal objection is probably the most common argument that the passage is not authentic. The claim is that the linkage of Ps. 110.1 and Dan. 7.13-14 reflects an early church midrashic teaching about Jesus.

47. A similar teaching appears in the response of the scribe in Lk. 10.25-29 to introduce the parable of the Good Samaritan, but the context is distinct enough that this may well reflect a distinct tradition, not a true parallel. See the discussion of the Lucan pericope in my *Luke 9:51–24:53*, pp. 1018–21.

48. Another example is Lk. 4.16–20, where Isaiah 61 and 58 are combined (but it is singly attested).

from reaching back to Jesus. In many cases the evidence that the expression goes back to him is stronger than that the church created it.

Because he has said it so clearly, I cite two of Raymond Brown's remarks about Mk 14.62.[49] One full citation presents his perceptive assessment of Perrin's claim that Mk 14.62 is Christian midrash, a common view echoed by Hampel and Boring. The second citation comes from his conclusion on the Son of Man in Mark 14:

> First, if it seems quite likely that the Gospel picture is developed beyond any single OT or known intertestamental passage or expectation, and that this development probably took place through the interpretative combination of several passages, any affirmation that all this development *must have* come from early Christians and none of it from Jesus reflects one of the peculiar prejudices of modern scholarship. A Jesus who did not reflect on the OT and use the interpretative techniques of his time is an unrealistic projection who surely never existed. *The perception that OT passages were interpreted to give a christological insight does not date the process.* To prove that this could not have been done by Jesus, at least inchoatively, is surely no less difficult than to prove that it was done by him. Hidden behind the attribution to the early church is often the assumption that Jesus had no christology even by way of reading the Scriptures to discern in what anticipated way he fitted into God's plan. Can one really think that credible?

Later he concludes:

> Jesus could have spoken of the 'Son of Man' as his understanding of his role in God's plan precisely when he was faced with hostile challenges reflecting the expectations of his contemporaries. Inevitably the Christian record would have crossed the *t*'s and dotted the *i*'s of the scriptural background of his words. Even though *all* of Mark 14.61–62 and par. is phrased in Christian language of the 60s

---

49. Brown, *The Death of the Messiah*, pp. 513–14 is the first citation, and the second appears on pp. 514–15. The emphasis in the citation is his.

(language *not* unrelated to issues of AD 30/33), there is reason to believe that in
14.62 we may be close to the mindset and style of Jesus himself.[50]

I agree and would like to push Brown's point. There is a far greater likelihood
that this text, with all of its sensitivity to Jewish background, goes back to Jesus
or, at least, reflects an earlier setting than Mark or the early church with which
he was associated.

Implications for Jesus' self-understanding

That Jesus used the Son of Man imagery from Daniel 7 of himself has several
points of significance.

First, it indicates that the line between Jesus and kingdom is not as great as

---

50.   Brown, *The Death of the Messiah*, p. 515, n. 55) adds one more point for authenticity in this Marcan text. He notes that the phrase 'you will see' is difficult and may favour
authenticity, because 'post factum, Christians producing such a statement might have been
clearer'. A variation on this kind of defence of authenticity, which I believe is less likely is
advocated by Bruce Chilton, who suggests that Jesus taught about the Son of Man as an angel
of advocacy in the divine court, who would defend and vindicate the accused because Jesus'
mission represented the programme of God. In this view, the Son of Man, though distinct from
Jesus, is inseparably bound with his mission. Thus, at the trial, the remark would still reflect
some authenticity and would still be seen by the leadership as a blasphemous rebuke of the
leadership's rejection of Jesus' divinely directed announcement of God's programme. The
Synoptics transform this close association into a purely Christological identity. See his 'Son of
Man: Human and Heavenly', in *The Four Gospels 1992: Festschrift Frans Neirynck* (BETL,
100C; Leuven: Leuven University Press, 1992), vol. 1, pp. 203–18. This reading does defend
the remark's essential historicity, but construes its force differently. Such a view, though possible, seems to leave the issue of the person of Jesus understated and unanswered as the reply
in effect becomes, 'I am who I claimed, whoever that is, and God will vindicate me through
his agent, showing this examination to be in grave error'. Chilton argues that Jesus' appeal to
the witness of heaven is like an appeal he engages in Mk 9.1, where the idiomatic phrase 'to
taste death' refers to the immortality of the witnesses Moses and Elijah, to whom Jesus appeals
through an oath in the midst of the transfiguration scene. My problem with this view of Mark
9 is that, despite the important linguistic evidence for the possibility of an idiom, it is not clear
that Moses was seen in Jewish tradition as one who was taken up while never experiencing
death. See the dispute over this in the Moses discussion in my *Blasphemy and Exaltation*,
pp. 133–37. For this view, see Chilton, '"Not to Taste Death": A Jewish, Christian and Gnostic
Usage', in *Studia Biblica 1978, II: Papers on the Gospels, Sixth International Congress on
Biblical Studies, Oxford, 3–7 April 1978* (ed. E. A. Livingston; JSNTSup, 2; Sheffield: JSOT
Press, 1980), pp. 29–36. For the reasons I am arguing, I think a more direct, personally focused
reply from Jesus is slightly more likely.

some suggest. The imagery in Daniel is primarily descriptive of the approach of God's kingdom made not with hands (Daniel 2). Jesus' kingdom presentation is a central feature of most scholars' treatments of Jesus. So Jesus' evocation of Son of Man before the Jewish leadership raises the issue of kingdom authority. Who speaks for God, Jesus or the leadership? The reaction of the Jewish leadership to Jesus in this scene shows that they got Jesus' point. What Jesus saw as vindication pointing to the support of his mission from God, they viewed as blasphemous, giving them a reason to take a political charge to Pilate. The evocation of a kingdom other than Rome as primary was competition that Rome would not take kindly. The central role of Jesus in the kingdom's disclosure and presence stands at the heart of what became the message of the emerging Jesus movement that eventually became the church. That message cost Jesus his life, and brought life to the subsequent message of his followers.

Second, there is a need to be careful of reading texts in a flat manner that attributes all key theological and Christological developments to the early church. The roots for the theological innovations within the Jesus movement appear far more likely to be rooted in him than in a nameless and faceless group of followers who made far more out of him than he gave them inclination to do, often in directions opposite of what these reconstructions suggest Jesus emphasized. One of the problems with views that see so much theological innovation in the early church alone is that it is hard to see what motivated these innovations, if Jesus did not seriously start them down this path. These claims brought intense opposition with them, even to the point of placing followers' lives at risk. To introduce them as a means of underscoring what many allege was a controversial call to reform in Judaism without a central role for Jesus appears to be an implausible case of theological overkill. On the other hand, if Jesus' role was as central as these texts from his followers suggest, and his confidence was that suffering and current rejection would lead to full vindication, then the lines of theological development we do see in the early church have roots that make sense of what grows out of it. It is important to recall that the sense of vindication the early movement attributed to Jesus was not merely a demi-god-like presence in the heavenly pantheon, like his Graeco-Roman divinely honoured contemporaries, but a full vindication to a status that was inseparably connected to God's throne and rule within the context of a Judaism that guarded God's unique honour (with only very rare exceptions even being entertained as possible by some Jews). A much easier path for theological creation by the community in this mixed Jewish and Greco-Roman context would have been for Jesus to be received in heaven, much like an emperor was perceived as being received. What we have here in Jesus' remarks was far more, because Jesus finds a place on God's throne, not just a place in his midst. The power of a highly regarded personality is far more likely to be responsible for such a conceptual breakthrough than a vague appeal to an amorphous community. Evidence for such a perspective from such a personality comes to us from this scene where Jesus identified himself as the Son of Man, a claim that forced the leadership's hand to oppose him to the full force of their powers, given that they did not accept his self-confession. Jesus, in his reply, was content to journey along the path he saw as his divine calling, and allow God's future actions to speak on his behalf.

THE USE OF THE SON OF MAN IDIOM IN THE GOSPEL OF JOHN

Benjamin E. Reynolds

Use of the expression 'the Son of Man' in the Gospel of John is normally absent from scholarly attempts to solve the Son of Man problem. Even Delbert Burkett, whose published thesis was on the Johannine Son of Man, is mostly silent on this topic in his second book, *The Son of Man Debate*.[1] Why this silence? Why is the Johannine Son of Man left out of most historical studies of the expression ὁ υἱὸς τοῦ ἀνθρώπου? The reason is essentially related to the questions surrounding the historicity of John. To cite Ernst Käsemann: 'We must admit that nowhere in the New Testament is the life story of Jesus so emptied of all real content as it already is here [in the Gospel of John], where it seems to be almost a projection of the present back into the past.'[2] A similar sentiment is expressed by A. J. B. Higgins in the concluding chapter of his book on the Son of Man: 'the Fourth Gospel . . . makes no positive contribution to the problem of Jesus

---

1.   D. Burkett, *The Son of Man Debate* (SNTSMS, 107; Cambridge: Cambridge University Press, 1999); Burkett, *The Son of the Man in the Gospel of John* (JSNTSup, 56; Sheffield: Sheffield Academic Press, 1991). However, Maurice Casey has recently included a chapter on the Johannine Son of Man in *The Solution to the 'Son of Man' Problem* (LNTS, 343; London: T&T Clark, 2007), pp. 274–313. See also the earlier work of F. H. Borsch, *The Son of Man in Myth and History* (Philadelphia: Westminster, 1967); B. Lindars, *Jesus Son of Man: A Fresh Examination of the Son of Man Sayings in the Gospels* (Grand Rapids: Eerdmans, 1984; first pub. London: SPCK, 1983); and D. R. A. Hare, *The Son of Man Tradition* (Minneapolis: Fortress Press, 1990), pp. 79–114.

2.   E. Käsemann, 'The Problem of the Historical Jesus', in *Essays on New Testament Themes* (trans. W. J. Montague; SBT, 41; London: SCM, 1964), p. 32.

and the Son of man'.[3] In contrast to John, the Gospels of Mark, Matthew and Luke are understood to contain at least some historical information about the actions and words of Jesus, and John, on the whole, is not.

So why include a chapter on the Johannine Son of Man in a book with the subtitle *The Latest Scholarship on a Puzzling Expression of the Historical Jesus*, even if the title *'Who is this Son of Man?'* derives from Jn 12.34? A good question and one that I think needs to be answered, even if briefly, before we proceed. First, although the Gospel of John may not carry the sort of historical credentials that satisfy contemporary scholarship, it still represents an early Christian understanding of Jesus' use of the phrase ὁ υἱὸς τοῦ ἀνθρώπου. The four Gospels are the primary witnesses to Jesus' use of the idiom, an idiom which quickly disappears from early Christian usage.[4] If some of these Son of Man sayings in Matthew, Mark and Luke are considered authentic sayings of Jesus (e.g. Mk 2.27-28; 10.45; pars.),[5] it is at least worth taking note of the other Gospel that also places the use of this idiom on the lips of Jesus, especially if the idiom is not as prevalent in later Christian writing.[6] In this sense, the sayings in John add further evidence for the authenticity of the use of ὁ υἱὸς τοῦ ἀνθρώπου by Jesus, whether or not these sayings themselves are considered to be authentic. They at least point to a common early Christian tradition of the words being spoken by Jesus, and as such it is at least worth discussing the Johannine Son of Man sayings with regard to the Son of Man debate.

Second, there has been a recent trend to reconsider the historicity of the

---

3.   A. J. B. Higgins, *Jesus and the Son of Man* (Philadelphia: Fortress Press, 1964), p. 185. See also more recently, P. M. Casey, *Is John's Gospel True?* (London: Routledge, 1996).

4.   The only other NT uses of the idiom are found in Acts 7.56 and Rev. 1.13; 14.14. The church fathers use it sparingly and usually in a contrast between Jesus' humanity and divinity (Ignatius, *Ephes.* 20.2; Justin, *Dial.* 100.3-4; Irenaeus, *Adv. Haer.* 3.10.2; 16.3, 7; 17; 18.3-4; 19.1-2). See also, *Barn.* 12.10. Note the use of the idiom by Jesus in the *Gospel of Thomas* 86 and the *Gospel of Mary* 8.12-22, where 'humanity' appears to be the meaning (see R. Doran, 'The Divination of Disorder: The Trajectory of Matt 8:20//Luke 9:58//*Gos. Thom.* 86', in B. A. Pearson [ed.], *The Future of Early Christianity: Essays in Honor of Helmut Koester* [Minneapolis: Fortress Press, 1991], pp. 210–19; and K. L. King, *The Gospel of Mary of Magdala: Jesus and the First Woman Apostle* [Santa Rosa, CA: Polebridge Press, 2003] pp. 59–62).

5.   Casey, *Solution*, pp. 121–25, 131–34. See M. Müller, *Der Ausdruck "Menschensohn" in den Evangelien. Voraussetzungen und Bedeutung* (Leiden: Brill, 1984).

6.   The logion in the Gospel of Thomas is parallel to Mt. 8.20 and Lk. 9.58.

Gospel of John.[7] This trend can be seen most recently in the work of the John, Jesus, and History Group of the Society of Biblical Literature, which is challenging the commonly held assumptions about John's lack of historicity.[8] Those in the Group are not necessarily claiming that John's account of Jesus is a purely historical portrayal untouched by Christian faith, but they are seeking to question the presuppositions concerning the 'dehistoricizing of John' and the 'de-Johannification of Jesus'. They have coined these phrases to refer respectively to the tendencies in scholarship to dismiss John simply as an unreliable historical source and to ignore the Johannine portrait of Jesus in historical Jesus studies. Paul Anderson, one of the organizers of the John, Jesus, and History Group, has pointed out that John has largely been dismissed because of the testimony of three witnesses: Matthew, Mark and Luke. However in response, Anderson argues that if Matthew and Luke are primarily relying upon Mark, as most scholars agree is the case, we really have only one witness and not three. John then should not be pitted as one tradition against three, but rather as one against one.[9] In which case, more weight should be given to John's portrayal of Jesus' words and deeds than has been given to them in the last century.[10]

Thus, we have two reasons for including an essay on the Johannine Son of Man sayings in a book on the historical use of the expression 'Son of Man'. First, John's Gospel is a witness to Jesus' use of the expression to refer to himself, and secondly, recent Johannine scholarship has been questioning the view that finds no historical value in the Gospel of John, the view prevalent since the rise of modern critical study of the Gospel. However, even with these

7. M. M. Thompson, 'The Historical Jesus and the Johannine Christ', in R. Fortna and T. Thatcher (eds), *Jesus in Johannine Tradition* (Louisville: Westminster John Knox, 2001), pp. 21–42; F. J. Moloney; 'The Fourth Gospel and the Jesus of History', *NTS* 46 (2000), pp. 42–58; C. L. Blomberg, *The Historical Reliability of John's Gospel* (Leicester: IVP, 2001).

8. P. N. Anderson, F. Just and T. Thatcher (eds), *John, Jesus, and History, Volume 1: Critical Appraisals of Critical Views* (SBLSymS, 44; Atlanta: SBL, 2007).

9. P. N. Anderson, *The Fourth Gospel and the Quest for the Johannine Jesus: Modern Foundations Reconsidered* (LNTS, 321; London: T&T Clark, 2006), pp. 102–26; Anderson, 'Why This Study Is Needed, and Why It Is Needed Now', in *John, Jesus, and History*, pp. 13–70.

10. M. A. Powell, 'The De-Johannification of Jesus: The Twentieth Century and Beyond', in *John, Jesus, and History*, pp. 121–32 (132).

reasons, the question of the relevance of the Johannine Son of Man sayings for understanding the historical use of the expression by Jesus still remains open, but we will leave aside that question for now and return to it after we have examined the Johannine use of the idiom ὁ υἱὸς τοῦ ἀνθρώπου.

I. *The Johannine Son of Man debate(s)*

Because most scholars have considered the Gospel of John to lack historical value, the study of the Johannine Son of Man has developed almost in isolation from studies of the Synoptic Son of Man.[11] As recently as 40 years ago, scholars began their studies of the Johannine Son of Man with references to the scarcity of literature written on the topic as compared to the volumes written on the Synoptic Son of Man.[12] The separation between the two scholarly discussions has resulted in the Johannine discussion being largely devoid of the questions about the Aramaic (א)שׁנ(א) רב and what the phrase may have meant to Jesus and his hearers. Rather, the Johannine debates primarily concern the possible origins of the idiom ὁ υἱὸς τοῦ ἀνθρώπου for the Evangelist and/or the Evangelist's community, the meaning of the idiom within the context of the Gospel, and/or the understanding of the phrase for the Johannine community.[13]

There are essentially four broad understandings of the meaning of ὁ υἱὸς τοῦ ἀνθρώπου within the context the Gospel of John: (1) 'Son of Man' in John

11.   See Note 1 for some exceptions.

12.   R. Schnackenburg, *The Gospel According to St. John* (3 vols; Tunbridge Wells: Burns & Oates, 1967), vol. 1, p. 529; S. S. Smalley, 'The Johannine Son of Man Sayings', *NTS* 15 (1969), pp. 278–301; B. Lindars, 'The Son of Man in the Johannine Christology', in B. Lindars and S. S. Smalley (eds), *Christ and Spirit in the New Testament: Studies in Honour of Charles Francis Digby Moule* (Cambridge: Cambridge University Press, 1973), pp. 43–60; R. Maddox, 'The Function of the Son of Man in the Gospel of John', in R. Banks (ed.), *Reconciliation and Hope: New Testament Essays on Atonement and Eschatology* (Grand Rapids: Eerdmans, 1974), pp. 186–204; F. J. Moloney, *The Johannine Son of Man* (BSR, 14; Rome: LAS, 2nd edn, 1978), p. 1.

13.   Some studies, however, have attempted to place the Johannine sayings within Synoptic Son of Man categories – earthly, suffering, and coming/glory/apocalyptic sayings. See C. Ham, 'The Title "Son of Man" in the Gospel of John', *Stone-Campbell Journal* 1 (1998), pp. 67–84.

highlights the humanity of Jesus.[14] (2) 'Son of Man' indicates that Jesus is a/ the divine-man.[15] (3) 'Son of Man' is simply synonymous with 'Son of God'.[16] (4) 'Son of Man' indicates that Jesus is a heavenly or divine figure.[17]

Now, although scholars variously arrive at these four broad understandings of the Johannine meaning of 'the Son of Man', they often argue for a specific meaning on the basis of differing methodologies. Also, some scholars who hold to similar understandings of 'the Son of Man' may have different views of the origin of the idiom. For some, the methodology begins with an examination of possible origins of the idiom – Wisdom, Hermetic literature, Philo, the Old Testament in general, Daniel 7 more specifically, and apocalyptic literature – and then they apply that to the understanding of the Johannine use.[18] Others focus primarily on the text of Gospel of John to discover the meaning.[19] This is essentially the question of whether or not the expression ὁ υἱὸς τοῦ ἀνθρώπου finds its meaning in its origin (diachrony) or in its use in its context

---

14. Moloney, *Johannine*, p. 213; E. Ruckstuhl, 'Die johanneische Menschensohnforschung 1957–1969', in J. Pfammatter and F. Furger (eds), *Theologische Berichte 1* (Zurich: Benziger, 1972), pp. 171–284; J. Coppens, 'Le fils de l'homme dans l'évangile johannique', *ETL* 52 (1976), pp. 28–81; C. H. Dodd, *The Interpretation of the Fourth Gospel* (Cambridge: Cambridge University Press, 1953, 1968), pp. 43–44, 243; M. Pamment, 'The Son of Man in the Fourth Gospel', *JTS* 36 (1985), pp. 56–66; R. Rhea, *The Johannine Son of Man* (AThANT 76; Zürich: Theologischer, 1990), p. 70; F. F. Ramos, 'El hijo del hombre en el cuarto evangelio', *Studium Legionense* 40 (1999), pp. 45–92.

15. T. Preiss, 'Le fils de l'homme dans le IVᵉ Évangile', *ETR* 28 (1953), pp. 7–61; E. Harris, *Prologue and Gospel: The Theology of the Fourth Evangelist* (JSNTSup, 107; Sheffield: Sheffield Academic Press, 1994), pp. 116–29.

16. E. D. Freed, 'The Son of Man in the Fourth Gospel', *JBL* 86 (1967), pp. 402–409; S. Kim, *The 'Son of Man' as the Son of God* (WUNT 30; Tübingen: Mohr Siebeck, 1983); Burkett, *Son of the Man, passim*; R. E. Brown, *An Introduction to the Gospel of John* (F. J. Moloney, ed.; New York: Doubleday, 2003).

17. S. Schulz, *Untersuchungen zur Menschensohn-Christologie im Johannesevan-gelium. Zugleich ein Beitrag zur Methodengeschichte der Auslegung des 4. Evangeliums* (Göttingen: Vandenhoeck & Ruprecht, 1957); Maddox, 'Function', pp. 186–204; J. Ashton, *Understanding the Fourth Gospel* (Oxford: Oxford University Press, 1991), pp. 337–73; J. Painter, 'The Enigmatic Johannine Son of Man', in F. Van Segbroeck, C. M. Tuckett, G. Van Belle and J. Verheyden (eds), *Four Gospels 1992. Festschrift Frans Neirynck* (BETL, 100; 3 vols.; Louvain: Peeters, 1992), pp. 1869–87; M. Sasse, *Der Menschensohn im Evangelium nach Johannes* (TANZ, 35; Tübingen, Basel: Francke, 2000); B. E. Reynolds, *The Apocalyptic Son of Man in the Gospel of John* (WUNT II, 249; Tübingen: Mohr Siebeck, 2008).

18. Burkett, *Son of the Man*, pp. 73–75, 77.

19. Moloney, *Johannine Son of Man*, p. 22.

(synchrony).[20] I believe that the origin of the expression can shed a beneficial light on the questions of meaning, and I have sought to show this elsewhere.[21] However, explorations of the origin of 'the Son of Man' do not automatically solve the problems, since disagreements over the meaning of possible background material (e.g. Daniel 7: a collective or heavenly messianic figure?) can and do affect scholarly understandings of 'the Son of Man' in John.[22] Because the topic of this paper is on *the use of the idiom in the Gospel of John*, the issue of origin will be left unaddressed, although, again, I do think it is important. Instead, our task here will be to discern the meaning of ὁ υἱὸς τοῦ ἀνθρώπου based on its use in the Gospel of John and then to compare that meaning with the portrait of 'the Son of Man' in the Synoptic Gospels.

II. *The Johannine Son of Man sayings: three significant themes*

As we approach the sayings, emphasis must be placed on all 13 sayings and not only on a select few.[23] In discussion of the Johannine Son of Man sayings (1.51; 3.13, 14; 5.27; 6.27, 53, 62; 8.28; 9.35; 12.23, 34 [2×]; 13.31), attention is often directed to aspects and themes that are distinctive to John – the ascent/ descent of the Son of Man, his lifting up and his glorification. In a similar manner, we will begin with these three themes, but then also move to address the other sayings.

A. *The ascent and descent of the Son of Man (3.13; 6.62)*
The Son of Man's ascent and descent have been understood to be the key to understanding the Johannine portrait of this figure.[24] This view arises most likely because of the uniqueness of this theme for John. At the same time, the

---

20.   See F. J. Moloney, 'The Johannine Son of Man Revisited', in G. Van Belle, J. G. van der Watt and P. Maritz (eds), *Theology and Christology in the Fourth Gospel: Essays by the Members of the SNTS Johannine Writings Seminar* (BETL, 184; Leuven: Leuven University Press, 2005), pp. 177–202 (182–85).

21.   Reynolds, *Apocalyptic Son of Man*, esp. pp. 215–28.

22.   Cf. Ashton, *Understanding*, pp. 337–73; and Lindars, *Jesus*, pp. 145–57.

23.   This is a weakness of Rhea, *Johannine Son of Man*; and Sasse, *Menschensohn*. See F. J. Moloney, 'A Johannine Son of Man Discussion?' *Salesianum* 39 (1977), pp. 93–102.

24.   Burkett, *Son of the Man*, p. 76; W. A. Meeks, 'The Man from Heaven in Johannine Sectarianism', *JBL* 91 (1972), pp. 44–72.

ascent/descent language appears only in 1.51; 3.13; and 6.62.[25] But 1.51 refers to the movement of angels and not the Son of Man, and in 6.62, only 'ascent' is mentioned (no 'descent'). Further, 6.62 is a hypothetical ('if') statement. So, although the theme of the Son of Man's ascent and descent is unique to John, it must be kept in perspective.

Yet, the ascent/descent sayings pose a difficulty for the view that 'the Son of Man' is an indication of Jesus' humanity. John 3.13 (especially) and 6.62 are commonly used as evidence that 'the Son of Man' is a heavenly figure and/or similar to 'Son of God'.[26] Jn 3.13 states: 'No one is able to ascend to heaven, except the one who descended, the Son of Man'. In the narrative context, Jesus is replying to Nicodemus, and by this statement he clearly indicates that the Son of Man descended from heaven. Jesus is explaining to Nicodemus that he can reveal heavenly things (3.12) because he has come from heaven. For Eugen Ruckstuhl and Francis Moloney who claim that 'the Son of Man' designates the incarnate Jesus, his descent from heaven is problematical.[27] They claim that the Son of Man's descent has nothing to do with his heavenly origin or pre-existence. Moloney states: 'Jn 3:13 is not about pre-existence or post-existence'.[28] For him, the descent is a 'literary *topos*' that suggests Jesus' uniqueness. But the Son of Man's descent from heaven seems to imply his prior existence before the incarnation, just as the ascent suggests the existence of the Son of Man after Jesus' earthly life.[29] It is not 'too much' to speak of the Son of Man's 'movement'.[30] In my view, movement (including ascent and descent) requires a person or object to be in existence both before and after the movement. Moloney is correct that the intent of 3.13 is to direct attention to the Son of Man's unique authority to reveal heavenly things (cf. 3.12). The Son of Man does have this authority because he is unique from other revealers, but

25.   The words ἀναβαίνω and καταβαίνω are also common words in John in relation to Jesus' travel (2.12, 13; 4.47, 49, 51; 5.1, 7; 6.16; 7.8, 10, 18; 10.1; 11.55; 12.20; 21.11).

26.   Ashton, *Understanding*, pp. 348–56; Sasse, *Menschensohn*, pp. 182–230.

27.   Ruckstuhl, 'Menschensohnforschung', p. 276; Moloney, *Johannine*, p. 213. See also Coppens, 'Fils de l'homme', p. 67.

28.   Moloney, 'Revisited', p. 192. Casey (*Solution*, p. 276) refers to this as Moloney's 'terrible tangles'.

29.   A. Y. Collins and J. J. Collins, *King and Messiah as Son of God: Divine, Human, and Angelic Messianic Figures in Biblical and Related Literature* (Grand Rapids: Eerdmans, 2008), p. 183.

30.   *Contra* Moloney, Editor's Note, in Brown, *Introduction*, p. 257 n. 87.

the Son of Man's uniqueness in revealing heavenly mysteries exists because he is from heaven and has descended from there.

Jn 6.61-62 draws even more attention to the Son of Man's heavenly origin. Jesus asks his disciples: τοῦτο ὑμᾶς σκαδαλίζει; ἐὰν οὖν θεωρῆτε τὸν υἱὸν τοῦ ἀνθρώπου ἀναβαίνοντα ὅπου ἦν τὸ πρότερον; Jesus' question raises another: is an actual ascent intended here or is it only hypothetical? Moloney thinks that the ascent is hypothetical, which is noticeable in his explanation of Jesus' statement which lacks the verb 'to see': '[Jesus] asks them if they would like "the Son of Man" to ascend "to where he was before (πρότερον)". For the Fourth Evangelist, there is no reason for Jesus to ascend, as other revealers have claimed as having done.'[31] But, contrary to what Moloney argues, what is actually hypothetical is not the ascent but the *seeing* of the ascent. Jesus seems to be saying: 'If you have difficulty with eating flesh and drinking blood, what will you do if you see the Son of Man ascend to where he was before?' The hypothetical aspect of the question is not about the ascent, but what the disciples will do if they see it. And even if the ascent was hypothetical, Jesus says that the Son of Man would ascend to where he was *before*. The use of πρότερον implies the Son of Man's pre-existence in heaven, and the 'ascent' itself, whether hypothetical or not, also suggests the post-existence of the Son of Man in heaven.[32]

B. *The lifting up of the Son of Man (3.14; 8.28; 12.34 [12.32])*

Another distinctive feature of the Johannine Son of Man is the use of the verb ὑψόω with this figure,[33] and the meaning of the lifting up of the Son of Man depends on one's understanding of this verb. The word has the literal sense of lifting something up, but in the LXX the metaphorical meaning 'to exalt' is more common. The Gospel of John is known for its use of words with double meaning, and ὑψόω is no exception. The first use of the verb in 3.14 makes this double meaning clear. Jesus says to Nicodemus: 'Just as Moses lifted up the serpent in the wilderness so must the Son of Man be lifted up.' Moses did

---

31. Moloney, 'Revisited', p. 195.

32. Painter, 'Enigmatic', p. 1883; H. Odeberg, *The Fourth Gospel* (Chicago: Argonaut, 1968; repr. Uppsala, 1929), p. 264.

33. Most scholars understand Isa. 52.13 to be in the background of the Johannine usage of the term, especially with the combined use of δοξάζω in Isa. 52.13 and in the Gospel.

not exalt the bronze serpent (unlike some later Israelites – 2 Kgs 18.4), but rather he placed it on a pole (Num. 21.9; cf. Wis. 16.7; *Barn.* 12.10). This gives the impression that the Son of Man is physically lifted up, i.e., on the cross, although this meaning is not obvious at this point in the Gospel, except to someone familiar with the crucifixion.

However, 8.28 and 12.32, 34 suggest that physical elevation is not the only meaning of ὑψόω in John. In 8.28, which is the only active use of the verb, Jesus tells 'the Jews': 'When you have lifted up the Son of Man, then you will know that I Am . . .' Since 'the Jews' are the subject of the verb ὑψόω, the physical lifting up on the cross appears to be the meaning again, but the knowledge that the Jews are said to gain cannot be seen to have come to them at the crucifixion – 'you will know that I Am'. Ἐγώ εἰμι should be understood here and in 8.24 as a referent to the divine name.[34] Jesus has just used the phrase previously in 8.24: 'If you do not believe that I Am, you will die in your sins.' The parallel between believing and knowing, added with the idea of dying in one's sins (8.24), suggests that this knowledge of Jesus as 'I Am' has salvific implications (cf. Isa. 43.10).[35] However, such a change of heart by Jesus' opponents is not apparent in the actions of the Ἰουδαῖοι at the cross. And in comparison, the disciples do not seem to believe or know at the crucifixion. Their belief does not begin until after the resurrection (20.8; cf. 2.19; 12.16). Therefore, this suggests that the metaphorical lifting up (i.e. exaltation) of the Son of Man stretches beyond the single event of the cross, while at the same time the literal meaning includes it.[36]

Jn 12.32, 34 also point in this metaphorical/exaltation direction. 'If I am lifted up from the earth, I will draw all people to myself'; 'We have heard in the law that the Christ remains forever. How do you say that it is necessary for the Son of Man to be lifted up? Who is this Son of Man?' Jesus says that the lifting up will bring about the drawing of all to himself. The events of the crucifixion do not indicate this drawing at the cross. Furthermore, the crowd's response

---

34. C. H. Williams, *I am He: The Interpretation of 'Anî Hû' in Jewish and Early Christian Literature* (WUNT II, 113; Tübingen: Mohr Siebeck, 2000), pp. 266–75.

35. See Schnackenburg, *Gospel*, 2.202–3.

36. R. E. Brown, *The Gospel According to John* (AB, 29 & 29A; 2 vols.; New York: Doubleday, 1966–70), p. 146; J. Blank, *Krisis. Untersuchungen zur johanneischen Christologie und Eschatologie* (Freiburg im Breisgau: Lambertus, 1964), p. 84.

in 12.34 does not suggest that they equated 'lifting up' with crucifixion. At the least, they sensed a contrast between 'lifting up' and 'remaining forever'. They appear to equate 'the Son of Man' and 'Messiah' to some extent, while treating 'lifting up' and 'remaining' as opposite actions.[37] This suggests that 'lifting up' in 12.34 refers to some sort of departure which may or may not include death. The following verses 12.35-36 further add to this idea of departure with Jesus' statement that he will only be with them for a little while. The phrase 'little while' (μικρόν) is used throughout the farewell discourse to indicate the time until Jesus' departure (13.33; 14.19; 16.16-18). Further, in 12.32 Jesus speaks of being lifted up 'from the earth'. This could be a reference to the physical lifting up on the cross, but as George Beasley-Murray, states the meaning appears to point beyond merely being lifted up six feet off the ground.[38] In sum, for John, the lifting up is not specifically the crucifixion, but it includes it. Lifting up occurs through the crucifixion, but it is not completed until after his resurrection.[39] There is a physical and metaphorical meaning of ὑψόω, but, in John, the metaphorical meaning is stronger.

C. *The glorification of the Son of Man (12.23; 13.31-32)*

Along with the ascent/descent and lifting up themes, another important Johannine Son of Man theme is the glorification of the Son of Man. The first mention of the Son of Man's glorification comes in Jn 12.23 after the Greeks request to see Jesus (12.21). Jesus says: 'The hour has come for the Son of Man to be glorified.' His statement points to the close relationship between the Son of Man's glorification and the hour of this event. Jesus' hour has been foreshadowed numerous times previously in the Gospel (2.4; 7.30; 8.20). The hour can be understood as a direct reference to the crucifixion, especially considering Jesus' statements about the kernel of wheat dying in 12.24 and Jesus' troubled

---

37. C. C. Caragounis, *The Son of Man: Vision and Interpretation* (WUNT, 38; Mohr Siebeck, 1986), p. 183; Hare, *Son of Man*, p. 108; Burkett, *Son of the Man*, p. 167.

38. G. R. Beasley-Murray, 'John 12,31–32: The Eschatological Significance of the Lifting up of the Son of Man', in W. Schrage (ed.), *Studien zum Text und zur Ethik des Neuen Testaments. Festschrift zum 80. Geburtstag von Heinrich Greeven* (BZNW, 47; Berlin: Walter de Gruyter, 1986), pp. 70–81.

39. See Schnackenburg, *Gospel*, p. 2.394.

soul in 12.27.[40] However, in 13.1, Jesus' hour is declared to be the time when he is to depart (μεταβαίνω) from this world to the Father. If, as it seems, Jesus' hour includes his going away and returning to the Father (7.33-34; 8.21-23), this suggests that the hour includes the crucifixion and the resurrection since Jesus does not ascend to the Father until after the resurrection (20.17).[41]

Likewise, the Son of Man's glorification is not merely a reference to the cross. The Son of Man is glorified through his crucifixion, resurrection and return to the Father.[42] In Jn 7.39, the narrator says: 'This he said concerning the Spirit, which those believing in him were about to receive, for the Spirit was not yet [given] because Jesus had not yet been glorified.' This statement implies that the Spirit is given following Jesus' glorification. Moloney argues that the Spirit is given at the crucifixion: παρέδωκεν τὸ πνεῦμα (19.30). But this view does not fully take into account Jesus' command to the disciples in 20.22 to receive the Spirit.[43] Further, in 16.7, Jesus says that the Spirit would come only after Jesus returned to the one who sent him. This appears to suggest that the glorification encompasses the crucifixion, resurrection and return to the Father, for Jesus returns to God following his resurrection (20.17). Again, 12.16 states that the disciples remembered the things done to Jesus at the triumphal entry after he was glorified. Earlier in the Gospel, the narrator informs us that

---

40.   Moloney, Johannine, p. 177; E. Thüsing, *Die Erhöhung und Verherrlichung Jesu im Johannesevangelium* (NTAbh, 21; Münster: Aschendorffsche, 3rd edn, 1979), p. 81.

41.   Blank, *Krisis*, p. 267; M. C. de Boer, 'Jesus' Departure to the Father in John: Death or Resurrection?', in G. Van Belle, J. G. van der Watt and P. Maritz (eds), *Theology and Christology in the Fourth Gospel: Essays by the Members of the SNTS Johannine Writings Seminar* (BETL, 184; Leuven: Leuven University Press, 2005), pp. 1–19.

42.   *Contra* Thüsing, *Erhöhung*, pp. 75–86. See W. Loader, *The Christology of the Fourth Gospel: Structure and Issues* (BBET, 23; Frankfurt am Main: Peter Lang, 1989), pp. 109–10; P. Ensor, 'The Glorification of the Son of Man: An Analysis of John 13:31–32', *TynB* 58.2 (2007), pp. 229–52.

43.   There is no strong consensus in Johannine scholarship on the moment of the Spirit's arrival, but most scholars see 20.22 as the giving of the Spirit or at least the completion of it. See Brown, *Gospel*, pp. 1037–39; G. Burge, *The Anointed Community: The Holy Spirit in the Johannine Tradition* (Grand Rapids: Eerdmans, 1987), pp. 123–31; T. R. Hatina, 'John 20,22 in Its Eschatological Context: Promise or Fulfillment?' *Bib* 74 (1993), pp. 196–219. C. Bennema ('The Giving of the Spirit in John's Gospel – A New Proposal?' *EvQ* 74.3 [2002], pp. 195–213) sees 19.30 as a symbolic giving and 20.22 as the realized giving. J. Swetnam ('Bestowal of the Spirit in the Fourth Gospel', *Bib* 74 [1993], pp. 556–76) argues for 19.30 and 20.22 as a two-phase giving. Loader (*Christology*, p. 109) refers to Moloney's interpretation of 19.30 as 'doubtful exegesis'.

the disciples remembered after he was raised from the dead (2.22). Speaking of 2.22 and 12.16, Josef Blank declares that Jesus' glorification encompasses his resurrection.[44] All of this evidence suggests that the hour and the glorification of the Son of Man do not refer solely to the crucifixion, but also include the resurrection and his return to the Father.

A second mention of the Son of Man's glorification is found in 13.31-32. The use of νῦν ('Now is the Son of Man glorified'; cf. 12.23) and its connection to Judas' exit into the night (13.30) may be seen to strengthen the connection of the glorification primarily with the crucifixion. The crucifixion *is* part of the glorification,[45] but it is not all of it. As shown above, there is evidence for the glorification encompassing the whole of Jesus' hour: death, resurrection and return to the Father.[46] In 13.33, Jesus says that he is going away, in other words, returning to the Father. The concept of his departure is an ongoing theme throughout the Farewell Discourse (chs 13–16), which begins in 13.31.[47] Jesus is going/returning to the Father. Both the immediacy of the future glorification (εὐθύς: 13.32) and his going away in a little while (μικρόν: 13.33; 14.19; 16.16-18) imply that this departure is part of his glorification.

If the glorification and the hour include the death, resurrection and return to the Father as has been argued, and if that glorification is said to have come (12.23) and is now (13.1, 31), then the realized and present aspects of the glorification refer to the whole of those events. God has glorified the Son of Man in these events and the Son of Man has glorified God in them. The future glorification – 'and God will glorify him in himself, and he will glorify him immediately' – then looks beyond the hour to the time after Jesus' return to the Father. Is it any coincidence that reference to Jesus' return to the Father follows directly after mention of the future glorification (13.33, 36; 14.2-4)? And again, although it is disputed that there is a connection between 13.31-32

---

44. Blank, *Krisis*, p. 267. Also Ashton, *Understanding*, p. 494.

45. *Contra* G. C. Nicholson, *Death as Departure: The Johannine Descent-Ascent Schema* (SBLDS, 63; Chico: Scholars Press, 1983), p. 149.

46. Brown, *Gospel*, p. 606; Ensor, 'Glorification', pp. 233–34.

47. μεταβαίνω: 13.1; ὑπάγω: 13.33, 36-37; 14.28; 16.5, 10, 17; πορεύομαι: 14.2, 28; 16.28.

and 17.1-5,[48] the same thought is present in both passages.[49] Jesus the Son and the Son of Man is glorified by God the Father.[50]

D. *The three Johannine Son of Man themes*

These three commonly discussed themes are important for understanding the Johannine Son of Man. They indicate the heavenly origin and pre-existence of the Son of Man, as evidenced by 3.13 and 6.62. The 'lifting up' sayings depict the beginning of the Son of Man's exaltation in the physical lifting up on the cross, and the exaltation also extends to include his resurrection and return to the Father. Similarly, the glorification of the Son of Man denotes the passion, resurrection and ascent. The Son of Man has already been glorified in these events and yet will be glorified again in heaven after his return to where he was before. However, there are other Son of Man sayings in John that too often play only minor roles in the debates and yet add more to our understanding of the Johannine Son of Man.

III. *The 'misfit' Johannine Son of Man sayings (1.51; 5.27; 6.27, 53; 9.35)*

A. *An apocalyptic introduction of the Son of Man: 1.51*

Too often focus is placed on the three themes of ascent/descent, 'lifting up', and glorification. Those sayings that do not fit nicely into these themes or any other categories for that matter commonly fall to the wayside. Jn 1.51 is one of the more frequently discussed of these 'misfit' sayings. Nevertheless, it is the first Son of Man saying in the Gospel, concludes ch. 1 and sets the stage for the beginning of Jesus' signs and teaching. In the narrative context, 1.51 is directly related to Jesus' dialogue with Nathanael.[51] The connection of

---

48. Moloney, *Johannine*, pp. 199–200.
49. Brown, *Gospel*, pp. 610–11; J. Frey, *Die johanneische Eschatologie. Bände 1–3* (WUNT, 96, 110, 117; Tübingen: Mohr Siebeck, 1997, 1998, 2000), vol. 2, p. 136.
50. For further detail, see Reynolds, *Apocalyptic Son of Man*, pp. 208–10.
51. Previous scholarship has seen 1.51 as an interpolation, esp. R. Bultmann, *The Gospel of John: A Commentary* (G. R. Beasley-Murray, R. W. N. Hoare and J. K. Riches, trans.; Philadelphia: Westminster, 1976), p. 105, n. 2.

the saying with Gen. 28.12 is almost universally recognized[52] and provides further links with the Jacob allusions in the passage.[53] Just as deceitful Jacob saw a vision of angels ascending and descending on a ladder so Nathaniel who is without deceit will see angels ascending and descending on the Son of Man. A cursory comparison of the two passages suggests that the Son of Man has replaced the ladder of Jacob's vision.[54] Exactly in the place where the pronoun for 'ladder' is in LXX Gen. 28.12, the phrase ὁ υἱὸς τοῦ ἀθρώπου is found.

Gen. 28.12 : καὶ οἱ ἄγγελοι τοῦ θεοῦ ἀνέβαινον καὶ κατέβαινον ἐπ' αὐτῆς.

Jn 1.51 : καὶ τοὺς ἀγγέλους τοῦ θεοῦ ἀναβαίνοντας καὶ καταβαινοντας ἐπὶ τὸν υἱὸν τοῦ ἀνθρώπου.

But one important piece of the saying has yet to be mentioned. The first thing the disciples will see is heaven opening, an event that does not take place in Jacob's vision. The opening of heaven reflects a larger apocalyptic theme (cf. Ezek. 1; T. Levi 2.6; 2 Bar. 22.1), and it introduces the Son of Man in John with heavenly and apocalyptic connotations, since it is the opening of heaven which allows this vision to be seen by the disciples. Heaven opening usually indicates that a connection is being made between heaven and earth, whether it allows for communication or travel between the heavenly realm and the earthly.[55] In the case of Jn 1.51, the Son of Man is being established as the connection between heaven and earth. Douglas Hare asserts that the Son of Man as the ladder is 'grotesque, apocalyptic imagery' that is 'not characteristic of the Gospel'.[56] But why should this be grotesque? As the ladder connects heaven to earth in

---

52. For one exception, see W. Michaelis, 'Joh. 1,51, Gen. 28,12 und das Menschensohn-Problem', *TLZ* 85 (1960), pp. 561–78.

53. J. H. Neyrey, 'The Jacob Allusions in John 1.51', *CBQ* 44 (1982), pp. 586–605; D. Tovey, 'Stone of Witness and Stone of Revelation: An Exploration of Inter-textual Resonance in John 1:35–51', *Colloquium* 38 (2006), pp. 41–58.

54. A number of scholars have argued that the Son of Man replaces various aspects of Jacob's vision, including the stone, the place and even Jacob himself. For further discussion, see Reynolds, *Apocalyptic Son of Man*, pp. 96–99.

55. W. C. van Unnik, 'Die „Geöffneten Himmel" in der Offenbarungs-Vision des Apokryphons des Johannes', in W. Eltester and F. H. Kettler (eds), *Apophoreta. Festschrift für Ernst Haenchen zu seinem Seibzigsten Geburtstag am 10. Dezember 1964* (Berlin: Alfred Töpelmann, 1964), pp. 269–80; F. Lentzen-Deis, 'Das Motiv "Himmelsöffnung" in verschiedenen Gattungen der Umweltliteratur des Neuen Testaments', *Bib* 50 (1969), pp. 301–27.

56. Hare, *Son of Man*, p. 83.

Jacob's vision so does the Son of Man in John. We know from 3.13 that the Son of Man has descended from heaven. Thus, this connection is not made by a human reaching up to heaven but by a divine being coming down. Jesus as Son of Man is the mediator between God and humanity. He communicates the message of God to humanity and humanity's response to God, as symbolized by the messengers/angels ascending and descending on him.

This vision is meant to be an explication of the greater things that the disciples will see (1.50). The disciples do not literally see this vision in the Gospel; angels do not appear again until the resurrection and even then none of the 12 disciples sees them (20.12-13). What the disciples will see is the link that Jesus creates between heaven and earth, not just in his signs, but in his ministry as a whole. However, they will not understand the significance of Jesus' ministry until after the resurrection (cf. 20.28).

B. *The Son of Man and judgement (5.27)*

John 5.27 has been used as an important support for the understanding of the Johannine Son of Man as a heavenly being because of the similarities it shares with Dan. 7.13. While J. Louis Martyn considers it the most 'traditional' of the NT Son of Man sayings,[57] Delbert Burkett does not think 5.27 is an actual Son of Man saying because the saying lacks the articles: υἱὸς ἀνθρώπου instead of ὁ υἱὸς τοῦ ἀνθρώπου.[58] Two possible meanings are suggested for the anarthrous phrase in 5.27. Either it means that the Son judges because he is 'a son of man', in other words a human being, or he judges because he is 'the Son of Man', the figure already mentioned previously in the Gospel (1.51; 3.13, 14).[59]

The phrase υἱὸς ἀνθρώπου can denote ὁ υἱὸς τοῦ ἀνθρώπου.[60] The evidence that is usually given for this view is either grammatical or the similarity with the anarthrous phrase in Dan. 7.13. The typical grammatical argument is

---

57. J. L. Martyn, *History and Theology in the Fourth Gospel* (3rd edn; Louisville: Westminster/John Knox, 2003), p. 133.

58. Burkett, *Son of the Man*, pp. 41–45.

59. The former view is essentially non-existent in German scholarship.

60. In this debate, the phrase with the article is usually referred to as definite and the anarthrous phrase as indefinite. However, it should be noted that the language of 'definite' and 'indefinite' is not entirely helpful since something can be indefinite even if it has articles. See C. Lyons, *Definiteness* (Cambridge Textbooks in Linguistics; Cambridge: Cambridge University Press, 1999), esp. pp. 1–46.

founded on E. C. Colwell's Rule: 'definite predicate nouns that precede the verb usually lack the article'. Colwell found this rule to be true almost 90 per cent of the time. The only catch, which proponents and opponents alike tend to miss, is that Colwell began his study by examining predicate nouns that he already found to be definite. Thus, since the point in question is whether or not υἱὸς ἀνθρώπου denotes 'the Son of Man' or 'a son of man', Colwell's rule is unhelpful.[61]

Context must be the determining factor. Strikingly, there is no indication in the Gospel of John of Jesus' humanity being the basis for his authority to judge, even though *T. Ab.* A 13.3 is often used as an example of a human being in the act of judging (see also the use of Hebrews 2.17-18 and 4.15).[62] In fact, Jesus' judgement in John is specifically not according to the flesh like that of his opponents (Jn 8.15-17). In contrast, the expression 'the Son of Man' is continually found in the context of judgement throughout John (8.28; 9.35-41; 12.30-36). Not only that but the similarities with Daniel – anarthrous phrase (Dan. 7.13), theme of judgement (Daniel 7), and the double resurrection of the righteous and the wicked (Dan. 12.2; Jn 5.28-29) – further suggest that the authority to execute judgement belongs to the Son because he is the Son of Man. This also indicates that 'Son' and 'Son of Man' function with separate and distinct meanings, a point we will return to later.

C. *Sealing, eating and drinking (6.27, 53)*

The saying in Jn 6.27 can sometimes slip through the cracks of Johannine Son of Man studies. Jesus tells the crowd: 'Do not work for food that perishes but for food that remains to eternal life, which the Son of Man will give you. For God the Father has sealed this one.' This verse highlights a distinctive feature of the Johannine Son of Man – his obvious role in salvation. The Son of Man is the one who gives the food that remains to eternal life. Later in ch. 6 it becomes clear that this food that will be given is the bread from heaven, the bread of life coming down from heaven, which is Jesus himself (6.32-35). The food that

---

61.   See D. B. Wallace, *Greek Grammar beyond the Basics: An Exegetical Syntax of the New Testament* (Grand Rapids: Zondervan, 1996), pp. 260–61; D. A. Carson, *Exegetical Fallacies* (Grand Rapids: Baker, 1984), p. 87.

62.   M. Casey, *Son of Man: The Interpretation and Influence of Daniel 7* (London: SPCK, 1979), p. 199; Burkett, *Son of the Man*, p. 44.

remains to eternal life that the Son of Man will give is himself. The Son of Man has this salvific role because God the Father has sealed him. The sealing of the Son of Man appears to indicate that God has authorized or verified the Son of Man to give this life-giving food.[63] Just as the Son of Man has the authority to judge, so he has the authority to save or give life (cf. 5.24-26).

In 6.51, Jesus clarifies that the food that he will give is his flesh for the life of the world. When 'the Jews' become upset about this, wondering how he can give his flesh, Jesus says to them: 'Amen, amen I say to you, if you do not eat the flesh of the Son of Man and drink his blood, you do not have life in yourselves' (6.53). As the bread of life coming down from heaven, attention is again drawn to the Son of Man's heavenly origin (6.32, 33, 38, 41, 42, 50, 51, 58). The Son of Man's flesh does not point to an equation of 'Son of Man' and humanity. Rather it only highlights what we have previously seen, namely, that the Son of Man has descended from heaven and become human. The eating and drinking of the Son of Man's flesh and blood are not meant to be taken literally any more than Nicodemus was to be born again in a physical sense.[64] Eating the flesh and drinking the blood is a metaphor for belief, believing in the Son of Man.[65] The language of 'remaining/abiding' highlights this emphasis on belief (6.56; cf. 15.4-5). Also, the result of both believing (6.40) and eating (6.54) is eternal life and being raised on the last day. 'The Spirit gives life; the flesh is of no value' (6.63).

D. *Belief in the Son of Man: the neglected saying (9.35)*
I find it extremely interesting that 9.35 silently disappears from a number of studies on the Johannine Son of Man. Siegfried Schulz relegated it to a footnote, and E. M. Sidebottom did not mention the saying at all.[66] The mysterious disappearance of this saying is most likely due in large part to the difficulty of placing

---

63. Brown, *Gospel*, pp. 261–62.

64. See Moloney, *Johannine*, p. 102.

65. J. D. G. Dunn, 'John VI – A Eucharistic Discourse?', *NTS* 17 (1970–71), pp. 328–38; D. M. Swancutt, 'Hungers Assuaged by the Bread from Heaven: "Eating Jesus" as Isaian Call to Belief: The Confluence of Isaiah 55 and Psalm 78(77) in John 6.22-71', in C. A. Evans and J. A. Sanders (eds), *Early Christian Interpretation of the Scriptures of Israel: Investigations and Prophets* (SSEJC 5; JSNTSup 148; Sheffield: Sheffield Academic Press, 1997), pp. 218–51.

66. Schulz, *Untersuchungen*, p. 118 n. 4; E. M. Sidebottom, 'The Son of Man as Man in the Fourth Gospel', *ExpTim* 68 (1957), pp. 231–35, 280–83.

9.35 into one of the Johannine Son of Man themes. Added to this, it is one of the most distinct of all the Son of Man sayings in all four of the Gospels because it is found in a statement of belief. Jesus asks the man born blind: 'Do you believe in the Son of Man?' Nowhere in the NT is ὁ υἱὸς τοῦ ἀνθρώπου found in a statement of belief. Not surprisingly, the textual tradition reveals a variant of ὁ υἱὸς τοῦ θεοῦ, but this variant makes the most sense as either a purposeful or accidental alignment with other Johannine statements about belief in the Son.[67]

The entire context of John 9 concerns the identity of Jesus, the one who gave sight to the man born blind. Although Jesus is never questioned, the blind man is interrogated about his new-found sight and specifically about the one who healed him. Since the man born blind moves from belief in Jesus as healer (9.11), to prophet (9.17), to one 'from God' (9.33), it is challenging to understand why Jesus would ask the man born blind to believe in the 'human one'. The Pharisees and scribes on the other hand see Jesus as a mere man (9.24) and cast the healed man out for thinking that Jesus is from God (9.33; cf. 9.16). If the entire passage has this crescendo of meaning concerning Jesus' identity as divine, how could the climax of the passage lead to a declaration of Jesus as the human one?[68] Edwin Abbott's defence of the humanity view for 9.35 captures the difficulty of this argument: 'The blind man, never having seen a man (or "son of man") before, could not be familiar with the sight, and would therefore be free from that kind of "familiarity" which "breeds contempt" for what we often call "a mere man".'[69]

The man born blind is either unaware of who the Son of Man is and wants to know his identity or the idiom is unclear to him.[70] Jesus' response implies that it is the identity of the Son of Man that the man seeks to know: 'You have heard him and the one speaking with you is *that one*' (ἐκεῖνος – 9.37; cf. 4.26). At the same time, this does not rule out the possibility that the man has no knowledge of the content of ὁ υἱὸς τοῦ ἀνθρώπου; yet his interest continues to be in the identity of this figure.

  67. B. M. Metzger, *A Textual Commentary on the Greek New Testament* (Stuttgart: Deutsche Bibelgesellschaft, 2nd edn, 1994), p. 194.
  68. *Contra* Pamment, 'Son of Man', pp. 63, 65; Ramos, 'Hijo', pp. 57, 90.
  69. Abbott, *Son of Man*, p. 538, n. 1. Casey (*Solution*, p. 307), who elsewhere says that 'Son of Man' refers to Jesus as a human being (p. 281), appears to modify this view in 9.35 to say that 'Son of Man' indicates 'the humanity of God incarnate who reveals himself through his σάρξ'.
  70. C. K. Barrett, *The Gospel According to St. John: An Introduction with Commentary and Notes on the Greek Text* (Philadelphia: Westminster, 2nd edn, 1978), p. 364.

Further, in Jn 9.39-41,[71] Jesus says: 'For judgement I have come into this world.' The connection of the Son of Man to judgement is brought again to the forefront. Judgement, since we last saw it in 5.27, is here an unsurprising function of the Son of Man. His heavenly origin is highlighted again by mention of his 'coming into this world'.[72] This suggests movement from outside this world and into it – such as a descent from heaven (3.13; 6.32, 51, 53).

Thus, Jn 9.35 is an important Johannine Son of Man saying, which is too often neglected. The saying may suggest similarity with the 'Son (of God)' sayings because of the theme of belief, but this does mean that they are equivalent titles in John.

E. *Summary of the Son of Man sayings in John*

Even though the sayings just discussed do not fit within the common thematic categories, they add significant insight into the characteristics of the Johannine Son of Man. The Son of Man in John is a heavenly, apocalyptic figure (1.51). He has a role in the final judgement, and 'Son of Man' appears distinct from 'Son' (5.27). Along with his role in judgement, the Son of Man acts in salvation giving himself as the life-giving food (6.27) and is a heavenly figure to be believed in (6.53; 9.35). All of these depictions raise questions about three of the four broad Christological understandings of 'Son of Man' in John's Gospel and help to clarify the fourth.

IV. *The Johannine Son of Man: humanity, divine-man, Son of God or heavenly figure*

So what does this examination reveal about the Son of Man sayings in the Gospel of John? How do the four broad Christological meanings hold up to scrutiny?

---

71.   That Jesus is speaking here as the Son of Man is reasonably clear since he has just declared himself 'Son of Man' in whom to believe (9.37). The possible narrative break between vv. 38 and 39 is non-existent since the themes of light/dark, blindness/sight and sin are repetition of themes at the opening of the narrative in 9.1-5 and conclude Jesus' discussion with the man born blind.

72.   Collins and Collins, *King and Messiah*, p. 185.

A. *Son of Man and Jesus' humanity*

Although the view that 'the Son of Man' indicates Jesus' humanity is the most common understanding of the use of the idiom in John, the evidence of the sayings suggests that this is not its meaning. I contend that references to the Son of Man's descent from heaven suggest that Jesus did not become the Son of Man at the incarnation, but rather existed as the Son of Man prior to his descent (3.13; 6.51-53). Similarly, the Son of Man's ascent involves existence after the ascent, since the Son of Man will ascend to where he was *before* (6.62). Despite claims otherwise, I posit that the Son of Man's descent implies pre-existence. For someone to move from one location to another requires the existence of that person in the first location prior to movement to the other.[73] Further, considering the Johannine emphasis on belief in the Son of God (3:16), the invitation to believe in the Son of Man suggests that the expression 'the Son of Man' refers to a heavenly being (9.35). The man born blind has come to understand that Jesus is from God (9.33) while the Pharisees believe Jesus to be a mere man (9.17, 24). There seems to be no reason why Jesus would tell the man to believe in the 'human one' or his humanity if Jesus is already understood to be a man by his opponents who do not believe in him (9.24).

Another argument put forward by the humanity proponents is that the crucifixion is a human event, and therefore, only a human could be crucified.[74] Although the lifting up and glorification of the Son of Man include the crucifixion, this does not mean that 'the Son of Man' expression designates Jesus' humanity. The point of John (and the Synoptics for that matter) is that Jesus the Son of God and Son of Man was crucified (cf. Mark 8.31; 9.31; 10.33; and pars.). The importance of the event is not that a human being died, but that the Son of Man and the Son of God could and did die.[75]

To be completely clear, *this is not an argument against the humanity of Jesus in the Gospel of John*. The Johannine Jesus is obviously human.[76] The

---

73. *Contra* Moloney, Editor's Note, in Brown, *Introduction*, p. 257, n. 87.

74. Moloney, 'Revisited', pp. 193, 201; Casey, *Solution*, p. 283.

75. See R. Bauckham, *God Crucified: Monotheism and Christology in the New Testament* (Grand Rapids: Eerdmans, 1998). Cf. Justin, *Dial.*, 31–32, where Trypho, according to Justin, expects the Son of Man to be the Danielic figure who will triumph and not suffer.

76. M. M. Thompson, *The Incarnate Word: Perspectives on Jesus in the Fourth Gospel* (Peabody, MA: Hendrickson, 1993; orig. *The Humanity of Jesus in the Fourth Gospel* [Fortress Press: 1988]).

Word became flesh and dwelt among us (1.14). Jesus' opponents refer to him as ἄνθρωπος (9.16, 24), and the crowd calls him the son of Joseph (6.42). But, at the same time, I contend that the idiom 'the Son of Man' is not used in John to emphasize Jesus' humanity.[77]

B. *'Son of Man' and 'Son of God'*

The Gospel of John's portrayal of the expressions 'the Son of Man' and 'the Son of God' raises questions about the relationship between them. These questions are non-existent in the Synoptic Gospels largely because of the comparative absence of 'Son (of God)' language, but in John we see overlap in context and sometimes meaning. The scholarly opinion about the relationship between the titles varies from synonymous meaning to stark contrast. Both extremes do not fit the evidence from the Gospel. First, there are obvious distinctions between the use and meaning of 'the Son of Man' and 'the Son (of God)'. In 5.27, the Son is able to execute judgement because he is 'the Son of Man'. The authority to judge here is thus dependent upon Jesus' being 'the Son of Man' and not on his status as 'the Son'.[78] Although Burkett claims: 'The fundamental signifi-cance of the title is thus relational: it expresses Jesus' Sonship, his relation to the Father',[79] there is no clear indication of the filial relationship between Father and the Son of Man. Furthermore, the Son is sent by the Father into the world and the Son of Man descends, indicating that there are definite distinctions between the uses of the two titles.

Yet with all of these distinctions, overlap between the titles remains. They are not entirely distinct from one another. Belief in 'Son' and 'Son of Man' leads to eternal life (3.16; 9.35; cf. 3.15). Both titles are used in the context of glory and glorification (12.23; 13.31-32; 17.1-5). And we find in an 'I' statement of Jesus, themes more often connected with 'Son (of God)' sayings – hearing the Father, being sent, doing the Father's will – alongside the theme of judgement, which is considered a 'Son of Man' theme (Jn 5.30). This suggests that the titles cannot be entirely separated from one another.

The expressions have distinguishable meanings and each further expands

---

77. The view that 'Son of Man' highlights Jesus' humanity and divinity simultaneously does not need a separate argument, since the above critique is relevant to this view as well.

78. Freed ('Son of Man', p. 404) fails to note this distinction.

79. Burkett, *Son of the Man*, p. 171.

our understanding of John's Gospel and the Johannine Jesus, but, at the same time, 'the Son of Man' and 'the Son (of God)' cannot be completely divorced from one another because they are attached to the same person.[80] There is distinctiveness between the two, but there is overlap due to the similar referent. Each expression, 'the Son (of God)' and 'the Son of Man', presents a distinct Christological understanding of the person of Jesus in the Gospel of John.

C. *The Johannine Son of Man as a heavenly figure in Johannine Christology*

Rather than 'the Son of Man' highlighting the humanity of Jesus or being synonymous with 'the Son (of God)', the expression draws attention to the heavenly nature of Jesus. The heavenly connotation of the expression can be seen in the Son of Man's appearance at the apocalyptic opening of heaven (1.51), his descent from and ascent to heaven (3.13; 6.62), and his coming into the world (9.35-41; cf. 12.32). Hints of the heavenly significance of the Johannine Son of Man can also be seen in the contextual understanding of the 'lifting up' and glorification sayings, since Jesus' return to the Father appears to be included in the Son of Man's lifting up and glorification (3.14; 8.28; 12.34; 12.23; 13.31-32). For John, '"Son of Man" points to a figure whose true home is in heaven'.[81]

Regarding the significance of 'the Son of Man' for Johannine Christology, scholars hold views at the two ends of the spectrum. Some see a Son of Man Christology as the central Christology of the Gospel,[82] whereas others see no Christological meaning of the expression.[83] It is by no means central to the gospel, as can be seen in its absence from important points in the narrative, such as Jesus' dialogue with the Samaritan woman (John 4), his disputes with the 'Jews' in John 7 and 10, and in the raising of Lazarus (John 11). Interestingly, it is at these junctures that the title 'Messiah' or 'Christ' is used by Jesus or others. However, the most telling evidence against 'the Son of Man' being the

---

80. M. M. Pazdan, *The Son of Man: A Metaphor for Jesus in the Fourth Gospel* (Zacchaeus Studies: New Testament; Collegeville, MN: Liturgical, 1991), pp. 79–81.

81. Ashton, *Understanding*, 337.

82. Higgins, *Jesus*, p. 155.

83. Barrett, *Gospel*, p. 73.

central Christology of the Gospel of John is the fact that it is missing from the author's statement about the reason for writing the Gospel in Jn 20.30-31.

Nevertheless, although it may not be the central emphasis of the Gospel, 'the Son of Man' still plays an important part in Johannine Christology. Together with 'Son of God', 'Messiah', the 'I Am' sayings, the theme of Jesus' kingship, etc., 'the Son of Man' adds to the overall depiction of the Johannine Jesus. The expression makes a distinctive contribution to John's Christological portrait of Jesus. For example, in John 'the Son of Man' draws attention to Jesus' ability to judge, his role in salvation, and his similarity with the Father in these actions. The expression also highlights the reason he can reveal heavenly mysteries, namely because he has descended from heaven, and clarifies that Jesus' death is the beginning of his exaltation and glorification. Borrowing a term from M.-É. Boismard, the titles of Jesus in John's Gospel form 'un bouquet' of titles.[84] 'The Son of Man' is not the dominant flower of the bouquet, but neither is it an insignificant flower, nor the same as any another flower. 'The Son of Man', along with the other titles, adds to the Christological presentation of Jesus and further enhances the Gospel's depiction of his identity.

V. *The Son of Man in John and the Synoptic Gospels*

The relationship between the Johannine Son of Man and 'the Son of Man' in the Synoptic Gospels requires assessment, not least because all four Gospels use the term to refer to Jesus. Moreover, in each Gospel, Jesus uses the idiom to speak of himself solely, and he is the only one to use the idiom (apart from the repetition of his words by the angels in Lk. 24.7 and the crowd in Jn 12.34). But do each of the Gospels use the term in the same way? Various opinions have been given on this; however, the majority see John as interpreting (or shall we say 'theologizing') 'the Son of Man' on the basis of the Synoptic portrayal(s). Markus Sasse has listed 11 differences between the Son of Man in John and the Synoptics.[85] A few such as Robert Maddox see closer similarity between

---

84.   M.-É. Boismard and A. Lamouille, *L'Évangile de Jean. Synopse des quatre évangiles* (Paris: Cerf, 3rd edn, 1977), p. 99.
85.   Sasse, *Menschensohn*, pp. 243–45. Although Sasse lists 11 differences, some of these are opposite sides of the same coin.

the descriptions.[86] Obvious differences exist between the four Gospels, but is John closer to the Synoptics than most think?

For those familiar with the Synoptic use of 'the Son of Man', some of the differences with the Gospel of John are stark. First, the Johannine Son of Man ascends and descends, while the Son of Man in Matthew, Mark and Luke does not engage in this movement. Second, there is no indication of a future coming (*parousia*) of the Son of Man in John, but in the Synoptic Gospels, the Son of Man is present on earth and will also come in the future with the clouds (Mk 13.26; 14.62; Mt. 24.30; 26.64; Lk. 21.27; 22.69?).[87] Consistent with the more realized eschatology of John, the Johannine Son of Man is presented as acting, judging and saving in the present. Third, the Son of Man's connection to the crucifixion is understood as part of a larger exaltation theme in John, whereas in the Synoptics this connection is spoken of in the language of suffering. For example, 'It is necessary for the Son of Man to suffer and to be persecuted by the elders and the high priests and the scribes . . .'. (Mk 8.31). Fourth, and related to the three previous differences, the Johannine Son of Man is glorified on earth (12.23; 13.31; cf. 12.28). In the Synoptics, glory is solely related to the Son of Man at the time of his future appearance with the clouds of heaven and the angels of God (Mk 13.62; Mt. 24.30; 25.31; Lk. 21.27). Fifth, the Son of Man in John is overtly depicted as having an active role in salvation. He is the one who gives the food that remains to eternal life (6.27), and those who believe have life in him (3.14-15). In the Synoptic Gospels, the Son of Man's role in salvation is not as clear. The nearest references are to the Son of Man giving his life as a ransom for many (Mk 10.45; Mt. 20.28) and his coming to seek and to save the lost (Lk. 19.10). Sixth, the Johannine Son of Man is one who is to be believed in. Belief in the Son of Man is absent in the Synoptics.[88]

Now while there are these obvious differences, there are some startling similarities that often go unnoticed or are considered unimportant due to the differences mentioned above. First, although the language surrounding Jesus' crucifixion in the Synoptic Gospels ('suffering', 'being rejected' and 'handed over') is different from that used in the Gospel of John ('lifting up' and 'glorification'), ὁ υἱὸς τοῦ ἀνθρώπου is the phrase the Johannine Jesus uses

---

86.   Maddox, 'Function', p. 203.
87.   Sasse, *Menschensohn*, p. 244. See Schnackenburg, *Gospel*, vol. 1, pp. 536–37.
88.   But cf. Lk. 18.8.

to refer to himself when speaking of his crucifixion, resurrection and return. This similarity is heightened by the fact that there are three Son of Man passion predictions in Matthew, Mark and Luke, and there are three Son of Man 'lifting up' sayings in John.[89] Further, the first passion prediction in each of the three Synoptics begins with the word δεῖ (Mk 8.31; Mt. 16.21; Lk. 9.22), and this same Greek word, which emphasizes the necessity of the Son of Man's passion, is found at the beginning of the first 'lifting up' saying in Jn 3.14.[90] So, similarity between John and the Synoptic Gospels is highlighted by the phrase ὁ υἱὸς τοῦ ἀνθρώπου in the context of Jesus' crucifixion, the three passion predictions and three 'lifting up' sayings, and the parallel use of δεῖ. The differences of language (πάσχω, παραδίδωμι, and κατακρίνω compared with ὑψόω and δοξάζω) can be explained as different perspectives and understandings of the same event. For the Synoptics and John, the resurrection is part of the prediction, although in John this is more implicit than in the Synoptic Gospels (see Jn 2.19; 12.16; 16.7; 20.22). Whereas the Synoptics speak of the Son of Man's suffering and death and being raised on the third day, the language of the Gospel of John portrays the entire event as his 'lifting up' or exaltation.[91]

Second, the Son of Man in Matthew, Mark, Luke and John takes part in judgement. The Matthean Son of Man sits on a throne of glory, separates the righteous from the wicked (25.31), and there is punishment for the wicked and eternal life for the righteous (Mt. 25.31–46). The Lukan Son of Man has come to cast fire on the earth (Lk. 12.49). Mark is not so explicit, but the Son of Man's role in judgement is still discernible (Mk 13.27). In John, the Son of Man has the authority to judge and has come into the world for judgement (5.27; 9.35-41; 12.30-36).[92]

Third, in the Synoptics and John, the Son of Man is involved in salvation. The Johannine Son of Man is more explicitly the giver of eternal life, but the Synoptic Son of Man is not devoid of salvific action. It was noted above that

---

89.   Thüsing, *Erhöhung*, p. 11; Blank, *Krisis*, pp. 82–83; Ashton, *Understanding*, p. 64.

90.   Intriguingly, δεῖ is also used in the two Son of Man sayings in the gospels not spoken by Jesus (Lk. 24.7; Jn 12.34).

91.   See P. Létourneau, 'Le quatrième évangile et les prédications de la passion dans les évangiles synoptiques', in A. Denaux (ed.), *John and the Synoptics* (BETL, 101; Leuven: Leuven University Press, 1992), pp. 579–86.

92.   Maddox, 'Function', pp. 203–204; Schnackenburg, *Gospel*, vol. 1, p. 535.

in the Synoptic Gospels the Son of Man came to give his life as a ransom for many (Mk 10.45; Mt. 20.28) and to seek and to save the lost (Lk. 19.10). Although there is some difference here over his involvement in, or manner of, the salvation, it is an important function of the Son of Man in each of the Gospels. This can also be seen in the relationship between 'the Son of Man' and the Eucharistic tradition. Each of the Synoptic Gospels has a Son of Man saying in conjunction with the breaking of bread and drinking of the wine. In Mark and Matthew, the institution of the Lord's supper follows the naming of Judas as the one who would betray the Son of Man (Mk 14.21-25; Mt. 26.24-29). In Luke, the Son of Man reference follows the breaking of the bread and passing of the cup (Lk. 22.19-22). In the Gospel of John, ch. 6 contains what is commonly recognized as Eucharistic language. Although I have argued above that this is primarily meant metaphorically as belief and not an overt reference to the Lord's Supper, it is extremely interesting that the Son of Man gives food that is himself (6.27, 32, 35). It is the flesh of the Son of Man that must be eaten and his blood that must be drunk in order for someone to have eternal life (6.53). Thus, all four Gospels present a connection between 'the Son of Man', the giving of himself in salvation, and the language of 'body'/'flesh' and 'blood'.

Fourth, Jesus the Son of Man is also depicted as the Messiah in the Synoptics and John. Some argue that 'the Son of Man' is used as a corrective in John (esp. 1.43–51; 12.34),[93] but this seems unlikely. Jesus is not actually correcting these Messianic pronouncements, but further defining who he is. Elsewhere in John, Jesus does not 'correct' messianic understandings of his identity (4.26; 11.27).

Fifth, glory is closely tied to the Son of Man in all four Gospels. In the Synoptics, the Son of Man's glory is noticeable at his return with the clouds and angels (Mk 8.38; 13.26; Mt. 16.27; 24.30; Lk. 9.26; 21.27). The Johannine Son of Man has already been glorified on earth (12.23; 13.31; cf. 12.28), yet he will also be glorified again in the future (13.32). Although there are timing differences, this is more likely due to John's realized eschatology than a difference in glorification. The Son of Man is still glorified.

---

93. Sasse, *Menschensohn*, pp. 77, 247; and more recently J. H. Ellens, 'Exegesis of Second Temple Texts in a Fourth Gospel Son of Man Logion', in I. Kalini and P. J. Haas (eds), *Biblical Interpretation in Judaism and Christianity* (LHBOTS, 439; London: T&T Clark, 2006), pp. 131–49.

Finally, the Son of Man is the one who will gather the righteous. In the Synoptics this gathering occurs when the Son of Man will 'gather his elect from the four winds, from the ends of the earth to the ends of heaven' (Mk 13.27; Mt. 24.31; cf. Lk. 12.35-40). The Johannine Son of Man will call the righteous and the wicked from the tombs (5.27-29) and will draw all people to himself when he is lifted up from the earth (12.32). This gathering, although expressed differently in the four Gospels, is a shared feature of the Son of Man.

These similarities suggest that the Son of Man has a number of similar functions and characteristics in each of the Gospels. There are some clear differences between John and the Synoptic portrayals, but these differences tend to be differences of nuance or timing rather than contradictory features. Even within the Synoptic Gospels, we do not find a completely uniform picture of the Son of Man. Mark has an emphasis on the Son of Man's authority. Matthew focuses on the figure's royal nature and role in apocalyptic judgement, whereas Luke highlights his path through suffering.[94] Although there are dissimilarities, the Son of Man in Matthew, Mark and Luke is more closely related to the Son of Man in John than is often noted. In the words of Robert Maddox, 'In spite of the considerable differences of vocabulary and imagery, the fundamental significance of the title "Son of Man" in John is not different from that which it has in the synoptic gospels.'[95]

VI. *The Johannine Son of Man and the Son of Man debate*

But what bearing, if any, does this have on the historical expression 'Son of Man' on the lips of Jesus? Has the Fourth Evangelist interpreted 'Son of Man' through the Synoptic tradition or does the Gospel of John provide evidence of a separate tradition (oral or written) about Jesus? The similarities between the Synoptics and John seem to suggest that these are the two most likely options for understanding their relationship.

---

94. For Mark, see M. D. Hooker, *The Son of Man in Mark: A Study of the Background of the Term 'Son of Man' and its Use in St Mark's Gospel* (Montreal: McGill University Press, 1967). For Matthew, see U. Luz, 'The Son of Man in Matthew: Heavenly Judge or Human Christ', *JSNT* 48 (1992), pp. 3–21; and for Luke, G. Schneider, '„Der Menschensohn" in der lukanischen Christologie', in R. Pesch and R. Schnackenburg (eds), *Jesus und der Menschensohn: Für Anton Vögtle* (Freiburg: Herder, 1975), pp. 267–82.

95. Maddox, 'Function', p. 203.

Schnackenburg takes the former view: 'As regards the Son of Man logia at any rate, one must not overlook the obvious links with the Synoptic tradition, though it may have been given a strikingly new interpretation.'[96] If, as Schnackenburg claims, the Johannine Son of Man derives from the Synoptic tradition, can we rule out the Gospel of John in the historical debates about Jesus' Son of Man sayings? The Gospel of John is still evidence of the sayings in the mouth of Jesus, but if there has been significant 'new interpretation', the historical value of the Johannine sayings becomes questionable and thus also their relevance for the debate.[97]

If, however, the Evangelist and the Synoptics drew from different streams of the Jesus tradition (as some in the John, Jesus, and History Group have recently proposed),[98] the Johannine sayings may carry their own weight against or in comparison with the Synoptic sayings in the Son of Man debate. Stephen Smalley made this argument 40 years ago. He stated:

> If the Johannine tradition is indeed historical and independent of the Synoptists, as surely it is, the authenticity of any part is open to question both ways. And if there is at the same time a sense in which John is also 'among the Synoptists', we need not assume the Johannine record (any more than the synoptic) is necessarily out of touch with the *earliest* strata of Christological tradition.[99]

Although there is not enough space to pursue the question of the historical relevance of the Johannine Son of Man sayings here, I would like to propose a way forward in exploring this matter. First, a helpful starting point would be to examine those Son of Man sayings that indicate similarities with those in the Synoptics, such as the 'lifting up' sayings. Do these comprise essentially the same sayings, one set being a reinterpretation of the other? If they are versions of the same sayings, either the Synoptic Gospels have reinterpreted the phrase

---

96.   Schnackenburg, *Gospel*, vol. 1, p. 538. See also Ashton, *Understanding*, p. 368 and Casey, *Solution*, p. 275.

97.   See M. M. Thompson, 'The "Spiritual Gospel": How John the Theologian Writes History', in *John, Jesus, and History*, pp. 103–107.

98.   See Anderson, *Fourth Gospel*, p. 38. This position is, however, not entirely new. See C. H. Dodd, *Historical Tradition in the Fourth Gospel* (Cambridge: Cambridge University Press, 1965).

99.   Smalley, 'Johannine Son of Man', pp. 300–301 (emphasis original).

'lifting up' with the specifics of suffering, death and resurrection, or on the other hand, as the majority of scholars see it, the hand of the Fourth Evangelist can be seen in the distinctive 'theologizing' of the passion events. However, if we say this is the same event, why do the disciples seem to be confused by the passion sayings in the Synoptics, while in John the disciples are not described as being in confusion about the Son of Man being 'lifted up' (cf. 12.34)? Other sayings that might be examined in this 'Synoptic-like' category include 5.27, 1.51, 6.53, and the glorification sayings (12.23; 13.31-32).

Second, such an examination would address those Johannine sayings that are unlike any of the Synoptic sayings.[100] These sayings are often ruled inauthentic because of their dissimilarity with Son of Man sayings in Matthew, Mark and Luke. But if John is viewed as one tradition alongside the Synoptics, the possibility exists that the Gospel of John provides evidence of another reliable historical tradition. If the Johannine sayings are evidence of early Jesus tradition – even if they were written down at a later date – they could be some of the earliest testimony that we have.[101] This might provide the possibility for the Johannine sayings being used in conjunction with the Synoptic tradition in the attempt to answer the historical questions surrounding the use of the idiom 'the Son of Man'. We may find, after all, that the non-Synoptic Johannine Son of Man sayings are compatible with those in the Synoptics. The criterion of dissimilarity may surprise us by implying that some of these sayings could be considered authentic, even if nothing like them is found in the Synoptic Gospels (especially Jn 6.27 and 9.35).[102]

This chapter by no means claims even to come close to providing a final answer to the question of the authenticity of the Johannine Son of Man sayings. However, the Johannine Son of Man's similarities with the Son of Man in each of the Synoptic Gospels should at least force us to pause before completely excluding these sayings from the discussion of this puzzling expression of the historical Jesus.

---

100.   A similar 'Synoptic'/'non-Synoptic' structure was used by Higgins (*Jesus*, pp. 153–84).

101.   See Smalley's statement above.

102.   For recent work on the authenticity of Jesus' Johannine sayings, see P. Ensor, 'The Johannine Sayings of Jesus and the Question of Authenticity', in J. Lierman (ed.), *Challenging Perspectives on the Gospel of John* (WUNT II, 219; Tübingen: Mohr Siebeck, 2006), pp. 210–34; Lierman, 'Glorification'.

THE ELECT SON OF MAN OF THE *PARABLES OF ENOCH*

Darrell D. Hannah

The eschatological heavenly mediator of the *Parables of Enoch*, alternatively termed the Elect One (or Chosen One), the Righteous One, the Messiah and the (or that) son of man, is quite probably the most exalted heavenly mediator to be encountered in the Judaism of the Second Temple period apart, that is, from Jesus the Messiah of early Christianity. The *Parables'* figure functions as *the* eschatological judge, sits on the very throne of God and receives homage which approaches, but is not to be equated with, worship. Early Christianity also professed its heavenly mediator to be *the* eschatological judge, often, although not always, envisioned him as exalted to the divine throne[1] and consistently offered him divine worship.[2] The two figures share other similarities: Both were held to be the Messiah, both were regarded as God's Elect, some of the same Old Testament Scriptures were interpreted as prophecies of

---

1. In my 'The Throne of Glory: The Divine Throne and Heavenly Mediators in Revelation and the Similitudes of Enoch', *ZNW* 94 (2003), pp. 68–96, I argue that the Book of Revelation, the Epistle to the Hebrews, and the Gospel of Matthew envision Christ seated on the throne of God. Other early Christian texts, such as Polycarp, *Phil.*2.1, *Apoc.Peter* 6.1 and probably *Asc.Isa.* 11.32-33, conceive of the exalted Christ occupying a throne next to the divine throne. Other early Christian texts which mention Christ's heavenly enthronement, e.g., Rom. 8.34; Col. 3.4; Eph. 1.20; Acts 2.33-34, are too concise to be sure just how their authors visualized the divine throne(s) and its/their occupants.

2. Cf. L. W. Hurtado, *One God, One Lord: Early Christian Devotion and Ancient Jewish Monotheism* (Edinburgh: T&T Clark, 2nd edn, 1998); Hurtado, *Lord Jesus Christ: Devotion to Jesus in Earliest Christianity* (Grand Rapids: Eerdmans, 2003); R. Bauckham, 'The Worship of Jesus', in *The Climax of Prophecy: Studies on the Book of Revelation* (Edinburgh: T&T Clark, 1993), pp. 118–49.

each, both were thought to pre-exist and both were believed to be the 'Son of Man' of Daniel 7. Although a comprehensive comparison of the *Parables'* Elect son of man with the Christ of Early Christianity lies beyond the scope of this essay, any understanding of ὁ υἱὸς τοῦ ἀνθρώπου of the Gospels must grapple with and come to terms with this other 'son of man'. In this chapter, after a brief discussion of the *Parables* themselves and the difficulties they present to interpreters, we will examine each of the key elements mentioned above: The four main 'titles' of the Elect son of man,[3] his exegetical basis in the Old Testament Scriptures, his eschatological role, his pre-existence and the problematic identification of this figure with Enoch.[4]

The Parables of Enoch: *their origin and significance*

Probably no text from Second Temple Judaism presents us with as many interpretative cruxes as do the *Parables of Enoch*. The *Parables* belong to the composite work known in scholarship as *1 Enoch* or the Ethiopic *Book of Enoch*. As the latter title suggests, this work has only been preserved, in its entirety, in Ge'ez or classical Ethiopic, the liturgical and canonical language of the Ethiopian Orthodox Church. In Ethiopia the *Book of Enoch* was (and is)

---

3.   Although 'Messiah' (48.10; 52.4) and 'Righteous One' (38.2; 53.6) are represented, the two 'titles' which predominate are 'Elect (or Chosen) One' and 'the (or that) son of man'. To reflect this and to keep the nomenclature from becoming too unwieldy, I have selected the term 'the Elect son of man', recognizing that this phrase never actually appears in the *Parables*. Cf. also H. S. Kvanvig, 'The Son of man in the Parables of Enoch', in *Enoch and the Messiah Son of Man: Revisiting the Book of Parables* (ed. G. Boccaccini; Grand Rapids: Eerdmans, 2007), pp. 179–215, esp. 200.

4.   In what follows the translation of the Ethiopic text of the *Parables* is my own. Consulted translations include: G. W. E. Nickelsburg and J. C. VanderKam (trans.), *1 Enoch: A New Translation, based on the Hermeneia Commentary* (Minneapolis: Fortress Press, 2004); M. Black, *The Book of Enoch or I Enoch* (SVTP, 7; Leiden: Brill, 1985); S. Uhlig (trans.), *Das äthiopische Henochbuch* (JSHRZ, V.6; Gütersloh: Gütersloher Verlagshaus, 1984); E. Isaac (trans.), '1 (Ethiopic Apocalypse of) Enoch', in J. H. Charlesworth (ed.), *The Old Testament Pseudepigrapha* (2 vols; Garden City, NY: Doubleday, 1983, 1985); M. A. Knibb (ed. & trans.), *The Ethiopic Book of Enoch: A New Edition in the light of the Aramaic Dead Sea Fragments* (2 vols; Oxford: Clarendon Press, 1978); R. H. Charles, *The Book of Enoch or I Enoch* (Oxford: Clarendon Press, 1912); G. Beer, 'Das Buch Henoch', in E. Kautzsch (ed.), *Die Apokryphen und Pseudepigraphen des Alten Testaments* (2 vols; Darmstadt: Wissenschaftliche Buchgesellschaft, 1975, orig. pub. 1900) and A. Dillmann, *Das Buch Henoch* (Leipzig: Vogel, 1853).

regarded as an authentic work of the prophet Enoch, 'the seventh from Adam', and thus included, along with *Jubilees*, in the Ethiopian Old Testament canon. Though tiny fragments of the original Aramaic were discovered at Qumran, and substantial fragments in Greek (as well as smaller extracts in Latin, Coptic and Syriac) are extant, *none* of these preserves material from the *Parables*. An Ethiopic version remains our only witness to the text of the *Parables*. The *Book of Enoch* was in all likelihood translated into Ethiopic from a Greek exemplar, although Syriac cannot be entirely excluded, sometime in the Askumite period, i.e., sometime between the fourth and seventh centuries. Our earliest Ethiopic manuscript of *Enoch*, Lake Tana 9, dates from the early fifteenth century.[5] Thus approximately a thousand years of copying separates our earliest manuscript of the *Parables* from its introduction into Ethiopia, and the Ethiopic manuscripts contain ample evidence of textual corruption. Moreover, the Ethiopic text represents, in all likelihood, a translation of a translation.[6] We cannot be certain whether the original language of the *Parables*, as opposed to the other portions of *Enoch*, was Aramaic or Hebrew; either way, we stand at two removes from

---

5. Other early manuscripts include EMML 7584 (late 15th), Paris Abbadianus 55 (15–16th), EMML 1768 (15–16th), EMML 2080 (15–16th), British Library Or. 485 (early 16th), and Berlin Or. Petermann II, Nachtrag 29 (16th). A handful of others date from the sixteenth or seventeenth centuries, but the majority belong to the eighteenth.

6. Maurice Casey (*The Solution to the 'Son of Man' Problem* [LNTS, 343; London: T&T Clark, 2007], pp. 95–97) argues that the *Parables* were translated into Ethiopic directly from the Semitic original, which he thinks was Aramaic. In fact, it is possible, but hardly probable, that the exemplar of the *Parables* was anything other than Greek. Greek was well known in the Aksumite kingdom, and the translators of the Ethiopic Bible worked primarily from Greek exemplars. By contrast, evidence for Syriac and/or Aramaic is slender at best. See M. A. Knibb, *Translating the Bible: The Ethiopic Version of the Old Testament: The Schweich Lectures of the British Academy* (Oxford: Oxford University Press, 1999), pp. 15–40. Moreover, Casey has also missed the significance of a text like *1En.* 46.1. The Ethiopic states that the son of man's face was 'full of grace like one of the holy angels'. It has been noted that the Aramaic fragments of *1 Enoch* from Qumran avoid the term מלאכא ('angel') and prefer terms like עירין ('watchers') and קדישין ('holy ones'), whereas the Greek fragments of *1 Enoch* translate both these terms with ἄγγελοι and tend to preserve ἐγρήγοροι ('watchers') for the fallen angels. See the excurses 'The Watchers and Holy Ones', in G. W. E. Nickelsburg, *1 Enoch 1* (Hermeneia; Minneapolis: Fortress Press, 2001), pp. 140–41. Since the Ethiopic behind 46.1 presupposes ἄγγελος, it follows that it is more likely a translation of a Greek *Vorlage* than an Aramaic (or Hebrew) one.

that original Semitic text of the *Parables*.[7] Of even greater significance is the fact that comparison of those portions of the *Book of Enoch* which are extant in Aramaic, Greek and Ethiopic reveal 'evidence of editorial intervention', that is, the Greek and Ethiopic versions are not simple translations of the Aramaic, but a reworking of the Aramaic text.[8] Thus real care is required when working the *Parables*: We do not possess the original text and not insignificant evidence suggests that the text which we do have should be treated with a certain degree of caution.[9]

Within the text of the *Book of Enoch*, the *Parables* (*1En*. 37-71) form the second major division of the Enochic pentateuch coming after the *Book of the Watchers* (6-36) and before the *Book of the Heavenly Luminaries* (72–82), the *Dream Visions* (83–90) and the *Epistle of Enoch* (91–105).[10] The *Parables*, however, are generally regarded as the last portion of the Enochic corpus to have been written. While the precise date of the *Parables*' composition remains a matter of some debate, both Charles' arguments for a date prior to 64 BC and Milik's arguments for 'around the year AD 270 or shortly afterwards' are now universally regarded as too early and much too late, respectively.[11] Today

---

7.   However, there is some limited, but not uncontroversial, evidence that the Ethiopic translators had access to a Semitic *Vorlage*, as well as the Greek. See E. Ullendorf, 'An Aramaic "*Vorlage*" of the Ethiopic Text of Enoch?' in *Atti del Convegno Internazionale di Studi Etiopici (Roma, 2–4 aprile 1959)* (Rome: Accademia Nazionale dei Lincei, 1960), pp. 259–67; and M. A. Knibb, 'The Date of the *Parables of Enoch*: A Critical Review', *NTS* 25 (1978–79), pp. 345–59, esp. 351.

8.   See M. A. Knibb, 'The *Book of Enoch* or *Books of Enoch*? The Textual Evidence for *1 Enoch*', in *Essays on the Book of Enoch and Other Early Jewish Texts and Traditions* (SVTP, 22; Leiden: Brill, 2009), pp. 36–55, esp. 36–44. The quoted material comes from p. 44.

9.   Cf. the conclusion of M. A. Knibb, 'Textual Evidence', p. 44: 'Thus the relationship between the Ethiopic and Greek on the one hand and the Aramaic on the other is not that of straight translation, but is rather comparable to that between the Hebrew of the Massoretic Text of Jeremiah and the Hebrew text that served as the *Vorlage* of the Greek of Jeremiah.'

10.   An Introduction (1–5) and two brief appendices, *The Birth of Noah* (106–107) and *Another Book which Enoch Wrote* (108), frame these five sections. I use the term 'Enochic pentateuch' in the general sense that it is a five-part work associated with Enoch, without meaning to imply that it was necessarily composed or edited in imitation or in competition with the Mosiac Pentateuch. Cf. also Knibb, 'The *Book of Enoch* or *Books of Enoch*?', p. 41, esp. n. 23.

11.   R. H. Charles, *The Book of Enoch or 1 Enoch* (Oxford: Clarendon Press, 1912), pp. liv–lvi, 67; J. T. Milik, *The Books of Enoch: Aramaic Fragments of Qumrân Cave 4* (Oxford: Clarendon Press, 1976), pp. 89–98, quoting p. 96.

most would place the *Parables* at the turn of the eras,[12] while a significant minority would argue for later in the first century AD.[13] The question cannot be settled here; the issues are too many and too involved. One issue raised by Milik should be addressed, albeit briefly. Milik pointed to the absence of any portion of the *Parables* among the 11 different copies of the *Book of Enoch*, or portions thereof, at Qumran. This fact is still cited from time to time, e.g. by Michael Knibb, as a primary reason for placing the *Parables* after AD 70.[14] This consideration loses much of its force, however, when it is remembered just how little text of the *Book of Enoch*, estimated to be about 5 per cent, has been preserved in the 11 Qumran manuscripts and when it is realized how many fragments from Qumran, 'running into the thousands', remain unidentified.[15] Other than this all too brief discussion, it will have to suffice for our purposes to record that no contemporary *Parables'* scholar would stray outside of the years 34 BC to AD 135. The *Parables*, then, come either from just prior to Jesus

12. Cf. e.g. J. C. Greenfield and M. E. Stone, 'The Enochic Pentateuch and the Date of the Similitudes', *HTR* 70 (1977), pp. 51–65; M. E. Stone, 'Enoch's Date in Limbo; or, Some Considerations on David Suter's Analysis of the Book of Parables', in Boccaccini, *Enoch*, pp. 444–49; G. W. E. Nickelsburg, *Jewish Literature between the Bible and the Mishnah* (London: SCM, 1981), pp. 221–23; Nickelsburg, 'Son of Man, *ABD* 6 (1992), pp. 137–50; Nickelsburg, *1 Enoch 1* (Hermeneia; Minneapolis: Fortress Press, 2001), p. 7; J. H. Charlesworth, 'Can we Discern the Composition Date of the Parables of Enoch?', in Boccaccini, *Enoch*, pp. 450–68; G. Boccaccini, *Beyond the Essene Hypothesis: The Parting of the Ways between Qumran and Enochic Judaism* (Grand Rapids: Eerdmans, 1998), pp. 144–49.

Cf. also J. J. Collins, 'The Son of Man in First Century Judaism', *NTS* 38 (1992), pp. 448–66 and Collins, *The Apocalyptic Imagination: An Introduction to Jewish Apocalyptic Literature*, (Grand Rapids: Eerdmans, 2nd edn, 1988), pp. 177–78, who would place the *Parables* in the early or mid-first century AD.

13. E.g. Knibb, 'The Date of the *Parables*', who argues for the end of the first century. However, it is important to note that Prof. Knibb has recently gone on record to affirm that while this late date makes sense, he 'would not rule out other possibilities, particularly the case' for the turn of the eras 'made by George Nickelsburg'. Knibb, *Essays*, p. 6. Cf. also his 'Messianism in the Pseudepigrapha in the Light of the Scrolls', *DSD* 2 (1995), pp. 165–84, esp. 171.

David Suter, on the other hand, would place the *Parables* in the first century before but 'as close as possible to the fall of Jerusalem'. See D. W. Suter, 'Enoch in Sheol: Updating the Dating of the Book of Enoch', in Boccaccini, *Enoch*, pp. 415–43, citing 440.

14. Knibb, 'The Date of the *Parables*', p. 358.

15. Stone, 'Enoch's Date in Limbo', p. 446.

of Nazareth and the emergence of the early Christian movement or are roughly contemporary with the latter.[16]

Milik's case for a Christian provenance has proved no more persuasive than his arguments for a late date. As Michael Knibb has noted, 'given the subject matter of the *Parables* it seems very hard to understand the absence of clear references to Christ if the *Parables* are Christian'.[17] Forceful evidence that the original language was either Hebrew or Aramaic further strengthens the case for Jewish provenance.[18] At the Third meeting of the Enoch Seminar, which was concerned with the *Parables of Enoch*, the 44 assembled Enoch specialists were at one point asked by the chair, Gabriele Boccaccini, if we could agree that the *Parables* were a Jewish, rather than a Christian, composition: Only

16.   In another context I have argued for a date in the first century BC. See D. D. Hannah, 'The Book of Noah, the Death of Herod the Great, and the Date of the Parables of Enoch', in Boccaccini, *Enoch*, pp. 469–77. My reasons for preferring the early date, which I still find compelling, focus on (1) what I and a number of other scholars regard as a possible allusion to the events leading up to the death of Herod in 4 BC at *1En.* 67.8-13, and (2) the fact that this passage occurs in the midst of what appears to be a long interpolation from a Noah Apocryphon (*1En.* 65.1–69.25). However, (3) it is only here in the Noah material that we encounter themes characteristic of the original text of the *Parables*. What are themes otherwise absent from the interpolated Noah material and characteristic of the original *Parables* doing in an interpolation? It would seem that the interpolator here brings his text up to date by referring to a well-known recent event, i.e. the death of Herod, and thereby 'tips his hand'. If this is accepted, the interpolator must have been active roughly contemporary with 4 BC, but the material with which he worked, both the original *Parables* and the Noah Apocryphon, must be earlier.

17.   Knibb, 'The Date of the *Parables*', p. 350.

18.   Knibb ('The Date of the *Parables*', pp. 350–51) mentions two mistranslations and a Semitic idiom. First, 45.3 ('On that day the Elect One will sit on the throne of glory, and *will choose* their works') where the Ethiopic word for 'to choose' (ኀረየ; *xarya*), is in all probability a mistranslation of בחר, which in both Hebrew and Aramaic can mean either 'to choose' or 'to test'; and, second, 52.9 ('All these things *will be denied* and destroyed from the face of the earth') in which the verb 'to deny' (ከሐደ; *keḥeda*) does not fit and is probably to be explained as a mechanical rendering of the Hebrew/Aramaic כחד (*kḥd*; 'to hide, to efface'). Finally, at various points throughout the *Parables* the Ethiopic word የብስ (*yabs*; 'dry ground') is used, instead of the more expected ምድር (*medr*; 'earth'), for the world. This recalls an idiom to be found in both Hebrew and Aramaic, and, thus, this choice of word is 'more readily explicable' if the *Parables* were written in either Semitic language than in Greek.

R. A. Kraft held out that a non-Jewish provenance was a possibility.[19] A work of Jewish provenance from the end of the first century would still provide valuable insights into the Judaism which served as the matrix in which early Christian ideas developed (cf. the use made of 4 Ezra and 2 Baruch by New Testament scholars). Of course, if the *Parables* date from the turn of the eras or early in the first century, their significance would be even greater. Either way, the dismissal of the *Parables* which followed Milik has now been rejected. No one can hope to come to terms with the New Testament 'Son of Man' without some understanding of the *Parables of Enoch*.

There also remains real disagreement over the *Sitz im Leben* of the *Parables* within Second Temple Judaism. Perhaps most would regard the *Parables* as a non-sectarian product of 'common Judaism', to borrow a term of E. P. Sanders.[20] Others of us would still wish to see 'the righteous and elect ones', with whose vindication the *Parables* are preoccupied, as a sectarian subset within Second Temple Judaism. However that debate is settled, it is clear that, in the words of John Collins, 'the major focus of [the *Parables*] is on the destiny of "the right-eous and chosen" and their wicked counterparts'.[21] Succinctly put, the group behind the *Parables*, whether or not they should be classed as a sect, regarded themselves as 'the righteous and the elect'. Their adversaries were 'the kings and the mighty', i.e., those who possessed political power when the *Parables* were composed. *The* principal concern of the *Parables* is to assure the faithful that despite appearances God will one day intervene, and at the resurrection and final judgement their faithfulness would be rewarded, while 'the kings and the mighty' will be dispatched to Sheol.

Finally, something must be said about the complicated problems surround-ing the composite nature of the *Parables* and the latter's structure. It has

19.   According to David Suter ('Enoch in Sheol', p. 427, n. 51), in a private conversation Kraft suggested 'that before settling for a Jewish provenance and a pre-70 dating, the pos-sibility of a Gnostic context needed further exploration'. I was not privy to that conversation, but I remember well the question concerning provenance put by Boccaccini and the almost complete unanimity – the only time we came as close to universal assent over any of the issues regarding the *Parables*.

20.   See esp. the case made by Pierluigi Piovanelli, '"A Testimony for the Kings and the Mighty Who Possess the Earth": The Thirst for Justice and Peace in the Parables of Enoch' and Daniel Boyarin, 'Was the Book of Parables a Sectarian Document? A Brief Brief in Support of Pierluigi Piovanelli', in Boccaccini, *Enoch*, pp. 363–79 and pp. 380–85, respectively.

21.   Collins, *Apocalyptic Imagination*, p. 181.

long been recognized that within the text of the *Parables* we find extraneous material which differs to no little extent from the rest of the *Parables*. Most of this extraneous material concerns not Enoch but Noah, and is probably to be explained as deriving from an otherwise unknown Noah apocryphon. R. H. Charles identified 54.7–55.2; 60; and 65.1–69.25 as fragments of a *Book of Noah*. Not all would follow him in every detail, but there is no question that at least parts of chapter 60 and most, if not all, of 65.1–69.25 are Noahic, rather than Enochic, in character and that 64.1–69.25 interrupts the narrative of 63.12 and 69.26-29. It is generally agreed that this material is to be regarded as a later interpolation into the text of the *Parables* and that it may well come from an otherwise lost *Book of Noah*.[22] Other passages may also be interpolations, most notably chapters 42 and 70–71. We will have occasion to return to the latter in due course. For now, it will be sufficient to remark that all of this material (42; 54.7–55.2; 60; 65.1–69.25 and 70–71) must be treated with caution. While all of it belongs to the final form of the text, at least the Noahic material is quite disruptive and should not be given the same weight as the rest of the *Parables*.

The Elect son of man

Nomenclature

As intimated above, the eschatological mediatorial figure of the *Parables* is variously termed the Righteous One (ጸድቅ፡ [*ṣādeq*]), the Messiah or Anointed One (መሲሕ፡ [*masiḥ*]), the Elect One (ኅሩይ፡ [*xeruy*]) and the (or that) son of man (ወልደ፡ ብእሲ፡ [*walda be'si*]; ወልደ፡ ሰብእ፡ [*walda sab'*] and ወልደ፡ እጓለ፡ እመሕያው፡ [*walda 'egʷāla 'emma-ḥeyāw*]). It hardly needs to be remarked that two of these terms correspond to the preferred nomenclature for the group behind the *Parables*. The group regarded themselves as the righteous (ጸድቃን፡; *ṣādeqān*) and elect (ኅሩያን፡; *xeruyān*). It is, therefore, not surprising in the least that they

---

22.   Cf. the recent treatments of Nickelsburg and Knibb and the responses to them in Boccaccini, *Enoch*: G. W. E. Nickelsburg, 'Discerning the Structure(s) of the Enochic Book of Parables', pp. 23–47; M. A. Knibb, 'The Structure and Composition of the Parables of Enoch', pp. 48–64; L. T. Stuckenbruck, 'The Parables of Enoch according to George Nickelsburg and Michael Knibb: A Summary and Discussion of Some Remaining Questions', pp. 65–71 and B. G. Wright, 'The Structure of the Parables of Enoch: A Response to George Nickelsburg and Michael Knibb', pp. 72–78.

referred to their champion as both the Righteous One (ጸድቅ፤ ṣādeq) and the Elect One (ኅሩይ፤ xeruy). The first two titles are the least frequent, occurring twice each: Righteous One at 38.2[23] and 53.6,[24] Messiah at 48.10 and 52.4. That the Hebrew and Aramaic מָשִׁיחַ (mašiḥa) could be used of *the* Messiah, of course, requires no defence, but at least Luke, in the New Testament, also treats 'the Righteous One' as a messianic title (Acts 3.14; 7.52; 22.14).[25] Both go back to the Old Testament Scriptures, and the *Parables'* use of them presupposes considerable preoccupation with the text of Scripture. It is, however, the other two designations, the Elect One and son of man, which predominate in the *Parables*. Elect One appears no less than 16 times,[26] while the three Ethiopic phrases rendered 'the (or that) son of man' together occur 14 times.[27] The latter two designations are clearly those preferred by the author(s), but the four complement one another and to a certain extend are interchangeable with one another. Note, for example, how Righteous One and Elect One are combined at 53.6. In the same way, righteousness is said to characterize the Elect One at 39.6 and the son of man at 46.3, while at 48.6 the son of man is said to be chosen, that

23.   A number of early and important manuscripts, however, read 'righteousness' (ጸድቅ፡ [ṣedq]) here rather than 'the Righteous One' (ጸድቅ፡ [ṣādeq]). The reading 'righteousness' has the superior manuscript support, but the transcriptional difference is very small and 'the Righteous One' is conceptually easier and arguably better fits the context. So also the translations of Nickelsburg & VanderKam, Black, Isaac, Knibb, Charles and Dillmann. *Contra*: Uhlig's translation, J. C. VanderKam, 'Righteous One, Messiah, Chosen One and Son of Man in 1 Enoch 37-71', in J. H. Charlesworth et al. (eds), *The Messiah: Developments in Earliest Judaism and Christianity* (Minneapolis: Fortress Press, 1992), pp. 169–91, citing 170; and Kvanvig, 'Son of Man', p. 187, n. 17.

24.   47.1, 4 also use the term ጸድቅ፡ (ṣādeq) in the singular, but the context indicates that it is being used as a collective and refers to the righteous ones.

25.   Cf. also 4Q252 vv. 3-4: 'Until the messiah of righteousness comes, the branch of David' (עד בוא משיח הצדק צמח דויד). Note also that the Messiah, according to the *Psalms of Solomon* 17.32, is characterised by righteousness: 'And he shall be a righteous king over them, taught by God, and there shall be no unrighteousness in their midst in his days; for all shall be holy and their king the Lord Messiah' (καὶ αὐτὸς βασιλεὺς δίκαιος διδακτὸς ὑπὸ θεοῦ ἐπ' αὐτούς, καὶ οὐκ ἔστιν ἀδικία ἐν ταῖς ἡμέραις αὐτοῦ ἐν μέσῳ αὐτῶν, ὅτι πάντες ἅγιοι, καὶ βασιλεὺς αὐτῶν χριστὸς κυρίος.

26.   39.6; 40.5; 45.3, 4; 49.2; 49.4; 51.3, 5; 52.6, 9; 53.6; 55.4; 61.5, 8, 10; 62.1. Cf. also 46.3 and 48.6.

27.   ወልደ፡ ሰብእ ፡ (walda sab'): 46.2, 3, 4; 48.2. ወልደ ፡ ብእሲ ፡ (walda be'si): 62.5, 69.29 (bis). ወልደ ፡ አጓል ፡ አመሕያዉ፤ (walda 'eg"āla 'emma-ḥeyāw): 62.6, 9, 14; 63.11; 69.26, 27; 70.1. I do not include the ወልደ ፡ ብእሲ ፡ of 71.14 nor the ወልደ ፡ አጓል ፡ አመሕያዉ፤ (walda 'eg"āla 'emma-ḥeyāw) of 71.17, since I hold 70.3–71.17 to be a later addition to the text. See below.

is, elect, in the presence of the Lord of Spirits.[28] No one today would demarcate different source material from the use of these 'titles' as Beer and Charles once did.[29]

On the other hand, the three distinct Ethiopic phrases traditionally rendered in the same way, 'son of man', have recently been the subject of varied interpretations. Translating with a slavish literalism **ወልደ፡ ሰብእ፡** (*walda sab'*) would mean 'son of humankind', in other words, a human being; **ወልደ፡ ብእሲ፡** (*walda be'si*) 'son of a man' or 'the son of a male';[30] and **ወልደ፡ እጓለ፡ እመሕያው፡** (*walda 'egʷāla 'emma-ḥeyāw*) 'son of the offspring of the mother of the living'. Some would urge that each phrase carries intended nuances of meaning. For example, Klaus Koch suggests that the last, **ወልደ፡ እጓለ፡ እመሕያው፡** (*walda 'egʷāla 'emma-ḥeyāw*), probably alludes 'to Eve as "mother of living" and her offspring', whose coming was 'prophesied' in the *protoevangelion* of Gen. 3.15-20, while **ወልደ፡ ብእሲ፡** (*walda be'si*) refers to Adam and contains the idea of a 'second Adam'. Koch also finds the literal meaning in **ወልደ፡ ሰብእ፡** (*walda sab'*), 'son of humankind' or 'a human being', particularly appropriate as an interpretation of Daniel 7. He notes that the last term only appears in *1En.* 46-48, an obvious reflection on and reinterpretation of Daniel 7 (see below), and it 'certainly' has 'the Aramaic *bar 'enash* as background'.[31] As exegetically fruitful as these nuances appear at first sight, they lose all credibility when the transmission of the text of *1 Enoch* in Ethiopic is taken into consideration. With regard to **ወልደ፡ እጓለ፡ እመሕያው፡** (*walda 'egʷāla 'emma-ḥeyāw*) it must be remembered that in the Ethiopic Bible **እጓለ፡ እመሕያው፡** (*'egʷāla 'emma-ḥeyāw*), without the **ወልደ፡** (*walda*; 'son of'), regularly renders υἱὸς ἀνθρώπου when the meaning is 'a human being'. For example, the statements of Num. 23.19, Jdt. 8.16, Ps. 8.5, 143.3 LXX, Jer. 2.6, 27.40 (ET 50.40), each of which parallel ἄνθρωπος with υἱὸς ἀνθρώπου, are consistently rendered **ሰብእ፡ . . . ን፡**

---

28.   The Ethiopic verb used here, **ኀርየ፡** (*xarya*), is cognate with the title 'Elect or Chosen One', **ኅሩይ፡** (*xeruy*).

29.   Beer, 'Das Buch Henoch', p. 227 and Charles, *Book of Enoch*, pp. 64–65. Beer's and Charles' theories in this regard were decisively answered by E. Sjöberg, *Der Menschensohn im Äthiopischen Henochbuch* (Lund: Gleerup, 1946), pp. 24–33.

30.   **ሰብእ፡** (*sab'*) serves as the plural form of **ብእሲ** (*be'si*).

31.   K. Koch, 'Questions regarding the So-Called Son of Man in the Parables of Enoch: A Response to Sabino Chialà and Helge Kvanvig', in Boccaccini, *Enoch*, p. 234. Kvanvig ('Son of Man', pp. 193–95), in the final form of his essay, takes up Koch's suggestions and develops them slightly.

አማሕያው፦ (sab'... 'egʷāla 'emma-ḥeyāw). If ሰብእ፦ (sab'; lit. 'humankind') and ኅለ፦ አማሕያው፦ ('egʷāla 'emma-ḥeyāw; lit. 'offspring of the mother of the living') are simply interchangeable, it is difficult to deny that the same is true for ወልደ፦ ሰብእ፦ (walda sab'; lit. 'son of humankind') and ወልደ፦ ኅለ፦ አማሕያው፦ (walda 'egʷāla 'emma-ḥeyāw; lit. 'son of the offspring of the mother of the living'). Moreover, the latter term, with or without the ወልደ፦ (walda), is simply too pervasive in Ethiopic to argue that it renders an underlying Aramaic, or Hebrew, phrase which contains an allusion to Eve. The vocative υἱὲ ἀνθρώπου, for example, at Dan. 8.17 and throughout Ezekiel, is consistently translated ወልደ፦ ኅለ፦ አማሕያው፦ (walda 'egʷāla 'emma-ḥeyāw) in the Ethiopic Bible.[32] If we are to suppose an allusion to Eve and the prophecy of Gen. 3.15 in the 'title' given the Enochic Elect son of man, we must do the same with the prophets Ezekiel and Daniel – at least in their Ethiopic dress!

A similar response must, I think, be made to Daniel Olson's more nuanced argument that Ethiopian scribes (including the original translator?) used ወልደ፦ ብእሲ፦ (walda be'si; lit. 'son of a man or male') at 71.14 because here Enoch was being addressed and, apparently, identified with the son of man of the previous visions. Since in the Ethiopic Bible, Son of Man passages which have Jesus Christ as their referent, including the Gospel Son of Man sayings,[33] Rev. 1.13 and 14.14,[34] and Dan. 7.13 invariably render the phrase with ወልደ፦ ኅለ፦ አማሕያው፦ (walda 'egʷāla 'emma-ḥeyāw), Olson argues that 'Ethiopian copyists who would have been anxious to dissociate Enoch and the walda

32. For Daniel I have consulted the edition of Oscar Löfgren, Die Äthiopische Übersetzung des Propheten Daniel (Paris: Geuthner, 1926). There is, as yet, no critical edition of Ethiopic Ezekiel, but one is currently in preparation. Michael Knibb, its editor, informs me that all the manuscripts of Ethiopic Ezekiel he has seen *always* use ወልደ፦ ተለ፦ አማሕያው፦ (walda 'egʷāla 'emma-ḥeyāw) for 'Son of Man'.

33. We are fortunate that critical editions of Ethiopic Mark, Matthew and John have recently been published: R. Zuurmond, Novum Testamentum Aethiopice. The Synoptic Gospels: General Introduction, Edition of the Gospel of Mark (ÄF, 27; Stuttgart: Harrassowitz, 1989); Zuurmond, Novum Testamentum Aethiopice: The Gospel of Matthew (ÄF, 55; Wiesbaden: Harrassowitz, 2001) and M. G. Wechsler, Evangelium Iohannis Aethiopicum (CSCO, 617; SA 109; Leuven: Peeters, 2005). There is, however, as yet no critical edition of either the Gospel of Luke or the Book of Acts. But given the unanimity of the rest of the Ethiopic Bible, it is highly unlikely that the situation differs with regard to these books.

34. Critical edition: J. Hofmann, Die Äthiopische Übersetzung der Johannes–Apokalypse (CSCO, 281; SA 55; Leuven: Peeters, 1967).

'egʷāla 'emma-ḥeyāw were only too happy' to use *walda beʾsi* for Enoch.[35] This also overlooks the significance of Daniel 8.17 and the whole of Ezekiel in the Ethiopic version. More importantly, as has been pointed out by Knibb, it also overlooks that fact that even *1En.* 71.14 is interpreted in Ethiopian traditional exegesis as a prophecy of Jesus Christ.[36] Ethiopian exegesis of *1 Enoch* consistently finds, in all three phrases, a reference to Jesus Christ.[37]

In the end, the three terms are in all likelihood nothing other than translation variants[38] of the same Greek phrase, (ὁ) υἱὸς (τοῦ) ἀνθρπώπου, which in turn renders an Aramaic or Hebrew original. If the latter, then that original was, in all probability, אדם בן (הדאם בן less likely, but perhaps still possible). If the former, then both בר (א)נש(א) and בר אדם (as in the Targum of Ezekiel) are candidates.[39]

---

35.   D. C. Olson, 'Enoch and the Son of Man in the Epilogue of the Parables', *JSP* 18 (1998), pp. 27–38, citing 36.

36.   M. A. Knibb, 'The Translation of *1 Enoch* 70:1: Some Methodological Issues', in *Essays on the Book of Enoch*, pp. 161–75, esp. 173.

37.   Cf. also Piovanelli's discussion in '"A Testimony for the Kings and the Mighty"', pp. 365–68. Although Piovanelli would like to find a pattern of the three terms in the text of *Enoch*, he nonetheless must admit that 'the Ethiopian scholars who produced the targumic Amharic version of 1 Enoch . . . systematically referred the three expressions to Christ' (p. 367, n. 12).

38.   Cf. the conclusion of Knibb ('*1 Enoch* 70:1', p. 173): 'In reality no distinction is drawn between the three expressions used for "Son of Man" within the *Parables of Enoch*, and the use of different terms has to be understood within the context of the wider problem of consistency and diversity in the use of translation equivalents in the Ethiopic Bible.'

39.   So also Black, *Book of Enoch*, p. 206.

The exegetical basis of the Elect son of man[40]

The author(s) of the *Parables of Enoch* clearly owed much to the Hebrew Scriptures for his or their depiction of the Elect son of man.[41] The Book of Daniel, especially the first vision (ch. 7), the so-called Servant Songs of Deutero-Isaiah and the prophecy concerning the Davidic Messiah, 'the shoot of Jesse' (Isa. 11.1-9) figure prominently, but the influence of other passages, especially certain Psalms, are also encountered. We may begin with Daniel 7. *1En.* 46-47 is widely and rightly seen as an interpretation of the vision recorded in Dan. 7. Enoch sees 'One who had a Head of Days', whose 'head was as white wool' (46.1) – a clear allusion to Daniel's 'Ancient of Days' (7.9). In the company of this 'Head of Days'[42] Enoch sees 'another whose face was as the appearance of a human and his face was full of graciousness as one of the holy angels'. Enoch asks his *angelus interpres* about 'that son of man, who he is and from where he comes (and) why he accompanies the Head of Days'. He is told, 'this is the son of man who is characterised by righteousness[43] and righteousness dwells with him; . . . for the Lord of Spirits has chosen him' (46.3). The

---

40.   The following section is heavily indebted to J. Theisohn, *Der auserwählte Richter: Untersuchungen zum traditionsgeschichtlichem Ort der Menschensohngestalt der Bilderreden des Äthiopischen Henoch* (SUNT, 12; Göttingen: Vandenhoeck & Ruprecht, 1975) esp. pp. 54-65 and 114-139 and M. A. Knibb, 'Isaianic Traditions in Apocrypha and Pseudepigrapha', in C. C. Broyles and C. A. Evans (eds), *Writing and Reading the Scroll of Isaiah: Studies of an Interpretive Tradition* (Leiden: Brill, 1997), pp. 2.633-50.

41.   That is not to say that the author's/authors' canon would have been identical with that which is familiar to us. It may well have included, for example, earlier Enochic works. Many interpreters would agree with Piovanelli ('A Testimony', pp. 363-64) that the *Parables* are 'a sort of midrashic rewriting of the Book of the Watchers (1 En 1-36) with the addition of many new motifs resonating with different parts of the Tanakh (especially Genesis, Isaiah and Daniel)'. Cf. esp. Nickelsburg, 'Discerning the Structure(s)', Knibb, 'Structure and Composition', and Kvanvig, 'The Son of Man', pp. 184-85. However, it is notable that the *Book of the Watchers* has no messianic or mediatorial figures, other than the four archangels. It is from the Hebrew Scriptures that our author(s) derive(s) the material out of which he/they constructed the Elect son of man.

42.   Here in 46.1 the nomenclature is 'One who had a Head of Days' or 'One to whom belongs a Head of Days' (ላዑተ፡ ርእሰ፡ መዋዕል፡; *za-lotu reʾsa mawāʾel*), but in the very next verse and elsewhere it is simply the/a 'Head of Days' (ርእሰ፡ መዋዕል፡; *reʾsa mawāʾel*). This nomenclature, 'Head of Days', is mostly found in these three chapters (46.1-2; 47.3; 48.2). Other than in this passage it occurs only at 55.1; 60.2 and four times in 71.10-14. Interestingly, all three of these passages may well be later interpolations. Elsewhere in the *Parables* the preferred title for the deity is 'the Lord of Spirits'.

43.   Lit. 'who has righteousness'.

language used to describe this figure obviously recalls Daniel's '(one) like a son of man' (כבר אנש; 7.13). Enoch's *angelus interpres* goes on to explain, utilizing a host of allusions to Old Testament Scriptures, that this son of man will oppose 'the kings and the mighty' and bring them to condemnation.[44] These kings and mighty are further described as 'those who judge the stars of heaven and lift up their hands against the Most High and tread upon the earth and dwell in it' (46.7). Although the text is undoubtedly corrupt at some points in this verse, the reference to Daniel 8.9-12 remains transparent. Then, after accusations that the kings and mighty practise idolatry and persecute 'the faithful who cling to the Name of the Lord of Spirits' (46.8), and a description of the intercession of the righteous and holy ones who dwell in heaven on behalf of the righteous who are being persecuted on earth (47.2), the author(s) return(s) to Daniel 7:

> In those days I watched as the Head of Days took his seat on the throne
> of His glory,
> and the books of the living were opened in His presence
> and all His hosts which are in the height of heaven and His council stood
> before Him (47.3)

All this, of course, recalls the enthronement of the Ancient of Days, the thousands of heavenly attendants, the heavenly court or council and the consulting of the heavenly books in Dan. 7.9-10. In light of this clear use of Daniel 7 it hardly needs to be emphasized that in the *Parables* 'son of man' is not used as a title comparable to 'Messiah' or even the 'Elect One'. The figure that Enoch sees accompanying the Head of Days in 46.1 is that son of man, i.e., that human figure, characterized by righteousness, whom Daniel also beheld. Whether or not our author(s) conceived of him as a human being is bound up with the question of the identification with Enoch found in 70.3–71.17 – a question to which we will return momentarily.

---

44.   Raising the kings and mighty from their thrones and couches (46.4b) recalls Isa. 14.9; the loosing of their loins (46.4c) picks up the language of Isa. 45.1 (cf. also Deut. 33.11); breaking the teeth of sinners (46.4d) harks back to Pss. 3.7 and 58.6; that the kings and mighty do not recognize that their sovereignty is a gift from God (46.5) alludes to Dan. 4.17, 25 and the worms and darkness which will serve as their bed in Sheol recalls both Isa. 14.11 and Job 17.12-16.

The next two chapters, 48–49, which are clearly part of the same section, move in a new direction. Here the exegetical inspiration is not Daniel 7, but Isaiah's Servant Songs and Isaiah's 'Shoot of Jesse'. From Deutero-Isaiah comes the explicit affirmation that the son of man will be 'the light of the nations' (Isa. 42.6; 49.6), but there are a few more, less obvious allusions to Isaiah's Servant of Yahweh. Isa. 42.6, for example, claims that Yahweh 'called' his servant 'in righteousness', and we have already seen that the son of man is characterized by righteousness (46.3). The naming of the son of man in the presence of the Lord of Spirits before all creation (48.2-3) takes up the call of the Servant, while still in his mother's womb (Isa. 49.1), and extends it to a pre-mundane existence (see below). In 48.6 the son of man is said to have been 'hidden in the presence [of the Lord of Spirits] before the world was created and forever'. Similarly, Yahweh hid his Servant 'in the shadow of his hand . . . (and) in his quiver he hid [his Servant] away' (Isa. 49.2bd). The reaction of the kings and mighty to the Lord of Spirits and His Anointed (*1En.* 48.8-10) recalls a similar response on the part of kings and princes to Yahweh and his Servant (Isa. 49.7). In addition to all this, the very title 'the Elect One' in all likelihood goes back to Isa. 42.1: 'Behold my servant, whom I uphold, my chosen, in whom my soul delights; I have put my Spirit upon him, he will bring forth justice to the nations (RSV)'. According to Deutero-Isaiah, the Servant of Yahweh is termed chosen or elect one (בחיר),[45] the title which is so prevalent throughout the *Parables*, and he is charged with the same task with which the Elect son of man is entrusted in the *Parables*: The phrase 'he will bring forth justice to the nations' (משפט לגוים יוציא) could also be rendered 'he will pronounce judgement on the nations'.[46] The indebtedness of our author(s) to Deutero-Isaiah's depiction of the Servant of Yahweh could not be clearer. In the mind of our author(s), the Elect son of man is not only the figure foreseen by Daniel, he is also the personage foretold by Isaiah.

---

45.   Cf. also Isa. 49.7: '. . . because of the LORD, who is faithful, the Holy One of Israel, who has chosen you' (יבחרך).

46.   Cf. allusion to Isa. 42.1 in 1QpHab. v.4: '. . . in the hand of his elect ones God will place the judgement over the nations' (וביד בחירו יתן אל את משפט כול הגוים). In the context it is clear that the *Habakkuk Pesher* understands the noun 'Elect One' (בחיר) as a collective referring to Israel as a whole, while the *Parables* takes it as a singular.

But it is also clear that our author(s) did not stop there. The Elect son of man is also the 'Shoot from Jesse', that is, the Davidic Messiah. Explicitly termed the Messiah or Anointed One (48.10; 52.4), he has also received the outpouring of the seven-fold Spirit of Yahweh (*1En.* 49.3; 62.2) and the ability to slay sinners with his spoken word (*1En.* 62.2), both prophesied of the descendant of Jesse by Isaiah (11.2, 4).[47] In addition to Isa. 11.1-9, our author probably also drew on the second Psalm, for it tells of 'kings of the earth who take their stand and princes who take counsel together against Yahweh and his Anointed' (2.2). In the formulation of our author(s) this has become, 'the kings of the earth and the strong ones who possess the dry ground . . . have denied the Lord of Spirits and his Anointed' (*1En.* 48.8, 10).[48] Much more could be said about the use of the Hebrew Scriptures in the *Parables*. From what we have seen, however, it is clear that the depiction of the Elect son of man has resulted from a profound reflection upon various passages deemed to foretell of God's deliverance through a future mediator.

The Elect son of man's eschatological office

The principal role of the Elect son of man in the *Parables* is that of eschatological judge; that is, the Elect son of man officiates at the great Assize, on behalf of the Lord of Spirits and as the latter's agent. At the beginning of the second parable, for example, the Lord of Spirits speaks concerning the 'lot of sinners':

On that day my Elect One[49] will sit on the throne of glory and he will *test*[50] their

---

47.   Isa. 11.1-9 was understood as a prophecy of the Davidic Messiah in a number of other texts roughly contemporary with the *Parables*, including the Qumranian *Rule of Blessings* (1QSb [1Q28] v.20-26); the *War Rule* (4Q285 + 11Q14) and the Isaiah *Pesher* (4QpIsaᵃ [4Q161] 8-10 iii. 11-25), and, outside of Qumran, the *Psalms of Solomon* (17.23-25, 29, 35, 37; 18.6-7), *4 Ezra* (13.10-11, 37-38) and the Isaiah Targum op. cit. Cf. also *Sib.Or.* iii. 788–95.

48.   Interestingly, the second psalm was understood as a prophecy of the Davidic Messiah in some of the same texts, mentioned in Note 47. Cf. e.g. *PssSol.* 17.23-25, 35; 18.6-7 and *4Ezra* 13.3-35. Cf. also 4Q246 and 4Q174 1 i.18-19.

49.   The Ethiopic manuscripts are divided between 'my Elect One' (ኅሩይየ; *xeruyya*) and 'the Elect One' (ኅሩይ; *xeruy*).

50.   See Note 18 for an explanation of this emendation.

works and their resting places[51] will be innumerable and their souls will be hardened within them when they see my elect ones and those who take refuge in my glorious name (45.3).

Similarly, 62.1-12 describes at some length the judgement and condemnation of 'the kings and the mighty, the exalted and those who possess the earth'.[52] This latter passage is significant in that the Elect son of man, in judging and condemning 'the kings and mighty', fulfils the office of the Davidic Messiah as foretold by Isaiah: 'the spirit of righteousness has been poured on him, and the word of his mouth slays all sinners and all the wicked are destroyed before his face' (62.2).[53] Moreover, we are told that nothing will escape the notice of the Elect son of man (69.29), no lie will be spoken in his presence (62.3), and his judgement will be comprehensive and final (49.2; 63.5-11; 69.27, 29). However, the Elect son of man will not only judge human sinners. He will also pronounce judgement on the Watchers who taught humankind to rebel at the dawn of history (55.4), and will even 'weigh in the balance' the deeds of the righteous (61.8). As mentioned above, the Elect son of man's judgement serves both to condemn 'the kings and the mighty' and to vindicate 'the righteous and the elect'. The two verdicts are of equal importance for our author(s). Indeed, it would appear that the one presupposes the other: because 'the kings and the mighty' actively persecute 'the righteous and elect' (46.4-8; 47.1-4; 48.8-9) they will be condemned, while the latter will be vindicated. In all this, as intimated above, the Elect son of man acts as the agent of the Lord of Spirits, judging 'by the word of the name of the Lord of Spirits' and 'by the way of the righteous judgement of the Lord of Spirits' (61.9). His appointment by the Lord of Spirits is repeatedly mentioned (61.8; 62.2; cf. 69.27).

It is clear that the Elect son of man accomplishes his task of rendering the final judgement while seated on the divine throne, the throne of the Deity himself. This throne is named throughout the *Parables* 'the Throne of Glory' (መንበረ፡ ስብሐት፡; *manbara sebḥat*) or 'the Throne of His Glory' (መንበረ፡ ስብ

---

51.   The text here appears to be corrupt. 'Resting places' hardly fits. See Black, *Book of Enoch*, p. 205 for possible emendations.

52.   The majority of manuscripts read 'and those who dwell on the earth', but two of the earliest, Tana 9 and EMML 2080, have the reading I have translated.

53.   Cf. Isa. 11.2, 4.

ሕትዕ፦; *manbara sebḥatihu*), which must go back to the Hebrew phrase כסא (ה)כבוד.[54] To be sure, Ethiopic has no definite article and so either phrase could be rendered 'a throne of (His) glory' or '(His) glorious throne'. Nonetheless, it is certain that the one divine throne is in view. I have examined this issue at length elsewhere.[55]

To summarize my arguments presented there, first, the phrase כסא כבוד is a technical term for the throne of God. In the Old Testament it is already used for the divine throne (Jer. 14.21; 17.12), although it is also used in the sense of 'a seat of honour' (1 Sam. 2.8; Isa. 22.23). In the rabbinic period כסא (ה)כבוד was a technical term for the throne of God and could mean nothing else. In between, in the Second Temple period, one can note a marked tendency in the same direction (Wis. 9.10; Dan. 3.54 LXX; *1En.* 9.4; *T. Levi* 5.1; *PssSol.* 2.19; 4Q405 23 i.23; 11Q17 x.7). Two possible exceptions do exist (Sir. 47.11; 4Q161 iii.20) but neither is textually certain. Second, within the text of the *Parables* it is notable that the Head of Days is himself situated on 'the Throne of Glory' (47.3).[56] The use of the same term for a different throne would have required some clarification, but none is ever given. Finally, *1En.* 62.3-5 is very significant. It describes how 'the kings and the mighty, the exalted and those who possess the earth' will be terrified and experience the pain of a woman in childbirth '*when* they see the son of man sitting on the Throne of His Glory' (v. 5) and *because* they 'recognize that he sits on the Throne of His Glory' (v. 3). Such an emphasis would be completely unnecessary if the Elect son of man merely occupied a glorious heavenly throne, one among many. That the Elect son of man sits on *the* divine throne in order to accomplish his eschatological role serves to validate his authority to render judgement. Because he fulfils a task usually reserved for the Deity, i.e., executing judgement, he is also granted the privilege of occupying the very symbol of that judgement.

In addition to his role as judge, there are other details which make clear the eschatological setting of the Elect son of man. His appearance will signal the end of warfare and the forging of weapons (52.8-9), as well as the

---

54. This is true even if the *Parables* were composed in Aramaic and the phrase used there was כורס(א) יקר, or something similar. For behind this would have been the biblical כסא כבוד.
55. Hannah, 'The Throne of His Glory', pp. 82–87.
56. Cf. also 60.2, although this passage belongs to the Noahic additions.

transformation of the earth (50.1-51.5). Moreover, the resurrection of the dead will take place on 'the day of the Elect One' (61.1-5). Finally, in the period of blessedness, which will follow the resurrection of the dead and the transformation of the heaven and the earth, the righteous and elect ones will be granted the privilege of dwelling (45.4-5) and feasting (62.14) with the Elect son of man.

The Elect son of man is an exalted figure, who enjoys certain privileges which elsewhere in Second Temple Judaism are reserved for the Deity. He occupies the divine throne and acts as *the* eschatological Judge. His appearance on earth will cause mountains consisting of various metals to melt as wax in a flame of fire (52.6; 53.7). The same is said of Yahweh in more than one of the Hebrew Scriptures (Mic. 1.3-4; Ps. 97.5; Nah. 1.5; cf. also *1En.* 1.4-6).[57] Despite all this and despite claims to the contrary,[58] the *Parables* never unambiguously depict the Elect son of man as a recipient of worship. While a number of passages unequivocally depict the worship of the Lord of Spirits (39.8-14; 61.9-11; 62.6; 63.2, 4-5), two could be read as depicting the worship of the Elect son of man, but it is more probable that the Lord of Spirits is the intended recipient (46.5; 48.5). Another passage, 62.9, describes how 'the kings and mighty and the exalted and those who rule the earth', after their condemnation, will seek mercy from the Elect son of man. Five verbs are used to describe their actions vis-à-vis the Elect son of man – falling on their faces, bowing down, hoping, pleading and asking for mercy – all of which convey supplication, but none needs to be understood in terms of worship. To be sure, the Elect son of man is exalted, he receives homage, at least at the Eschaton, but to conclude that he was given cultic veneration by the group behind the *Parables* goes beyond the evidence.

Pre-existence

Four passages taken together indicate that, in the mind of our author(s), the Elect son of man enjoyed a pre-mundane pre-existence. Not one of the four, in isolation from the others, makes the case without any ambiguity. Taken together, however, it is clear the Elect son of man existed from before creation.

---

57.   Similarly, in 46.4 the Elect son of man crushes the teeth of sinners; an action of Yahweh in Pss. 3.7 and 58.6.

58.   E.g. L. W. Walck, 'The Son of Man in the Parables of Enoch and the Gospels', in Boccaccini, *Enoch*, pp. 299–337, citing 304.

In the first passage we are told that before the creation of sun, constellations and stars 'that son of man was named in the presence of the Lord of Spirits and his name (was named) before the Head of Days' (48.2-3). A little later it is stated that although 'the Elect One had been chosen and hidden in the presence [of the Lord of Spirits] before the world was created and for ever, the wisdom of the Lord of Spirits has revealed him to the holy and righteous ones' (48.6-7). It is possible to read the first of these as merely a statement of an ideal exist-ence in the mind of God, i.e., foreknowledge on the part of God, rather than an ontological pre-existence on the part of the Elect son of man. Rabbinic literature provides lists of 'the seven things created before the creation of the world: the Torah, repentance, the Garden of Eden, Gehenna, the Throne of Glory, the Holy Place (i.e., the temple) and the name of the Messiah' (*bPes.* 54a = *bNed.* 39b).[59] Here the phrase 'the name of the Messiah' probably indicates not that the Messiah was himself created before the world, but rather that his name, i.e., his identity, was already in the mind of God before the creation of the world. The statement of 48.2-3, taken in isolation, could be understood in a similar manner. The second statement, that the son of man was hidden in the presence of the Lord of Spirits, does not lend itself so easily to a mere affirmation of God's foreknowledge. To be hidden presupposes some kind of existence. This latter passage poses a real difficulty for those who would argue that the *Parables* know only a divine foreknowledge of the Elect son of man. James VanderKam, for example, is left with contrasting 48.6-7 with 'the Lord's subsequent act of revealing [the son of man] to the holy and righteous ones', and lamely concludes '[p]erhaps, then, the choosing and hiding refer to no more than pre-mundane election and concealment of [the son of man's] identity'.[60] VanderKam has, in my opinion, missed the significance of 70.1: 'And after this it happened that *his name*, while living, was raised up to that son of man and to the Lord of Spirits.'[61] Here it cannot be merely Enoch's identity, as opposed to his person, which is exalted to heaven. Here rather we have to do with the phenomenon, not unknown in biblical literature, in which 'name' (שֵׁם; ὄνομα) stands for 'person' (Num. 1.18, 20; 26.53, 55; Acts 1.15; Rev. 3.4; 11.13; cf. also Ignatius, *Smyrn.* 13.2; *Polyc.* 8.3). The use of 'name'

---

59. In both passages the tradition is identified as a *baraita*.
60. VanderKam, 'Righteous One', p. 180.
61. For a defence of this translation and the text which lies behind it, see below.

in this manner at 70.1 does not guarantee an equivalent use in 48.2-3, but it does tip the balance in that direction.

It is much more difficult to ascribe an 'ideal pre-existence' or divine fore-knowledge to the next passage. Here an ontological pre-existence seems to be affirmed:

> For from the beginning the son of man was hidden
>
> and the Most High preserved him in the presence of his host,
>
> and he revealed him to the elect ones. (62.7)

That the Most High kept or preserved the Elect son of man before his revela-tion to the kings and mighty (cf. 62.1-6) in the company of the heavenly host strongly implies an ontological pre-existence. The reference to the angelic host rules out merely an idea in the mind of God; such could not be preserved *with* or *in the presence of* the angelic host. It is true that the middle line is often rendered differently. Nickelsburg and VanderKam, for example, translate it as 'and the Most High preserved him in the presence of *his might*'.[62] What 'in the presence of his might' might mean, however, is not at all clear. While the phrase occurs nowhere else in the *Book of Enoch*,[63] the word rendered by Nickelsburg and VanderKam as 'might', ኃይል: (*xāyl*), regularly refers to the angelic host in the text of *Enoch*.[64] For example, in close proximity to 62.7, we read of the Lord of Spirits summoning 'the host of heaven' (ኃይለ ሰማያት:, *xāyla samāyāt*), 'the host of God' (ኃይለ እግዚአብሔር:, *xāyla 'egzi'abḥēr*) and 'the other host who are on the earth and over the water' (ወካለ ኃይል እለ ስተ የብስ ወዲበ ማይ:, *wa-kāle' xāyla 'ella westa yabs wa-diba māy*), as well as various other classes of angelic beings and other denizens of heaven, including the Elect One (61.10-11).[65] This latter passage offers an apt parallel to 62.7: The Elect son of man, as a denizen of heaven, is closely associated with the various classes of angels. On the other hand, there is no parallel in *Enoch* which offers

---

62. So also the translations of Charles, Knibb and Uhlig.

63. The Ethiopic is በቀድመ ኃይል: (*ba-qedma xāyl*). A single manuscript, Abbadianus 55, has በኃይሉ: (*ba-xāylu*; 'by his might'), but this is clearly a secondary attempt to clarify the text.

64. Cf. Black, *1 Enoch*, p. 236, who plausibly suggests the Hebrew original was לפני צבאו and Casey, *Solution*, p. 102, who suggests the Aramaic קדם חילה.

65. Cf. also 18.14; 47.3; 60.1, 4; and 82.7 for ኃይል: (*xāyl*) as the, or a, 'host' of angels.

support for the translation 'in the presence of his might'. Further, it is true, as VanderKam argues,[66] that the Ethiopic phrase rendered above 'from the begin-ning' (አምቀድሙ፥; *'em-qedmu*), *could* be translated 'prior to this' or something similar. Nonetheless, the phrase undoubtedly is used elsewhere in *Enoch* to indicate 'from the beginning' (39.10). Moreover, even VanderKam accepts that 62.7 is an allusion to the prophecy of the Ruler who is to come from Bethlehem (Mic. 5.2). Now, while the Hebrew text of Micah can be understood to assert that this Ruler's origin is in the ancient past, not necessarily pre-mundane, the LXX rendering ($\dot{\alpha}\pi$' $\dot{\alpha}\rho\chi\hat{\eta}\varsigma$ $\dot{\epsilon}\xi$ $\dot{\eta}\mu\epsilon\rho\hat{\omega}\nu$ $\alpha\dot{\imath}\hat{\omega}\nu o\varsigma$)[67] proves that Mic. 5.2 could also be taken to refer to a pre-mundane pre-existence, even if only in an ideal sense.[68] The Elect son of man's preservation in the presence of the angelic host in 62.7, thus, affirms a real, as opposed to an ideal, existence and strongly suggests a pre-mundane setting (cf. Job 38.6-7).

The last passage which implies some kind of pre-existence is the most subtle and, therefore, potentially the most revealing. In 39.4-9 Enoch observes the righteous dead in their heavenly dwellings interceding for 'the sons of men' (39.4-5) – obviously, this must mean for those who are still living on earth. In this context, Enoch also sees 'the Elect One of righteousness and faithfulness' (39.6). The pre-eschatological setting means the Elect son of man must have ontological existence before his revelation and the fulfilment of his role as eschatological judge, for he is seen by Enoch.[69] A *pre-mundane* pre-existence is not necessarily included, but the passage coheres with what we have seen above. It is, therefore, best to understand these four passages as affirming both an ontological and a pre-mundane pre-existence: Before his revelation at the

66.   VanderKam, 'Righteous One', p. 181.

67.   Cf. Gen. 1.1 LXX!

68.   Tg. Micah on 5.1(2) makes explicit that it is the Messiah who will come from Bethlehem, 'he whose name was mentioned from of old, from ancient times'. Cf. also Tg. Zech. 4.7.

69.   VanderKam's arguments ('Righteous One', pp. 184–85) that (1) this is an eschatologi-cal vision and so the prayers belong to the future period and that (2) the only verb used with regard to the Elect One is imperfect ('there *will be* righteousness in his days') can only be termed special pleading. First, the setting is clearly pre-eschatological; the intercession of the holy ones will have been brought to an end at the Eschaton. Second, the imperfect verb is used because the Elect son of man will only establish righteousness in the future. Nonetheless, he is clearly seen by Enoch in heaven prior to the End. The fulfilment of his office belongs to the future, but his existence is already a reality.

Eschaton, before his revelation to the holy and elect, indeed before the creation of the world, the Elect son of man was known, named and preserved in the company of the host of heaven. Chapter 48 makes clear his *pre-mundane* origin, just as 62.7 and 39.4-9 affirm his *ontological* existence prior to his revelation.

Later identification with Enoch

The *Parables* conclude with a surprising ending. We are told, in the third person, that Enoch was raised up, while living, in a chariot of wind to 'the presence of the son of man and the presence of the Lord of Spirits'. He has now left, for a final time, those who dwell on the earth (70.1-2). The text then switches to first person. Enoch recounts his journey to Paradise, in the north-west of the earth where he sees the first fathers and the righteous (70.3-4). After this Enoch is taken to heaven where he sees 'the sons of the holy angels' and two rivers of fire (71.1-2), is then taken on a tour of the heavenly treasuries by Michael (71.3-4), and then is taken up into the heaven of heavens and is brought to just outside the heavenly throne room (71.5-8). There, at the door of the heavenly throne room, he is met by the four archangels, innumerable lesser angels and the Head of Days himself, before whom he falls down in worship (71.9-12). An angel, probably Michael,[70] informs him, 'You are the son of man who was born to righteousness and with you righteousness dwells, and the righteousness of the Head of Days will not forsake you' (71.14).

Given that throughout the *Parables* Enoch has seen in visions the Elect son of man and there has been no indication that he was viewing himself, this identification is unexpected – to say the least. It is surely one of the most surprising endings in the whole of ancient literature; for many interpreters, *too* surprising to be accepted at face value. The distinction between Enoch and the Elect son of man runs throughout the text and is maintained as late as 70.1, according to the majority of manuscripts.

A significant textual variant, however, has occasioned of late no little discussion in scholarly circles and, thus, demands our attention. Of the manuscripts

---

70. Although some manuscripts merely read 'that one', the best text asserts 'that angel' spoke to Enoch. The identity of 'that angel' is not made explicit, but the context, especially vv. 3-5, suggests Michael. Casey's (*Solution*, p. 109) attempt to make the Head of Days the speaker is unconvincing. The speech which follows, whether it extends to the end of v. 17 or just v. 16, speaks about the Head of Days and so is not likely to have been spoken by him!

known at the time of R. H. Charles' edition, one relatively early witness, Abbadianus 55 (late fifteenth or early sixteenth century), contained a text which omitted the preposition በኀቤሁ፡ (*ba-xabēhu*; 'the presence of') prior to the phrase 'that son of man' (ለወአቱ፡ ወልደ፡ እጓለ፡ እመሐያው፡; *la-we'etu walda 'egʷāla 'emma-ḥeyāw*).[71] The resulting text should probably be translated 'the name of that son of man was raised up, while living, to the Lord of Spirits'.[72] Much has been made of the fact that the text of Abbadianus 55 is now known to be supported by other early manuscripts only recently made available to scholars, especially EMML 1768, EMML 2080, and EMML 7584 (all from the late fifteenth or early sixteenth centuries).[73] It is worth emphasizing a number of facts concerning the Ethiopic manuscript tradition, especially in light of claims made by Olson and Casey.[74]

First, the original text of EMML 2080 has been erased at this point and is no longer legible. Only the corrected text of EMML 2080 supports the omission of the preposition. Given what we know about the wider textual tradition of this verse and the space available between the words ሐያው፡ (*ḥeyāw*; 'while living') and ለወአቱ፡ (*la-we'etu*; 'to that'), it is reasonable to suppose that EMML 2080 originally contained the preposition.[75] Second, Olson asserts that EMML 2080 'may be the oldest Ethiopic MS of *1 Enoch* extant, possibly dating from the twelfth century'.[76] This is very debatable and almost certainly incorrect. Siegbert Uhlig, in his definitive study of Ethiopic palaeography, places EMML 2080 in his third period, that is, the second half of the fifteenth to first half of the sixteenth centuries. He, moreover, is inclined because of certain 'well-developed

71.   The exact form of the preposition varies in the manuscripts which attest it (በኀቤሁ፡ [*ba-xabēhu*], በኀበ፡ [*ba-xaba*], and በቅድመ፡ በኀበ፡ [*ba-qedma ba-xaba*], but these variations make no difference to the meaning of the passage. Such variation is quite common in Ethiopic manuscripts. Two nineteenth-century manuscripts, Abbadianus 99 and 197 (Charles' v and w), support Abbadianus 55 (Charles' u) in the omission of the preposition.

72.   It should be acknowledged, however, that because the ለ- (*la-*) preposition can function similarly to the preposition በኀቤሁ፡ (*ba-xabēhu*), the shorter text could still be rendered as the longer text. This is less likely, but not impossible. See also VanderKam, 'Righteous One', p. 184 and Knibb, '*1 Enoch* 70:1', p. 165, n. 21.

73.   Olson, 'Enoch and the Son of Man', pp. 30–32 and Casey, *Solution*, p. 108.

74.   In what follows, I have followed and summarized the arguments of Michael Knibb's article on this verse, '*1 Enoch* 70:1'.

75.   This is admitted by Olson, 'Enoch and the Son of Man', pp. 37–38, but Casey, *Solution*, p. 108, neglects to mention either the erasure or the correction.

76.   Olson, 'Enoch and the Son of Man', p. 31.

essential characteristics' to place it in the second half of that period.[77] It is, then, perhaps a century later than the earliest Ethiopic witness to the text of *1 Enoch*, Tana 9.

Third, that manuscript, our earliest witness to the text of the *Parables*, supports the longer reading, with the preposition.[78] Fourth, it has long been known that Abbadianus 55 is characterized by important omissions from chapter 83 onward, and so 'the significance of any omission in this manuscript is diminished'.[79] Fifth, Knibb, who has worked with these manuscripts closely, is of the opinion that Abbadianus 55 is closely related to EMML 1768; it is possible, then, that their witness should count as one, not two, manuscripts. Thus, perhaps only EMML 7584 remains as a new early supporter of Abbadianus 55. Finally, it is just as probable that the omission of the preposition at 70.1 resulted merely from a transcriptional error. Ethiopic manuscripts are full of variants of this sort and it is unlikely that much should be made of them. In light of all this, that the original Ethiopic reading of this verse made a distinction between Enoch and the Elect son of man should not be doubted. In other words, the tension between 70.1 and 71.14 remains, despite the efforts of Casey and Olson to remove it.

It should be added that the change from third to first person at 70.3 looks suspiciously like an editorial seam. In light of these two facts, it would appear that 70.3–71.17 is best regarded as a latter addition to the text of the *Parables*.[80] An inconsistency of detail between 70.3–71.17 and the text of the rest of the *Parables* adds further weight to this conclusion. According to 70.3-4 the realm of the righteous dead lies on earth, in the north-west. This agrees with the *Book of the Watchers* (*1En.* 22.1-9; cf. also 32.3 and 77.3), but contradicts the *Parables* themselves which situates the righteous dead in the heavens (39.3-8; 47.2; 58.5).[81] The author of 70.3-4 has, it would seem, mistakenly understood 61.1-5 to locate the realm of the dead in the North. And, finally, the ontological

---

77. S. Uhlig, *Äthiopische Paläographie* (ÄF, 22; Stuttgart: Franz Steiner, 1988), pp. 419–20.

78. In fact, Tana 9 has an even longer reading with two prepositions: በቅድመ፡ በኀበ፡ (*ba-qedma ba-xaba*).

79. Knibb, '*1 Enoch* 70:1', p. 165.

80. So also Nickelsburg, 'Discerning the Structure(s)', pp. 42–43.

81. 61.12 should probably be added here; its parallelism would seem to indicate that 'the garden of life', in which the elect dwell, is situated in the heavenly realms.

and pre-mundane pre-existence of the Elect son of man, discussed above, confirms such a conclusion. Since he was named in the presence of the Lord of Spirits and was preserved with the angelic hosts before the creation of the world, he cannot be the same person as Enoch, 'the seventh from Adam' (Jude 14; *1En.* 60.8; cf. Gen. 5.1-24; *1En.* 37.1; 93.3; *Jub.* 7.39). The ontological, pre-mundane pre-existence of the Elect son of man is an insurmountable obstacle to viewing their identity proclaimed in 71.14 as original.[82]

All of the above makes a strong case that in 70.3–71.17 we have an addition, made at a later time, whose sole purpose was to give an identity to the otherwise mysterious Elect son of man. This position remains popular and has many supporters.[83] It has, however, been challenged. VanderKam, for example, who has dismissed the evidence for a real pre-existence, but in my opinion has missed the significance of both 62.7 and 39.4-6, has suggested that either the Elect son of man functions as Enoch's heavenly *doppelgänger* or that Enoch merely 'sees the son of man in visions of the future, not in disclosures of the present. [In chapters 38–69, h]e is seeing only what he will become'.[84] Both of these propositions lose all force once it is allowed that in the *Parables* the Elect son of man possesses a real and pre-mundane pre-existence.

However, even if one does not accept that the Elect son of man enjoys real pre-existence, significant problems remain with both of VanderKam's proposals. First, there is no contemporary evidence of a seer observing his own heavenly doppelgänger in a vision and neither example which VanderKam offers, of Uriel/Jacob in the *Prayer of Joseph* nor the features of Jacob 'engraved on high' according to *GenR* 68.12, provide this. More to the point, as Collins has noted, the words of the angel to Enoch in 71.14 are 'You are the son of man',

---

82.   Casey (*Solution*, p. 101) seems to accept the son of man's pre-existence. He nonetheless never addresses how Enoch can be both pre-existent and the seventh from Adam. Does he suppose that the author of the *Parables* preceded Christians in attributing two natures, human and heavenly/angelic/divine, to their heavenly mediator?

83.   So, among others, Nickelsburg, 'Discerning the Structure(s)', pp. 42–45; Knibb, 'Structure and Composition', pp. 62–63; Collins, 'Enoch and the Son of Man', and his earlier 'The Heavenly Representative: The "Son of Man" in the Similitudes of Enoch', in J. J. Collins and G. W. E. Nickelsburg (eds), *Ideal Figures in Ancient Judaism* (Chico, CA: Scholars Press, 1980), pp. 111–33; and S. Chialà, 'The Son of Man: The Evolution of an Expression', in Boccaccini, *Enoch*, pp. 153–78, citing 162.

84.   VanderKam, 'Righteous One', pp. 182–84.

not 'This is your heavenly "double."'[85] Second, as Collins has also noted, Enoch's observation of himself without any recognition is both odd, requiring an explanation which is never given, and without parallel.[86]

Maurice Casey has offered three instances of 'hints' within the main text of the *Parables* which prepare for the identification of the Elect son of man with Enoch in the final chapter. First, he claims that since Enoch was held in Enochic literature to have been a paragon of righteousness (*1En*. 12.4; 14.1; 15.1; cf. also *Jub*. 10.17; *T. Levi* 10.6; *T. Jud*. 18.1), the characterization of 'that son of man' as having righteousness and that 'righteousness dwells with him' (46.3) would have been 'instantly recognized' by members of an Enochic community as an allusion to Enoch. Moreover, the major function attributed to Enoch in Second Temple literature is, in this same verse, applied to 'that son of man': 'He reveals all the treasures of the mysteries.'[87]

Righteousness, however, characterizes all the members of the group behind the *Parables*; 'righteous ones' appears throughout the text as a title for the adherents of the Elect One. This is not just true of the *Parables*; in Enochic literature the community (*1En*. 10.16; 93.10; 91.11-17), Noah (*1En*. 106.18) and God himself (*1En*. 22.14) are all characterized by righteousness. Moreover, it is striking that in the *Parables* themselves, as well as the *Animal Apocalypse*, Enoch functions primarily as the *recipient* of revelations, not as the *revealer* of heavenly mysteries.[88] Second, Casey believes that 69.26 ('because the name of that son of man was revealed to them') points forward to 71.14 when it is made clear that his name is 'Enoch'.[89] However, given 70.1 where, as we have seen, our author(s) use 'name' for 'person', there is no difficulty in supposing

---

85. Collins, 'Enoch and the Son of Man', p. 223.

86. Collins, 'Enoch and the Son of Man', p. 223 and 'Heavenly Representative', p. 122. In 'Enoch and the Son of Man', pp. 218–19, Collins also rightly dismissed as unfounded Kvanvig's ('Son of Man', pp. 200–201) attempt to interpret *1En*. 12-14 as another instance of Enoch viewing himself in a vision. Casey (*Solution*, pp. 110–11) offers two other parallels: Levi in *Testament of Levi* 7.4–8.1 and Enoch in the *Animal Apocalypse* (*1En*. 85-90). Admittedly, in both of these the seer sees himself in a dream. But Casey overlooks the central point: In neither of these does the seer fail to recognize himself, as Enoch would do in the *Parables*, if he is indeed identified with the Elect son of man.

87. Casey, *Solution*, pp. 99–100.

88. Contrast his function in the *Book of the Watchers* (esp. *1En*. 15); the *Book of the Heavenly Luminaries* (esp. *1En*. 81.1–82.2); *Jubilees* 4.16-19; and *2 Enoch* in all of which Enoch both receives and passes on revelations.

89. Casey, *Solution*, p. 105.

the same meaning here. Thus, 69.26 says no more than what is implied in 62.7. Finally, Casey introduces at 69.27b the questionable translation '(the son of man) will not pass away and he will not perish from the face of the earth'. He then argues that this refers to Enoch, who did not die but was translated while still living (Gen. 5.24).[90] Casey here follows the text of a single manuscript, Tana 9, which is our oldest and often our best. However, none of our manuscripts of Ethiopic *Enoch* is particularly good and Tana 9 should be regarded as corrupt here. The majority of manuscripts, with support from Berlin Petermann II Nachtrag 29 (sixteenth century), offer the only text which makes any sense: '(the son of man) will cause sinners to pass away and be destroyed from the face of the earth'.[91] Nonetheless, even if one were to accept the reading of Tana 9, it must be admitted that it does not fit Enoch at all. Enoch may not have died, but he did pass (or vanish or depart) from the earth. In the end, none of Casey's preparations for 71.14 can stand up to scrutiny and the ending remains contradictory, unexpected and surprising: simply too contradictory to be regarded as original.

Another defender of the originality of 70.3–71.17, Helge Kvanvig, has insisted that '[s]cholars who assume a later addition cannot escape the troublesome question that at one stage in the growth of the book readers actually were invited to identify Enoch and the Son of Man'.[92] He rightly observes that '[t]his section [which] not only adds new material, but [also] alters the basic meaning of the book' demands some explanation.[93] Nonetheless, it does not follow that the identification was made by the original author(s). Would not the original author(s) have at least attempted to explain how Enoch had not recognized himself or his heavenly double? More importantly, how did they conceive that Enoch could be both pre-existent and 'the seventh from Adam'? An interpolator, who is intent, in changed circumstances, to give new meaning to an old text, need not be bothered with such niceties. An original author is much less likely to leave them unexplained. Moreover, a later interpolator is much more likely than the original author(s) to have been guilty of the incongruity of placing

---

90. Casey, *Solution*, p. 105–106.
91. So also the translation of Nickelsburg and VanderKam and that of Knibb.
92. Kvanvig, 'Son of Man', p. 199.
93. Kvanvig, 'Son of Man', p. 199.

the realm of the righteous dead on earth, after repeatedly situating it, in the
proceeding chapters, in the heavens.

Kvanvig's challenge that the reasons for a late addition must still be explained
should be taken seriously, even if, in the end, it proves unanswerable. The
transformation of Enoch into a heavenly being in *2 Enoch* and the identification
of Enoch with Metatron, which we encounter in *Sefer Hekhalot* or *3 Enoch*,
appears to have developed out of *1En.* 71. It is clear that some Jews came to
regard Enoch as an exalted heavenly mediator. One, admittedly, uncertain piece
of evidence suggests that this development had already occurred before the end
of the first or the beginning of the second century. *Asc.Isa.* 9.7-9 looks like an
allusion to *1En.* 70.4. If this is correct, then, 70.3–71.17 must have been added
to the text of the *Parables* before the *Ascension of Isaiah* was composed, late
in the first century or in the opening decades of the next. That the addition
was made to counter claims made about Jesus by Christians is only a guess,
but a plausible one.[94] One can easily imagine an 'Enochic' Jew, that is, a Jew
who valued the Enochic corpus and whose hope was set on its Elect son of
man, disturbed by the all too similar assertions being made for the crucified
Messiah of early Jewish Christians, responding with an identification of his
own. Kvanvig is certainly right that the identification of the Elect son of man
with Enoch probably resulted from a brilliant intertextual reading of *1En.* 14-15
and Daniel 7. He may well be right that *1En.* 90.37-38 also played a role.[95]
What Kvanvig, in my opinion, cannot explain is the reason(s) which led an
'Enochic' Jew to make such a move, so out of step with the rest of *Parables* – to
say nothing of the rest of *1 Enoch*. On the other hand, Jesus of Nazareth, the
crucified and risen Messiah, and Son of Man of Jewish Christianity, offers a
plausible catalyst for just such an innovation.

94.   Collins, 'Heavenly Representative', pp. 125–26.
95.   Kvanvig, 'Son of Man', pp. 207–10. I am less convinced by his arguments for *1En.*
32.6.

SUMMARY AND CONCLUDING OBSERVATIONS

Larry W. Hurtado

Part of my task in this concluding chapter is to note where we are in discussion of the thorny issues connected with 'the Son of Man' expression in the Gospels, especially in light of the foregoing contributions to this book. I will also offer a few observations of my own, and conclude by indicating what I think is the most reasonable proposal as to origins of this expression. As an entrée, it may be helpful to review the main data that provoke and puzzle, and continue to generate the efforts of scholars to propose solutions for them. As I will argue below, I think that a clear and sustained engagement with the data is essential, and may enable some progress in understanding things.

'Just the facts, ma'am'[1]

As with any really important problem, so in the case of the one before us there are data that require to be engaged and explained. Especially in light of the many theories and proposals generated, it is well to have these data clearly in mind. We are concerned essentially with usages of key expressions in certain ancient Greek texts. Even though Semitic-language constructions typically underlie (or are commonly thought to underlie) all the Greek expressions

---

1.   I beg the indulgence of readers in this allusion to the most famous ever detective series on American radio and TV, 'Dragnet'. For those unfamiliar with the series and the unforgettable Jack Webb, see http://en.wikipedia.org/wiki/Dragnet_(series).

in question, it is the usage of these latter that provides the starting point for analysis.[2]

To clarify one point at the outset, ὁ υἱός τοῦ ἀνθρώπου is not an expression that is native to, or common in, ancient Greek. With the benefit of the *Thesaurus Linguae Graecae*, it is possible to verify this readily. Simply put, there is no instance of the singular or plural form of this construction, anarthrous or articular, in extant Greek literature outside of the LXX, the NT, Philo (*Vit. Mos.* 1.283), and subsequent texts that show the influence of the LXX and/or NT. That is, all uses of this particular Greek expression appear in texts of ancient Jewish provenance or influenced heavily by Jewish texts.[3] To be sure, these expressions are all framed in understandable Greek vocabulary and syntax, but they are simply not ones that came naturally on the lips of native Greek speakers/writers uninfluenced by the Greek OT and Jewish tradition.

The Greek Old Testament

By contrast, in the LXX I count some 166 instances of various forms of the singular or plural 'son of man' and 'sons of men'.[4] These all reflect, either directly (translation) or indirectly (Semitic phrasing exerting influence on writers of Greek), equivalent Hebrew or Aramaic expressions, which are thoroughly idiomatic in both Semitic languages. Nearly all the LXX uses are in texts known to have been translated from Hebrew or Aramaic.[5] This is a boon for any interest in how the relevant Semitic expressions were handled when translated. The *general* observation to make is that the various LXX translators appear to have

---

2.   See also my previous discussion of these matters in *Lord Jesus Christ: Devotion to Jesus in Earliest Christianity* (Grand Rapids: Eerdmans, 2003), pp. 290–306.

3.   Our editions of the LXX rest mainly upon Christian copies of the Greek OT writings (from the third century CE and later), and we have only limited evidence of the pre-LXX Greek OT. But there is no reason to think that 'Old Greek' translators differed greatly in their rendering of the phrases in question. Hence, for economy of expression, in the following discussion I shall refer to LXX translators, meaning the translators whose work is preserved for us in our editions of the LXX.

4.   In the following discussion, I draw upon results using *BibleWorks for Windows* (version 4.0), counting instances found in standard printed editions of the LXX and Greek NT.

5.   The few possible exceptions include Wis. 9.6 ('sons of men'), on the common assumption that Wisdom of Solomon was composed in Greek. In this case, we have here an instance of someone writing in Greek but consciously or unconsciously reflecting a Semitic idiom.

rendered the underlying Hebrew and Aramaic expressions faithfully, sometimes even somewhat woodenly.

For example, the singular and plural forms of the Semitic expressions are carefully rendered by corresponding forms in Greek. So, the 54 instances of the plural '(the) sons of men' (υἱοὶ ἀνθρώπων / οἱ υἱοὶ τῶν ἀνθρώπων) in the LXX all seem to translate equivalent Hebrew plural forms. The typical Hebrew expression translated is the plural, בְּנֵי אָדָם, but in a number of instances it is בְּנֵי הָאָדָם (i.e. with the article, Pss. 33.13; 145.12, and 10× in Ecclesiastes), and occasionally בְּנֵי אִישׁ (Pss. 4.2; 62.10 [LXX 61.10]). The LXX translators typically preferred to translate these Hebrew plural expressions with οἱ υἱοὶ τῶν ἀνθρώπων (i.e. with definite articles before each noun, 27×), less frequently using υἱοὶ ἀνθρώπων (i.e. without any article, 17×), and one instance of υἱοὶ τῶν ἀνθρώπων (Odes Sol. 8.82, perhaps a rather wooden translation of the underlying Hebrew construct form). However, in LXX Ecclesiastes we find υἱοὶ τοῦ ἀνθρώπου (6×) and οἱ υἱοὶ τοῦ ἀνθρώπου (4×), the underlying Hebrew in all these ten instances being בְּנֵי הָאָדָם. As to why the LXX translators preferred one or the other Greek phrasing, the matter need not detain us here. Basically, it seems that the alternative Greek expressions carried a sufficiently similar sense, the choices reflecting efforts by LXX translators to render Semitic constructions for which there were not already direct equivalents in use native to Greek.

There are some 112 instances of the singular forms for '(a) son of man' in the LXX, each of these faithfully rendering a corresponding Hebrew (or Aramaic) singular form. Ninety-four of these are the vocative singular (υἱε ἀνθρώπου) in Ezekiel, rendering the peculiarly frequent use of 'son of man' as the expression by which *Yahweh* addresses the prophet. It is noteworthy that each of these 112 singular forms in the LXX is 'anarthrous' (no definite article), e.g. υἱός ἀνθρώπου in Ps. 8.4/LXX 8.5, accurately reflecting in each instance the Hebrew (or Aramaic) expressions. In nearly all instances the Hebrew is בֶּן אָדָם (e.g. Num. 23.19; Ps. 8.4; Jer. 2.6), the exceptions being Ps. 80.16/LXX 79.16 (בֶּן אִמַּצְתָּה, 'the son you have reared'), Ps. 144.3/LXX 143.3 (בֶּן אֱנוֹשׁ), Jer. 2.6 (אָדָם), and of course the Aramaic expression in Dan. 7.13 (בַּר אֱנָשׁ).

We can now draw some summarizing observations from these details. First, the singular form, 'son of man', is consistently without an article in the Hebrew texts of the OT (and in its few OT instances in Aramaic does not have the final *aleph* that would give a corresponding definite sense to a noun).[6] Thus, as far as the evidence of the Hebrew OT and other Second Temple Jewish literature is concerned, it appears that the articular form 'the son of man' was not a familiar expression, in Hebrew, Aramaic or Greek, in the period in which these writings were composed.[7] There is certainly no basis for thinking that the Semitic articular/definite forms were used somewhat interchangeably with the anarthrous/indefinite forms of the expressions involved. Instead, the impression given is that the articular/definite singular expression, 'the son of man', would have been regarded as highly unusual, perhaps even peculiar.

Second, and perhaps as interesting, although the LXX translators often supplied definite articles in rendering plural forms ('the sons of men'), including instances where the Hebrew construction has no article (e.g. Ps. 11.4/LXX 10.4), they rather consistently refrained from doing so in translating these many instances of singular forms. Even in cases where it would seem fully appropriate to have supplied the definite article in the interest of conveying the connotation of a given sentence, and where subsequent translators often have done so (e.g. Ps. 8.4; 80.17/LXX 79.16; 144.3/LXX 143.3), the LXX translators scrupulously refrained from adding a definite article to 'son of man', retaining the indefinite forms of the various underlying Semitic expressions. Perhaps the articular form, 'the son of man', seemed still more strange in Greek than the indefinite (anarthrous) form. In any case, based on this evidence we should be cautious in ascribing to ancient Greek translators of Hebrew and/or Aramaic a readiness to supply a definite article to instances of 'son of man' where there was none in the underlying Semitic being translated.

---

6. There is one apparent instance where a copyist has added the definite article in the Qumran manuscript, 1QS (11.20), producing בֶּן הָאדם. For discussion, see Joseph A. Fitzmyer, 'The New Testament Title "The Son of Man" Philologically Considered', in *A Wandering Aramean: Collected Aramaic Essays* (SBLMS 25; Missoula: Scholars Press, 1979), pp. 143–60, esp. 146.

7. See the evidence cited by Paul Owen and David Shepherd, 'Speaking Up for Qumran, Dalman and the Son of Man: Was *Bar Enasha* a Common Term for "Man" in the Time of Jesus?' *JSNT* 81 (2001), pp. 81–122, esp. 104–20. Note also that in the Aramaic fragments of *1 Enoch* there are no instances of the definite-singular form of 'son of man'. J. T. Milik (ed.), *The Books of Enoch: Aramaic Fragments of Qumran Cave 4* (Oxford: Clarendon Press, 1976), p. 371, s.v. בר.

The New Testament

Now let us turn now to the data pertaining directly to NT texts. The first thing to note is the surprising frequency of, and preference for, the articular-singular expression 'the son of man' (ὁ υἱός τοῦ ἀνθρώπου), some 80 instances, 79 of them in the Gospels and once in Acts (7.56). In addition, we have a few uses of the anarthrous singular form, υἱός ἀνθρώπου (in Heb. 2.6, where it is part of a quotation of Ps. 8.4, and in Rev. 1.13; 14.14, both of these likely allusive to Dan. 7.13). Clearly, we are looking at an expression that is very unusual and plays some sort of important role in the vocabulary of the intra-canonical Gospels in particular.[8]

Moreover, nearly all of these articular-singular instances are in sayings ascribed to Jesus, and 'the son of man' is his typical self-designation, especially prominently in the Synoptic Gospels. Other characters in the Gospels, however, basically do not use the expression, with reference to anyone. No one ever acclaims Jesus as 'the son of man'. Nor does his use of the expression ever generate controversy or accusation. The closest that we have to an exception is Jn 12.34, where the Jewish crowd is portrayed as asking Jesus what he means by referring to 'the son of man'. But the impression given here is that the crowd simply finds the expression novel and they are unsure what to make of it. 'The son of man' is not itself an honorific claim here that the crowd recognizes or contests.[9] Among the several positive estimates of Jesus ascribed to people in the Gospels narratives (e.g. Mk 8.27-29, John the Baptist, Elijah, a prophet, Messiah), 'the son of man' is totally absent as an option. Nor is 'the son of man' among the confessional titles accorded Jesus elsewhere in the NT (e.g. 'Lord', 'Christ', 'the Son of God').[10] So, we cannot account readily for the expression as some regular feature of early Christian kerygmatic or confessional usage that was retrojected back into the narratives about the earthly Jesus.

It is also interesting to note the variation in frequency and usage of the expression among the Gospels. Matthew leads in frequency (30×), and deploys the expression uniquely in some sayings with parallels in the other Synoptics

---

8. The plural form, 'the sons of men', is used only twice in the NT (Mk 3.28; Eph. 3.6).

9. Cf. e.g. the excited questions over whether Jesus might be a prophet or even 'the Christ' (Jn 7.40-44; 10.24) and the accusation that he 'made himself the Son of God' (19.7).

10. The statement ascribed to Stephen in Acts 7.56 is not a real exception. In the wider context of Luke-Acts, 'the son of man' is already known to readers as Jesus' characteristic self-designation. So Stephen is pictured here as claiming that the one known (to readers and to the opponents in the scene) by the sobriquet 'the son of man' has been exalted to heavenly glory.

where the expression is not used. Compare, in particular, Matthew's use of 'the son of man' in Jesus' question to his disciples near Caesarea Philippi concerning what people are saying about him (16.13) with the use of the first-person pronoun in the parallels in Mk 8.27; Lk. 9.18. Compare also the reference to 'the son of man' enthroned in Mt. 19.28 with the Lk. 18.30 parallel, which lacks this image (referring instead to 'my table' and 'my kingdom'). Matthew alone refers to 'the coming of the son of man' (ἡ παρουσία τοῦ υἱοῦ τοῦ ἀνθρώπου, 24.27, 37, 39; and cf. also 10.23; 25.31), and to 'the sign of the son of man' (τὸ σημεῖον τοῦ υἱοῦ τοῦ ἀνθρώπου, 24.30). In addition, though most of the relevant sayings in Matthew have parallels in one or more of the other Synoptics, there are a few other sayings unique to Matthew in which 'the son of man' features: 10.23; 13.37; 26.2b.

On the other hand, whereas Lk. 12.8 promises that 'the son of man' will acknowledge those who confess Jesus, Mt. 10.32 simply has Jesus give this assurance using the first-person pronoun and verb (ὁμολογήσω κἀγὼ), and where the other Synoptics have Jesus teach his disciples 'that the son of man must suffer many things' (Mk 8.31; Lk. 9.22), Mt. 16.21 has 'Jesus' show them 'that he must go to Jerusalem and suffer many things'. Nevertheless, the expression 'the son of man' is clearly prominent in Matthew's presentation of Jesus, and serves as the author's favoured way of representing Jesus' self-designation.

Next in frequency is Luke (23×). Here again, there are interesting distinguishing features to the Lukan usage of the expression. Luke alone refers to 'the day(s) of the son of man' (17.22, 30). Lk. 6.22 uniquely refers to persecution of Jesus' followers 'on account of the son of man' (cf. Mt. 5.11). In addition, there are a few other sayings about 'the son of man' exclusive to Luke (18.8; 19.10; 22.48; 24.7, the angels at the tomb here echoing Jesus' saying from 9.22).

The 14 son-of-man sayings in Mark nearly all have parallels in Matthew and/ or Luke, which is consistent with the common view that Mark was the principal source and precedent for the authors of the other Synoptics, Markan material heavily appropriated by the other two Synoptic Evangelists.[11] The possible

---

11.   Mk 2.10/Mt. 9.6/Lk. 5.24; Mk 2.28/Mt. 12.8/Lk. 6.5; Mk 8.31/Lk. 9.22 (cf. Mt. 16.21); Mk 8.38/Lk. 9.26; Mk 9.9/Mt. 17.9; Mk 9.31/Mt. 17.22/Lk. 9.44; Mk 10.33/Mt. 20.18/ Lk. 18.31; Mk 10.45/Mt. 20.28; Mk 13.26/Mt. 24.30/Lk. 21.27; Mk 14.21/Mt. 26.24/Lk. 22.22; Mk 14.41/Mt. 26.45; Mk 14.62/Mt. 26.64/Lk. 22.69.

exception is in 9.12, where Jesus says that 'it has been written concerning the son of man' that he should suffer. There is no Lukan parallel, and Mt. 17.13 has a comparable saying about 'the son of man' but worded differently.

For its size, John uses the expression less intensively (12×, plus one anarthrous construction in 5.27), and the explicit emphasis on Jesus' divine sonship is clearly more prominent.[12] Nevertheless, 'the son of man' still plays a significant role in John. Indeed, in John the expression is used quite distinctively.[13] None of the Johannine sentences in which 'the son of man' features has an obvious or direct parallel in the Synoptic Gospels. In John, we have sentences referring to angels descending and ascending on 'the son of man' (1.51), the descent (from heaven) and ascent of 'the son of man' (3.13-14; 6.62), his giving food of eternal life and his own flesh and blood (6.27, 53), 'the son of man' being 'lifted up' (8.28) and glorified (12.23; 13.21), and even a probable reference to belief in 'the son of man' (9.35).[14] Clearly, the sentences in which the author deploys the expression 'the son of man' comprise a unique body of material in this unique Gospel.

Indeed, I suggest that this sharply distinctive use of 'the son of man' in John is perhaps particularly valuable in demonstrating for us the function and significance of this expression in the NT writings. We have noted already that, even among the individual Synoptics, there are some distinctive sentences or phrases in which the expression is deployed. But in John it is more boldly and thoroughly used in a body of statements that reflect explicitly the distinctive emphases of this Gospel. The variations in the usage of 'the son of man' in the Synoptics, including particularly the apparent freedom of Synoptic authors to use 'the son of man' and the first-person pronoun somewhat interchangeably in sayings of Jesus, suggests that in these texts it functions simply (or at least primarily) as a unique self-referential expression. I propose that this is rather

12. In contrast to the 12 uses of 'the son of man' in John, I count at least six uses of 'the son of God', and another 15 references to 'the Son' (of course, the latter all affirmations of Jesus' divine sonship).

13. Cf. the essay on use of 'the son of man' in John by Benjamin E. Reynolds in this volume; and also Delbert Burkett, *The Son of Man in the Gospel of John*, JSNTSup 56 (Sheffield: JSOT Press, 1991).

14. The widely supported variant, 'the son of God', in 9.35 is quite likely an effort to align Jesus' question here with a more common early Christian confessional claim.

more obviously shown in John, where the expression is deployed entirely in sayings that reflect this author's particular Christological emphases.

That is, I submit that the diversity of sentences/sayings in which 'the son of man' is used in the Gospels leads to the conclusion that in these texts the expression's primary linguistic function is to *refer, not to characterize*.[15] The expression refers to Jesus (and almost entirely in sentences where it is used as a self-designation), but does not *in itself* primarily make a claim about him, or generate any controversy, or associate him with prior/contextual religious expectations or beliefs. 'The son of man' can be used in sayings that stake various claims about Jesus (e.g. Jesus' authority, or humble situation, or heavenly provenance, or eschatological significance), but it is the *sentence/saying* that conveys the intended claim or statement, *not 'the son of man' expression itself.*

With genuine respect for the many scholars who have done so, it is, nevertheless, a linguistic fallacy to impute to the expression 'the son of man' the meanings of the various statements in which it is used. Instead, we are to attribute to *the referent*, Jesus, the import of these sentences. As an analogy, let us consider the statement, 'The professor is compassionate'. In this statement, compassion is ascribed to a particular figure referred to as 'the professor'; but the word 'professor' itself does not thereby carry (or acquire) the meaning 'compassionate'. 'The professor' designates and even classifies a given person as holding a particular professional role, but the term itself does not acquire the attribute ascribed to this particular professor. So, for example, to treat 'the son of man' as if in itself it 'means' a figure of authority (on the basis of sayings such as Mk 2.10), or of humility (on the basis of sayings such as Mt. 8.20/ Lk. 9.58), or eschatological judge (on the basis of Mt. 25.31), or a heavenly being (on the basis of Jn 3.13-14), or even the figure of Dan. 7.13 (on the basis of Mk 14.62/Mt. 26.64) would all represent the fallacious move that I identify here. For emphasis, I repeat that in all the Gospels sayings, the function of 'the son of man' expression is essentially to refer to Jesus as the figure about whom the sentence says something. The particular 'meaning' of each statement/saying lies in the statement, not in the expression 'the son of man'. In short, Jesus (as

15.   I employ here some elementary insights about language from linguistics, a subject with which NT remain surprisingly ill-informed. For a helpful entrée, see John Lyons, *Language and Linguistics: An Introduction* (Cambridge: Cambridge University Press, 1981).

portrayed in the sayings/sentences in question) defines 'the son of man'; 'the son of man' designates but does not define Jesus.

Of course, 'the son of man' is a particularizing form of an idiomatic expression with broad inherent meaning. Any study of the uses of the singular and plural forms of 'son of man' in the OT will show readily that in the relevant Semitic languages these expressions connoted, singly or collectively, human beings, members of the human species (and so the mysterious figure in Dan. 7.13 likened to a human in the phrase, 'one like a son of man'). The unusual articular-singular form so frequently and consistently used in the Gospels, 'the son of man', probably connotes further a certain particularity or specificity. So, in the Gospels 'the son of man' may convey something like 'the man' or even 'this man'.[16] If this seems an unusual expression in English, especially as a self-designation, it appears that it was equally unusual and curious in biblical Hebrew, in the Aramaic of Jesus' time, and in Koine Greek, to judge from the scarcity of any occurrence of the fully equivalent expression in any of these languages outside of the Gospels.[17]

But the sheer diversity of sentences in which the Evangelists used 'the son of man', and the instances where they felt free to use the personal pronoun interchangeably with the expression, surely show that it did not have for them some precise and fixed meaning (or fixed set of meanings). Instead, these authors knew the expression essentially (and in all likelihood solely) as the distinctive way that Jesus typically referred to himself, and so deployed it accordingly when they sought to represent Jesus uttering sayings that included a self-reference. The imprint of this peculiar expression as distinctive to Jesus' usage is found frequently in all four Gospels, and even in sayings that are widely thought to derive from the sayings-source, Q.[18] But other than this function of the expression as Jesus' unique self-referential device reflecting some

16. The Greek definite article, which originated as a demonstrative pronoun, retains something of this quasi-demonstrative sense in Koine Greek. See e.g. C. F. D. Moule, *An Idiom Book of New Testament Greek* (Cambridge: Cambridge University Press, 1963), pp. 106–17, esp. 111.

17. Given the controversy over relevant Aramaic expressions, I emphasize here that we have no instances of the definite-singular *in Aramaic texts of the Second Temple period*. I do not consider instances in texts of several centuries earlier or later to be probative of Aramaic usage of the time of Jesus and the Evangelists.

18. Cf. the single instance of the equivalent Coptic expression in *Gospel of Thomas* 86, which is a version of the saying found also in Mt. 8.20/Lk. 9.58.

sort of emphasis on him as a particular human being, the expression 'the son of man' has little by way of inherent Christological meaning.

In later/other early Christian texts, to be sure, 'the son of man' takes on more confessional significance.[19] In early orthodox circles, for example, it was used to emphasize Jesus' human nature in comparison with his divine nature (typically expressed by use of the title 'the Son of God').[20] But I contend that 'the son of man' does not really function as a Christological title in first-century Christian texts, and that it is a mistake to seek to assign to it some precise 'meaning' or set of meanings.[21] Instead, it functions essentially as a unique self-designation of Jesus and is deployed in sentences which ascribe this or that action, significance or attribute to the figure referred to as 'the son of man'.

Origins

The obvious other question is how to account for this expression and its prominence in the Gospels. I suggest that there have been two types of scholarly proposals about the origins of 'the son of man' expression, some attributing it to Jesus, others to the early church, and both types remain advocated in current discussion.[22] In what follows, I assess briefly main current options of each type, especially taking account of the other contributions to this volume.

Several decades ago, Norman Perrin argued that the expression 'the son of man' arose through a creative early Christian exegetical move in which the 'one like a son of man' in Dan. 7.13 was identified as the risen/exalted Jesus.[23] Perrin found his evidence in the rather obvious allusion to Dan. 7.13 in Mk 14.62 and

---

19. Frederick H. Borsch, *The Son of Man in Myth and History* (London: SCM Press, 1967) surveys uses of the expression in early orthodox and heterodox Christian circles/texts.

20. As noted also by Reynolds in his essay in this volume, who cites Ignatius (*Eph.* 20.2), Justin (*Dial* 100.3-4), Irenaeus (*Adv. Haer* 3.10.2; 16.3, 7; 18.3-4; 19.1-2), and *Barn.* 12.10.

21. It will be clear, thus, that I do not find persuasive the sort of approach taken, e.g., by Reynolds in his study of Johannine uses of 'the son of man' in this volume.

22. See the fuller review of previous scholarship by Delbert Burkett, *The Son of Man Debate: A History and Evaluation* (Cambridge: Cambridge University Press, 1999), who similarly judged that 'the bulk of scholarship is now divided between two basic alternatives': the expression originated either with Jesus' own use of an Aramaic equivalent, or as a messianic title applied to Jesus either by himself or the early church (122).

23. Norman Perrin, 'Mark 14:62: The End Product of a Christian Pesher Tradition?', *NTS* 12 (1965–1966), pp. 150–55.

parallels, where Jesus is portrayed as affirming that 'the son of man' will be seen seated at God's right hand and 'coming with the clouds of heaven'. Perrin argued that this saying was put into the mouth of Jesus, but actually originated in early Christian '*pesher*' activity driven by Christological interests. Then, from this initial move, 'the son of man' expression quickly came to be deployed more widely in a variety of sayings in the Jesus tradition. More recently, in his survey of scholarship on the expression, Delbert Burkett seems to lean towards a somewhat similar view, with some slight hesitation.[24]

But all such proposals that 'the son of man' originated in early Christian circles and expressed some Christological conviction about Jesus seem to me to ignore, and so to founder on, a rather important datum. As we have noted already, there is no evidence that 'the son of man' functioned in the proclamation, confession or liturgical practices of any first-century Christian circle, at least to judge from the available texts. Instead, the sole place of the expression is in sayings of Jesus, where it seems to serve simply as a distinctive self-referential formula. By contrast, in the case of 'Messiah/Christ' or 'Son of God', we clearly have Christological titles that were central in early Christian discourse, and that also laid claims about Jesus that were recognizable in the settings of first-century Christian circles. In principle, therefore, it is fully reasonable to consider whether one or both of these latter titles may have been heightened in the Gospels narratives of Jesus (or even read back into them), the Evangelists thereby linking these narratives somewhat with the discourse and beliefs of the first readers.[25] But in the case of 'the son of man' we are not dealing with the same sort of item. 'The son of man' is a fixed expression and has a prominent and distinctive function in the Gospels, but it is simply not a Christological title.

Burkett suggested that the absence of the expression in the NT outside of the Gospels (and the one Acts passage) could be accounted for 'if the title had currency primarily in Palestinian Christianity'. Granting that the NT generally reflects 'Hellenistic Christianity outside of Palestine', nevertheless, he judged that the Gospels and early chapters in Acts 'retain traces of Palestinian

---

24. Burkett, *The Son of Man Debate*, esp. pp. 122–24.
25. I neither offer nor imply any judgement about whether this happened, only that it is reasonable to consider the matter.

tradition'. So, he contended, 'the son of man' appears in the NT precisely where we should expect it.[26]

But this argument does not convince. Certainly, the Gospel narratives are set in Roman Judea (Palestine), but it is dubious to suggest that they therefore reflect and preserve the beliefs and supposedly distinctive discourse of 'Palestinian Christianity'. The Gospels are late-first-century accounts of Jesus that are each intended to be meaningful for readers of that time and in the various settings in which they were read.[27] The authors sought to connect these readers with Jesus, not particularly with 'Palestinian Christianity'. So, they deployed the expression 'the son of man' apparently because in the traditions they drew upon it was already a distinctive mark of Jesus' own sayings, not because it was supposedly a feature of 'Palestinian' Christian Christological confession.

The early chapters of Acts are presented as reflecting the earliest days of the young Christian movement in Jerusalem and related areas, which makes it all the more interesting that 'the son of man' does not feature in the representations of early Jewish-Christian proclamation and confession. The one instance of the expression on the lips of Stephen in Acts 7.56 is obviously one feature of the author's larger presentation of Stephen's martyrdom as echoing Jesus' interrogation and death. So, in 7.56 we have an allusion back to Lk. 22.69, where Jesus predicts that 'the son of man' will be seen at the right hand of God in heavenly glory. This sole instance of the expression scarcely suffices to show that it functioned as a Christological title in 'Palestinian' Christian circles of the time. In short, Burkett actually presupposes the very thing that needs to be shown – that 'the son of man' was ever used as a Christological title in confession and/or proclamation, among early Jewish believers or any others.

Perrin, Burkett and others who ascribe the expression to the early church tend to posit Dan. 7.13 as the crucial biblical text that provided the exegetical point of origin. Unquestionably, Dan. 7.13-14 was drawn on and alluded to in

26. Burkett, *The Son of Man Debate*, p. 123.

27. I side-step here the issue raised by Richard Bauckham over whether the Gospels were originally written for some specific church or geographical/cultural setting. See Richard Bauckham, 'For Whom Were the Gospels Written?', in *The Gospels for All Christians: Rethinking the Gospel Audiences*, ed. Richard Bauckham (Grand Rapids: Eerdmans, 1998), pp. 9–48. Whatever the force of Bauckham's argument, the Gospels quickly circulated among various churches, but clearly among Greek-reading circles and well beyond 'Palestinian Christianity'.

several NT texts (esp. Mk 14.62/Mt. 26.64; Mk 13.26/Mt. 24.30; Lk. 21.27; Rev. 1.7). But it does not seem to me that Dan. 7.13 was quite as crucial in framing the Christological convictions of the early church as would seem to be required/presumed in the sort of proposal supported by Burkett. Other OT texts seem to have been far more crucial (especially Ps. 110).[28] Moreover, if 'the son of man' originated via pondering OT texts, there are actually other texts as well that could have served to suggest the expression. These include Ps. 8.4; 80.18/ LXX 79.18, the latter interestingly combining a reference to 'the man at your [God's] right hand' and 'the son of man'.

Other scholars, e.g. Darrell Bock in his contribution to this volume, have proposed that Dan. 7.13 was particularly important *to Jesus* in framing his self-understanding, and that 'the son of man' may have originated as his somewhat veiled device for linking himself with the mysterious figure in Daniel 7. I grant that it is entirely appropriate to explore how Jesus might have drawn upon his biblical heritage in framing his understanding of his own particular mission and role in the divine plan. Also, I think that it is fully plausible that Jesus could have made the sort of claim, involving an allusion to Dan. 7.13-14, which we have reflected in the scene of Jesus' interrogation by the Jewish authorities (Mk 14.62). But I am not persuaded that the expression 'the son of man' originated through Jesus perceiving Dan. 7.13 as the crucial text in forming his self-understanding and his use of the expression.

One important reason, again, is the lack of evidence that 'the son of man' functioned as a claim made by believers about Jesus' significance in first-century Christian texts. If 'the son of man' originated in Jesus' pondering of Dan. 7.13-14 and served in particular as his device to affirm his identify as the human-like figure of that passage, it is very curious that this expression was not then taken up in early Christian proclamation and confession. Why would early Christians have dropped or ignored the expression, if it had served in Jesus' own teaching to identify himself as the exalted being in the Daniel passage? If the expression was a 'veiled' way of making this claim in the time of Jesus' own ministry, in the post-Easter situation of overt proclamation of Jesus we should expect a clear and forthright proclamation that Jesus is specifically 'the son of man' of

---

28. David M. Hay, *Glory at the Right Hand: Psalm 110 in Early Christianity* (Nashville: Abingdon Press, 1973).

that passage. But there is scant indication that the expression 'the son of man' functioned in making any such claim in early Christian proclamation. Jesus' allusion to Dan. 7.13-14 in the scenes of his interrogation before the Jewish authorities will hardly serve by itself as sufficient evidence of early Jewish Christian confessional use of 'the son of man'.

The other major approach in contemporary scholarly discussion is to take ὁ υἱός τοῦ ἀνθρώπου as deriving from Jesus' use of one or more equivalent expressions in Aramaic, but not as a pointer to Daniel 7. There are different options offered. One option is to posit that Jesus used an idiomatic Aramaic expression that was putatively a common way of referring to someone else or to oneself. Among current exponents of this sort of view, Maurice Casey is probably the most prominent, and certainly the most vigorous.[29] This is reflected in the attention given to his work in several of the chapters in this volume (especially the contributions by Albert Lukaszewski, Paul Owen, David Shepherd and P. J. Williams). The particular wrinkle in Casey's approach is his insistence that the definite singular form, בר אנשא, was an Aramaic idiomatic expression that did not necessarily carry a particularizing force, and was simply a common way for a speaker to refer to someone (including oneself) as a human person. Casey further proposes that the Greek expression ὁ υἱός τοῦ ἀνθρώπου originated as a rather literal translation of this definite-form Aramaic expression, the early Christian translators thereby introducing innocently a particularizing force into the Greek phrasing that was not connoted in the Aramaic equivalent. This, Casey further proposes, then contributed to the Greek for 'the son of man' becoming a title as applied to Jesus, as it came to reflect the kind of uniqueness that early Christians quickly wished to ascribe to him.

But, as was pointed out forcefully by Owen and Shepherd several years ago, it is a major problem for Casey's argument that there is no evidence for a common use of the definite-singular expression בר אנשא in extant Aramaic texts of the Second Temple period and Palestinian provenance.[30] The essays

---

29.   See now, especially, Maurice Casey, *The Solution to the 'Son of Man' Problem* (London: T&T Clark, 2007), which consolidates work from a number of his earlier publications. Casey's confidence in his proposal is reflected in the title of this book: *'The Solution'*! This basic approach was brought to renewed attention by Geza Vermes, initially in his essay, 'The Use of *Bar Nasha/Bar Nash* in Jewish Aramaic', in Matthew Black, *An Aramaic Approach to the Gospels and Acts* (3rd edn; Oxford: Oxford University Press, 1967), pp. 310–30.

30.   Owen and Shepherd, 'Speaking Up for Qumran'.

by Owen and Shepherd in this volume reiterate their forceful argument, and engage Casey further and effectively in my view. This lack of evidence of the definite-singular form in Second Temple Aramaic texts is also consistent with the lack of any instance of the articular-singular form of the Hebrew equivalent (הָאָדָם בֶּן) in the Hebrew OT. For reasons that are not entirely clear, thus, it seems that the definite-singular in Aramaic (as the case for the equivalent in Hebrew) in fact was *not* in use, or at least not used with sufficient frequency to have left instances in the available evidence of Aramaic of Jesus' time.

Casey points to instances from centuries before or after the Second Temple period, and insists that in this particular idiomatic expression Aramaic remained constant across several hundred years and various locales. This is, of course, a possibility, but assertion does not comprise evidence, and repeated assertion does not increase the probative force of the claim. It would be equally plausible to think that, as with living languages generally, Aramaic changed across centuries of time. It is certainly the case that there were various regional dialects of Aramaic. Moreover, although the extant body of Aramaic texts from roughly Jesus' time and geographical setting is frustratingly limited, we cannot ignore or downplay the absence of evidence that the definite-singular equivalent of 'the son of man' was a common idiom. Indeed, Casey's claim that this expression was common and unremarkable in Aramaic usage of Jesus' setting actually makes the absence of supporting evidence all the more serious for his position. Instances of an unusual and infrequently used expression might not have been preserved in the modest-sized body of first-century Aramaic. But the total lack of any instance of a supposedly common idiomatic expression is very strange indeed, and I do not think that Casey's efforts to deflect the force of this deficiency have been persuasive.

Williams' essay reflects doubt about Casey's position similar to that expressed by Owen and Shepherd. Williams makes the further valid point that one can connote particularity in various ways, in ancient Aramaic and other languages. So, even if Casey were correct in his claims about the usage of the definite-singular form, בַּר אֱנָשָׁא, there were other means by which Jesus could have connoted a particularizing force in his self-references. Lukaszewski expresses a broader hesitation regarding our ability to make confident claims about the details of first-century Aramaic, the effect of his argument being to cast doubts on the sort of efforts that Casey and others before him have made to retro-translate the Gospels sayings back into Aramaic. Given the sort of caution expressed by Lukaszewski, these efforts can be regarded as interesting exercises, but they carry very limited probative force. Further, the very weak basis for these efforts should make us cautious about pronouncing on the historicity of individual sayings, or positing some distinctive meaning of them, on the basis of retro-translation. But this point takes us beyond 'the son of man' debate and into the wider efforts of Casey and others to use retro-translation as a basis for critical judgements about the Jesus tradition.[31]

In light of the linguistic data we have surveyed, therefore, I am led to give renewed support for the proposal I offered in a previous discussion of 'the son of man' issue published in 2003.[32] That proposal is that ὁ υἱός τοῦ ἀνθρώπου likely represents a careful translation of an equivalent, unusual and distinctive Aramaic expression, probably בר אנשא. This singular-definite form of the more familiar Semitic idiom for referring to someone as a human, בר אנש ('a son of man'), was retained and deployed exclusively in sayings ascribed to Jesus in the early decades, because the expression was regarded reverentially as Jesus' own distinctive way of referring to himself. It did not represent some established title in Jewish tradition, nor did it comprise some new Christological title, and so did not claim for Jesus some honorific status. Instead, it functioned in the tradition drawn upon in the Gospels simply as Jesus' preferred self-referential device.[33] In Aramaic, there was a particularizing force to this unusual singular-definite expression, as there was in the articular-singular Greek translation, ὁ υἱός τοῦ ἀνθρώπου. That is, the expression designated Jesus in particular, and it could be deployed in any statement intended to make reference to Jesus.

I further propose that the most likely reason that the Jesus tradition linked Jesus so closely and uniquely with the expression is that he actually used it. That is, Jesus likely made בר אנשא his preferred self-designation, which

31. See also the earlier cautionary discussion by Loren T. Stuckenbruck, 'An Approach to the New Testament through Aramaic Sources: The Recent Methodological Debate', *Journal for the Study of the Pseudepigrapha* 8 (1991), pp. 3–29.

32. Hurtado, *Lord Jesus Christ*, pp. 290–306.

33. As I noted in *Lord Jesus Christ* (p. 305, n. 119), a speech-formula is not the same thing as a 'title', for the latter term typically designates some office or honoured status.

formed a salient feature of his own speech-practice, his 'voice' or manner of speaking, in linguistic terms, his 'idiolect'.[34] This would be an example of what competent users of languages often do, adapting idiomatic expressions, either in form or connotation, to serve some new and particular semantic purpose.[35]

The obvious next question is what might have prompted Jesus to formulate and deploy so regularly this apparently unusual expression with its particularizing implication. We have already noted the proposal that 'the son of man' originated through Jesus identifying himself with the human-like figure of Dan. 7.13-14, and I have indicated why this seems to me unlikely. I propose, instead, that the expression simply reflected Jesus' sense that he had a particular, even unique, vocation in God's redemptive purposes. That is, I suggest that Jesus saw himself as having a special role and mission, and that he used the expression for 'the son of man' self-referentially to express this conviction. It did not indicate what that mission was, and did not lay claim to any office or previously defined status. Instead, 'the son of man' functioned to express his sense of being chosen for a special purpose before God.

I emphasize that this is a historical, and not a confessionally based, claim.[36] To consider that Jesus saw himself as having a unique significance and role does not require that he did or did not see himself in terms of the specific post-Easter claims about him. Nor does it require that one assent to him having any such special significance. Also, it is not so strange an idea as bourgeois moderns might at first think. A sense of being divinely called to a unique mission or role is neither unique in history, nor in itself indicative of mental health problems.[37]

---

34.   I refer to my discussion in *Lord Jesus Christ*, p. 292, where I provide further distinctive features of Jesus' speech-practice ascribed to him in the Gospels. For the notion of 'idiolect', see e.g. Lyons, *Language and Linguistics*, pp. 26–27.

35.   See e.g. Lyons, *Language and Linguistics*, pp. 22–23; Ruth M. Kempson, *Semantic Theory* (Cambridge: Cambridge University Press, 1977), pp. 50–74.

36.   I plead guilty to the charge of being a Christian (take me to the lions!), but my proposal does not depend upon or in itself promote a Christian stance on Jesus.

37.   See e.g. Rodney Stark, 'Normal Revelations: A Rational Model of "Mystical" Experiences', in *Religion and the Social Order: Vol. 1, New Developments in Theory and Research*, ed. David G. Bromley (Greenwich, CT: JAI Press, 1991), pp. 239–51; Bromley, 'How Sane People Talk to the Gods: A Rational Theory of Revelations', in Michael A. Williams, Collette Cox and Martin S. Jaffee (eds), *Innovations in Religious Traditions* (Berlin/New York: Mouton de Gruyter, 1992), pp. 19–34.

We know of other figures who firmly believed that they were divinely commissioned for a unique role. Paul is perhaps the most obvious example from the NT, in his conviction that he had been destined by God before birth to fulfil his apostolic vocation (esp. Gal. 1.15-16). Although we have no comparable first-hand testimony, we should also presume that John the Baptist saw himself as specially called by God to announce eschatological judgement and salvation to Israel, in the mould of the OT prophets. If we broadened the survey, we could also include figures such as 'the Teacher of Righteousness', commonly thought by Qumran scholars to have had a sense of unique calling, and others across the centuries and in various religious traditions.

The specifics of Jesus' own sense of his vocation need not detain us, and it would require much more space than is available to explore adequately and defend any proposal about what it was. For the purpose of accounting for his use of the expression 'the son of man', it is sufficient to posit here that Jesus thought of himself as having a particular, probably even unique, divine vocation and mission, and that this sense of being a particular mortal called to a special role in the coming of the kingdom of God found expression in the use of that distinctive way of referring to himself.

Conclusion

This book does not address all matters concerning 'the son of man', and will probably not settle all minds on the issues included for discussion in it. But I believe that it brings together a collection of studies that consolidate and confirm some important points for further exploration and debate. Among other points made, several contributions combine to show that Casey's confidently proposed solution to 'the son of man' problem has significant problems itself. The origin of the expression ὁ υἱός τοῦ ἀνθρώπου probably does lie in some Aramaic expression. But the Greek phrasing and probably the underlying Aramaic equivalent were both unusual, and were each intended to connote a particularizing sense. The most economical explanation for the restricted pattern of usage of 'the son of man' in the Gospels is that it reflects a reverential attitude towards Jesus' own distinctive use of an Aramaic equivalent, and an effort to convey that use in the Greek rendition of Jesus' sayings. The evidence of choice in the retention and deployment of the expression in the Gospels probably reflects the aim of the authors (and the tradition on which they drew) to give the sayings of Jesus a certain recognizable verisimilitude, using what had become known as a key feature of Jesus' speech-practice.

Index to Scripture and Other Ancient Sources

SUBJECT INDEX

AUTHOR INDEX